MW01225711

Fighting the Diseases of Poverty

About International Policy Network

International Policy Network (www.policynetwork.net) is a UK-based charity which coordinates policy activities to broaden public understanding of issues relating to sustainable development, health, technology, trade, and economics. To achieve that goal, IPN sponsors events and publications, coordinates activities at international meetings, and promotes greater media awareness of public policy issues.

IPN also works with numerous organisations and individuals in developing countries to enhance their capacity to participate and engage in public policy activities.

About the Campaign for Fighting Diseases

The Campaign for Fighting Diseases (CFD) seeks to raise awareness of the realities of diseases suffered in the poorest regions of the world, and the need for viable solutions for these diseases. Members of the CFD, including academics, NGOs and think tanks, argue for prioritisation of action at local, national and international levels, to ensure that time and money are used most effectively to save lives and achieve the best results with limited resources.

About International Policy Press

International Policy Press is a division of International Policy Network.

Fighting the Diseases of Poverty

Edited by
Philip Stevens

Published by International Policy Press
a division of International Policy Network

Fighting the Diseases of Poverty
Edited by Philip Stevens

First published in Great Britain in 2007 by
International Policy Press
3rd Floor, Bedford Chambers
The Piazza, Covent Garden
London WC2E 8HA, UK

ISBN 1-905041-14-4

Designed and typeset in Oranda by MacGuru Ltd
info@macguru.org.uk
Cover design by Sarah Hyndman

Printed and bound in Great Britain by
Sunshine Promotions
PO Box 31
Westham
BN24 6NZ

A CIP catalogue record for this book is available from the British Library.

Contents

The authors

Johan Biermann is a planning consultant and policy researcher in Pretoria, South Africa. Over the last decade he has undertaken research for the Free Market Foundation of Southern Africa on the impact of government planning and regulation on economic development and service delivery, including the effect of legislation, regulation and government policy on the delivery of health-care. His published articles on healthcare include *Government can reduce medicine prices overnight* (2003), *Certificates of need are a recipe for chaos* (2004), and *Health charter perpetuates fallacies* (2005). He is the author of the occasional paper *Undermining Mineral Rights: an International Comparison* (2001) and the briefing paper *Town Planning and the Market* (2002), both published by the Free Market Foundation, of which he is a Council member. Conference papers include *Planning, Prosperity and the Market* (1992), and *A Critique of Social Health Insurance* (2004).

David Bloom is Clarence James Gamble Professor of Economics and Demography at the Harvard School of Public Health. Professor Bloom has published over eighty articles and books in the fields of economics and demography, and his current research interests include labour economics, health, demography, and the environment. Professor Bloom has served as a consultant to the United Nations Development Programme, the World Bank, the World Health Organization, the International Labor Organization, the National Academy of Sciences, and the Asian Development Bank. In addition, he is a member of the American Arbitration Association's Labor Arbitration Panel, and a faculty research associate at the National Bureau of Economic Research, where he participates in the programs on labour studies, health economics, and aging.

David Canning is Professor of Economics and International Health at the Harvard School of Public Health. His research focuses on the role of demographic change and health improvements in economic development. Before taking up his position at the Harvard School of Public Health, Professor Canning held faculty positions at the London School of Economics, Cambridge University, Columbia University, and Queen's University Belfast. Professor Canning has served as a consultant to the World Health Organization, the World Bank, and the Asian Development Bank. In addition, he was a member of Working Group One of the World Health Organization's Commission on Macroeconomics and Health.

Indur Goklany is a researcher and manager of science and policy issues at the U.S. Department of the Interior's Office of Policy Analysis. Dr Goklany has written extensively in peer-reviewed literature, has authored and contributed to several books on issues such as climate change, biodiversity and the relationship between economic growth and the environment. He was the first Julian Simon Fellow at the Property and Environment Research Center in Bozeman, Montana, in the summer of 2000. He also has been a Visiting Fellow at the American Enterprise Institute. His most recent book, *The Improving State of the World: Why We're Living Longer, Healthier, More Comfortable Lives on a Clean Planet* was published in 2007. The views expressed in his chapter are his own.

Dr Maureen Lewis is a health and development economist for the Center for Global Development in Washington, DC. Prior to this, she was chief economist of the World Bank's Human Development Network. She led the team that designed the Bank's first major HIV project, in Brazil in 1993. Previously she established and directed the Urban Institute's International Health and Demographic Policy Unit. An Adjunct Professor at the George Washington University,

Maureen has published dozens of articles in peer-reviewed journals on health and population. She has a PhD from John Hopkins University, and an MA and BSFS from George Washington University.

Julian Morris founded International Policy Network in 2001. He was previously the Director of the Institute of Economic Affair's Environment and Technology Programme. He has two Masters Degrees in economics and a Graduate Diploma in Law from the University of Westminster. He is also a Visiting Professor at the University of Buckingham.

Philip Stevens is the director of the health programme at International Policy Network, a UK-based development think tank. He is the author of numerous health policy publications, including *The real determinants of health*, and *Free trade for better health*. His writings on health policy have appeared in a wide range of international newspapers, and he is a frequent commentator on TV and radio. Philip has also held research positions at the Adam Smith Institute and Reform in London, and spent several years as a management consultant. He holds degrees from the London School of Economics and Durham University.

Richard Wagner is Hobart R. Harris Professor of Economics and Graduate Director of the Economics Department of George Mason University. He received his Ph.D. in economics from the University of Virginia in 1966. He joined the faculty of George Mason University in 1988, after having held positions at the University of California, Irvine, Tulane University, Virginia Polytechnic Institute and State University, Auburn University and Florida State University.

Mark Weston is an independent policy consultant specialising in international development. His interests include public health, HIV/AIDS, demography, education and corporate social responsibility.

Introduction

By Philip Stevens

In many public health and journalistic circles, it is taken for granted that globalisation and market-lead economic growth are undermining people's health, particularly in the poorest countries. HIV/AIDS dominates discussion to the extent that the casual observer would be forgiven for believing it to be the only health problem in Africa. Commentators, academics and activists routinely accompany their gloomy prognostications with calls for greater intervention by governments and global health agencies in the supply and management of healthcare in less developed countries, to be funded lavishly by wealthy countries.

It is certainly true that far too many people around the world are dying unnecessarily from preventable or curable diseases. But is it true that the world's health is deteriorating as economic globalisation accelerates? Are the grand plans and strategies executed by international intergovernmental organisations such as the UN the best way to tackle the myriad health problems faced by the world's poorest people? And why exactly is it that millions of children still die every year from easily preventable illnesses that have long been consigned to history in the West? Are governments the most efficient and equitable suppliers of healthcare, or does the market have a role? This book is an attempt to shed some light on these questions.

Good news: the world is getting healthier

At this point in history, we appear to be in the grip of a cultural pessimism that implies not only that things were better in the past, but also that things are set to get much worse unless governments take drastic action. Such thinking underpins much of the debate about health in less developed countries. Surely with scourges such as HIV/AIDS, malaria and tuberculosis rampant in many parts of the world, we have no reason to be optimistic about human health outside of a few cosseted pockets of the West?

Indur Goklany's chapter demonstrates that such pessimism is unwarranted. At the beginning of the 21st Century, human beings live longer, healthier lives than at any other time in history. This trend is set to continue, as living standards continue to rise and technology improves and spreads around the world. Using human development data from across time and over many countries, Goklany shows how, with some minor hiccoughs, the lot of humanity has steadily improved since modern economic growth began in the early nineteenth Century.

Since around 1820, infant mortality rates and life expectancy have improved dramatically around the world, and food is more abundant and inexpensive than ever before. These indicators of human well-being improved particularly noticeably in rich countries from the mid to late 19th century, as water supplies were cleaned up and basic public health measures, such as sanitation, pasteurization, and vaccination were introduced. Then, in the first half of the twentieth century, antibiotics, pesticides, and an array of vaccines were added to the arsenal of weapons against disease.

Once the traditional infectious and parasitic diseases were essentially conquered, richer countries turned their ingenuity and wealth to dealing with so-called diseases of affluence: cancer, heart diseases and strokes (plus HIV/AIDS, a non-traditional infectious disease). While these have not yet been entirely defeated, a vast array of new treatments, drugs and technologies now exist to mitigate their effects.

During the second half of the twentieth century, the diffusion of technology from the rich to lower-income countries, as well as greater wealth in the lower-income countries, led to what has been described as the third of three great waves of mortality decline (Gwatkin, 1980).

This period saw an increase in access to safe water and sanitation services in lower-income countries. Such access, coupled with increases in per capita food supplies, basic public health services, greater knowledge of basic hygiene, and newer weapons (such as antibiotics and tests for early diagnosis) were instrumental in reducing mortality rates.

As a result of these advances, life expectancies lengthened worldwide, not just in the richest nations. Globally, average life expectancy increased from 46.6 in 1950–1955 to 66.8 years between 1950–1955 and 2003, as technology and knowledge was diffused around the world (World Bank, 2005).

Economic growth, technology and free trade – a cycle of progress

This amazing story has at its roots what Goklany describes as the "mutually reinforcing, co-evolving forces of economic growth, technological change and free trade." Economic growth is a particularly potent force for improving health, as was demonstrated by a seminal 1996 study by economists Lant Pritchett and Lawrence Summers. Their research demonstrated a strong causative effect of income on infant mortality, showing that if the developing world's growth rate had been 1.5 percentage points higher in the 1980s, half a million infant deaths would have been averted.

When economic growth translates into higher incomes, it allows people to invest in cleaner drinking water, proper sewage and sanitation, clean fuel and better nutrition. Currently, water-borne diseases, chest infections caused by using biomass fuels in unventilated dwellings and malnutrition constitute a large proportion of the disease burden in the world's poorest countries. If a country is wealthy, these diseases can easily be overcome by upgrading water and electrical infrastructure, and by ensuring the population is well nourished.

The improvements in health that prosperity brings can also help to further reinforce and accelerate economic growth. Good nutrition, for example, allows working adults to be more productive at work and to spend more time generating income. Proper nutrition amongst children improves their cognitive and physical ability as adults, helping to ensure that the future adult population is economically productive.

Healthier people who live longer also have stronger incentives to invest capital in developing their skills, because they expect to accrue the benefits over longer periods. So, for example, if a child is more likely to make it to adulthood, the risk of investing in its education is reduced. So parents are more likely to make such investments, which tend to raise productivity, and hence income, in adulthood. Improved child health can also reduce the economic burden on both families and governments, freeing up resources for investment elsewhere (Karoly *et al.*, 1998).

Free trade and health

Free trade is the final part of this 'cycle of progress.' Increased cross-border trade is directly and causatively associated with economic growth (Dollar, 1995; Dollar & Kraay, 2001; Frankel & Romer, 1999; Sachs & Warner, 1995), which, as we have seen, is directly beneficial to health. International trade also expands competition, forcing companies to innovate and drive costs down in order to gain new competitive advantages. This helps to bring newer, better products to more people at lower costs, a process which also explains why medical technology continues to advance at an incredible pace.

Free trade also facilitates the spread of ideas, knowledge and technology across borders. The discovery by John Snow in London in 1854 that cholera is spread by contaminated water was to have significant implications for the prevention of infectious diseases throughout the world. This knowledge gradually filtered from London throughout Europe, leading city authorities to upgrade their water and sewage systems in order to prevent human waste contaminating water supplies (Williamson, 1990). Today, germ theory is widely understood and recognised by public health authorities all over the world as an important tool for fighting disease.

Similarly, lowering the costs of trade can speed up the rate at which proven medical technologies can be adopted by other countries. Some of the most effective and simple medicines such as antibiotics and vaccines were first developed in richer countries, but the international manufacture and trade of such technologies has allowed them to become readily available and inexpensive in most parts of the world.

The progress made in Asia in the 20th century is a particularly powerful testament to the ability of trade to improve health. In the 1940s, most countries in the region ended several decades of relative economic and cultural isolation and began to integrate into the global economy. Alongside trade in goods came the transfer of knowledge, technologies and techniques from richer countries, and led to the development of public health programmes. The 1920s to 1940s had seen huge advances in pharmacology, including the development penicillin, sulfa drugs, bacitracin, streptomycin and chloroquine. With the arrival in Asia of these and other drugs, effective treatments for the diseases which had once killed millions were now available at low cost. Furthermore, DDT, invented in 1943, offered a powerful weapon in the fight against malaria, enabling the eradication of the disease from the US and Europe, and near eradication (caseloads reduced by over 99 per cent) in parts of Sri Lanka and India (Gramiccia & Beales, 1988).

As a result of the widening availability and decreasing cost of such interventions – made possible by freer trade – crude death rates dropped steeply, particularly in eastern Asia in the late 1940s. By the 1960s, far fewer children and young people were succumbing to the easily preventable diseases which had historically impacted the health of the region's people and life expectancy was on the rise (Bloom & Williamson, 1997).

This process continues today as new drugs and medicines that are invented in one place are made available on international markets. Even though nearly all drugs start their life protected by patents, these eventually expire, opening the market for generic competition. As a result, many off-patent medicines are available throughout the world at extremely low prices – allowing people in poorer countries to benefit from the knowledge and innovation of more affluent parts of the world. More recent examples of this would include antiretroviral drugs and statins, as well as items such as neonatal intensive care units, kidney dialysis equipment, screening equipment and myriad other modern medical devices. Of course, many drugs that are on-patent are also subject to competition from other medicines in the same class. Moreover, with price differentiation, patent drugs are often made available to poorer people at prices close to the cost of production.

What about inequality?

A frequently cited objection to the arguments made above is that although economic globalisation may indeed improve matters for a small proportion of the world's population, it leads inexorably to a widening level of inequality across countries. The fear is that globalisation is causing the poor in many countries to become poorer and, as a consequence, less healthy. Such reasoning has underpinned a number UN Human Development Reports and countless NGO campaigns calling for greater redistribution of wealth from rich to poor countries.[1]

Does the evidence support such concerns? Indur Goklany's research shows that income disparities between countries have widened since the early 19th century but that these gaps are now narrowing – especially as economic growth in China and India has begun to lift hundreds of millions out of poverty. The numbers of people living in absolute poverty in sub-Saharan Africa have not declined, however, mainly because of political mismanagement. As a result, diseases such as malaria, tuberculosis and other common infectious diseases remain rampant, and HIV/AIDS has exploded. This notwithstanding, the health indicators that really matter – life expectancy, infant mortality and hunger – are continuing to converge globally, making the world a far more equal place health-wise than it was in 1950, despite the continuing divergence of incomes (Kenny, 2005). Although life expectancy has fallen slightly in sub-Saharan Africa as a result of the reasons outlined above, modest progress is being made with infant mortality rates.

Another sub-species of the inequality argument is that income disparities within countries are bad for health *per se*, even if those at the lowest end of the socio-economic scale are relatively well-fed, housed and have access to public services, as is the case in most OECD countries. According to this reasoning, broader economic policies have an important role to play in improving health, especially those which reduce inequality by facilitating the redistribution of wealth. Such thinking underpins much of the work of the World Health Organisation, which in 2005 established a Commission on the Social Determinants of Health, which is due to report in 2008.

The premise that economic inequality is deleterious to health stems from an influential series of studies on health outcomes in the British civil service in the 1980s and 1990s. These "Whitehall studies" found a strong association between grade levels of civil servant employment and mortality rates from a range of causes. Men in the lowest grade (messengers, doorkeepers, etc.) were found to have a mortality rate three times higher than that of men in the highest grade (Marmot *et al.*, 1984; 1991)

The "Whitehall studies" gave empirical backing to the idea that *relative* rather than *absolute* poverty can be a significant determinant of health. This, it is argued, is largely attributable to negative psychosocial factors such as stress, which are heightened amongst individuals further down the social hierarchy in industrialised countries. Stress has been associated with a wide range of health problems, including cardiovascular disease – which imposes a great health burden on both rich and poor countries alike. As a country becomes wealthier, income inequalities often also increase, which gives rise to the idea that economic growth *per se* is undesirable unless it is accompanied by strong government measures to ensure greater income equality.

Proponents claim that these studies challenge the idea that the best way to improve health is to maximise economic growth. Such an approach, it is argued, will do nothing to tackle income and social inequality, which is in itself a significant determinant of health. Instead, policymakers should aim to foster greater income equality through expanding welfare systems and restricting private employment policies. The theory suggests that subsequent improvements in the social environment due to reduced income stratification will improve a population's psychosocial welfare as well as social cohesion. This will see concomitant improvements in a wide range of physical disorders and thereby contribute to improvements in population health (Wilkinson, 1999).

However, such an approach could, in fact, be counterproductive, not least because there is a paucity of evidence that actually links income inequality (rather than social stratification) with health inequalities. This is especially true of lower-income countries. Early cross-country correlations between life-expectancy and income inequality were driven by flawed measures of inequality and are impossible to reproduce with more credible data (Deaton, 2003).

The relationship between income inequality and poor health is more complex than it appears at face value. For instance, in his analysis of data from 42 countries, Adam Wagstaff (2002) finds that in both rich and poor countries health inequalities rise with rising per capita incomes. This is probably due to in part to the rapid improvements in health technology that accompany economic growth, which are often taken up more speedily by the rich than the poor. However, it is important to note that the poorest levels of society do not get *less* healthy as the society's wealthier elements get healthier. Rather, they become healthier at a slightly slower rate.

As such, it is not clear that policies which forcibly redistribute wealth from the rich to the poor will actually have a net beneficial effect on health. As we have already seen, economic growth is strongly and causatively associated with improved health (Pritchett & Summers, 1996). So, although rising incomes appear to be associated with rising health inequalities, they are also associated with rising overall levels of health. As Wagstaff writes, "the force that makes for higher health inequalities – higher per capita incomes – is precisely the same that makes people healthier on average" (Wagstaff, 2002). There is a danger that aggressively redistributive policies will stifle economic growth, undermining the very process that is most associated with improving health.

A study conducted by Issidor Noumba (2004) reinforces this hypothesis. Like Wagstaff, Noumba found that the higher the inequality in health and income in a number of African countries, the lower the infant mortality and crude death rates and fertility index: "In other words, for African countries, income is relatively more important for the health of the population than income inequality and inequality in health status. Consequently, it is a priority to take measures that accelerate income growth rather than those directed to the reduction in inequalities."

Is the state the best provider of healthcare?

It is now both clear and generally accepted that the best way to ensure economic prosperity is to allow the operation of free and open markets. Nevertheless, the provision of healthcare is typically assumed by politicians and commentators to be too important to be left to the caprices of the market. As a result, in most countries the majority of formal healthcare provision is controlled by the government. This ranges from direct state funding, to mandatory insurance, to regulation. Governments around the world own and manage hospitals, employ doctors and nurses, control the supply of pharmaceuticals, and finance healthcare collectively through taxation, social insurance or other mechanisms.

The justifications for such intervention are many. Privately provided healthcare is portrayed as divisive and inequitable. Private health insurance is assumed to suffer from 'adverse selection.' By contrast, state-provided healthcare is seen as an important means of achieving "universal" access to healthcare, thereby fulfilling the human "right" to health,[2] and achieving "social justice." It is also often assumed that the state can achieve better health outcomes at lower financial cost.

In recent years, national governments from Accra to Washington, DC have been centralising and collectivising large parts of their healthcare systems. An example is South Africa, which has recently enacted legislation to centralise and bolster the poorly-performing state health sector, placing significant restrictions and controls on the freedom of private sector. Johan Biermann evaluates these reforms in chapter two, and concludes that they will emasculate South Africa's world-class private sector while leaving the poor in much the same position as they are now.

Biermann argues that the South African government has ignored the problems faced by centrally-planned, state-owned health systems the world over. These include: rationing in the form of waiting lists; cost-containment through the use of outdated medical technology and pharmaceuticals; shortages; inefficiency; increased corruption; decisions made according to political rather than clinical needs; an absence of patient choice and capture by producer interests. At a broader level, state healthcare can lead to higher taxes and reduced productivity, which may even feed through into lower economic growth, thereby negatively impacting health – especially in poorer countries where the association between health and wealth is stronger.

Biermann argues that the government should instead be encouraging a massive expansion of the successful private sector so that it can be accessed by all levels of society – not just the rich. Universal access could be accomplished by establishing medical savings accounts, by providing vouchers, or by through competition between medical aid funds. Such a reform would remove the daily management and allocation of healthcare from the purview of the government, which has consistently proved incapable of efficiently managing the extremely complex and costly business of delivering healthcare.

Corruption in healthcare

South Africa's movement towards a more fully socialised healthcare system is in tune with the strategy being promoted by the UN to achieve its Millennium Development Goals, as well as the various anti-poverty campaigns that have been calling for increased foreign aid. These campaigns are based largely on the premise that the poor health and education in lower-income countries is a root cause of their poverty, so massive public investments in health and schools are needed to make the population more productive, which would then stimulate economic growth.[3]

While there is a positive feedback effect between health and wealth, there is little evidence that the "big push" government healthcare approach can actually achieve results. A multi-country study by Filmer and Pritchett (1999) showed that public spending on health in lower-income countries has only a minute impact on mortality. The authors showed that a significant proportion of deaths of children below five years could be averted for as little as US $10 each, yet even in the poorest countries, the average amount spent by governments per child death averted is a staggering US $50,000–$100,000.

One of the prime movers behind this failure has been the high levels of corruption in public health agencies in less developed countries. As a result of this corruption, the proportion of a donor's contribution that actually results in delivery of healthcare services (whether they are vaccines or nurses' salaries) is often very low. Unfortunately, donor and recipient governments have historically responded to healthcare funding needs without first considering effectiveness and outcomes. As a result, corruption within the various bureaucracies and ministries that administer healthcare in less developed countries has gone largely unaddressed, thereby severely blunting the effectiveness of donor funding.

This is the issue raised by Maureen Lewis in her chapter on "corruption in public health," which examines the role of government institutions in healthcare delivery. Her conclusion is that the improvements in mortality envisaged by the Millennium

Development Goals will be extremely difficult to achieve unless governments pay more attention to the institutional factors in healthcare systems that incentivise corruption. Lewis looks at evidence from a range of countries over the last decade, and examines many of the forms of corruption that impede the delivery of health services – ranging through bribery, absenteeism, the purchasing of public positions, drug mismanagement and leakage, corruption in the supply chain, and informal payments. She then goes on to suggest some strategies for strengthening accountability and transparency. In the end, she concludes, the issue of governance can only be addressed by empowering consumers of healthcare by providing them with better information, by incentivising health staff through such things as targeted training and performance related pay, and by importing commercial management and accounting techniques into health systems.

What is the greatest health challenge: pharmaceutical innovation or distributing existing medicines?

The controversy surrounding the role of markets in healthcare does not stop at the provision of hospitals and doctors. There is also a considerable degree of scepticism about the ability of the market to deliver the drugs that are needed to fight diseases that are specific to lower-income countries. Health activists make much of the fact that billions of dollars are spent researching cures for erectile dysfunction and baldness, while tropical diseases and other diseases of poverty have been relatively neglected by commercial research and development. This alleged imbalance has become formalised in a construct known as the "10/90 gap," the premise of which is that 90 per cent of all health research benefits only 10 per cent of the world's population. The implication of the activists' campaigning is that profit-driven markets are incapable of meeting the needs of the poor, who can only be catered for by state-sponsored collectivist measures. Such thinking was behind the creation in 2003 of the World Health Organization's Commission on Intellectual Property

Rights, Innovation and Public Health (CIPIH), and the subsequent and (at the time of writing) ongoing Intergovernmental Working Group on Public Health, Innovation and Intellectual Property.

This view has become practically orthodox in public health circles, but is it justified by the evidence? My chapter reviews the publicly available data on the global burden of disease (much of which is collated by the World Health Organization) and concludes that the 10/90 gap is a deeply flawed interpretation of the market's ability to deliver innovative medicines. The data shows that there are only a handful of diseases that have been truly neglected by medical research, and that – contrary to popular belief – the disease burden of poorer countries increasingly resembles that of rich countries, with chronic diseases accounting for an ever bigger proportion of mortality. New drugs for these diseases are being developed in large numbers, a fact which somewhat undermines those who reflexively cry 'market failure.'

In fact, the biggest problem faced by lower income countries is not a lack of suitable drugs, but the widespread inability to distribute already existing, off-patent drugs to the sick. There are many factors which actively impede access to medicines, a range of which are examined by the authors of the chapter on "Increasing Access to Medicines," a version of which was originally drafted by a coalition of civil society groups as a response to the CIPIH. In their analysis, the authors discovered that a number of self-generated public policy failures are responsible for the fact that up to 50 per cent of people in parts of Africa and Asia have no access to essential medicines. These include, amongst other things, weak healthcare infrastructures, regulatory environments that are hostile to health insurance markets and other risk pooling mechanisms, and taxes, tariffs and price controls on medicines.

This notwithstanding, there is still some need for new medicines for less developed countries. Bacterial and viral resistance to existing medicines is a major problem in treatments for diseases such as malaria and tuberculosis (Zumla *et al.*, 2001; Ridley, 2002). In addition, specific subpopulations such as pregnant women and children are most at risk from diseases such as malaria, and require medicines with specific formulations (Bremen, 2001).

The manifold failures in drug distribution are directly related to the fact that few commercial companies are willing to shoulder the risk of developing these new medicines. If a medicine stands little chance of actually reaching its intended consumer, there is little point in risking large amounts of capital in developing a drug specifically designed for a poorer market. If the barriers to access were lifted, there would be far greater demand for new medicines, which would make them a more enticing commercial proposition.

Grand plans and political diseases

Since the early 1990s, the United Nations and its various subagencies have assumed a leadership role in coordinating and managing the global response to the HIV/AIDS and malaria pandemics, as well as many other of the health problems that beset less developed countries. More often that not, however, the UN has failed to achieve its self-imposed targets and goals.

Moreover, it has failed to contain and reverse pandemics such as HIV/AIDS and malaria, despite being given both a mandate and generous resources. Both of these diseases appear to be getting worse. The UN spent $8.3bn on HIV/AIDS in 2005, yet global HIV prevalence had risen to an estimated 40.3 million people by the end of 2005 (UNAIDS, 2006), from a figure of 34.9 million in 2001 (UNAIDS, 2004). 4.1 million people were infected in 2005 alone, an increase from 3.9 million in 2003. The UN's efforts to tackle malaria have been equally ineffectual: despite launching the Roll Back Malaria initiative in 1998 with the aim of halving global malaria incidence by 2010, malaria incidence is likely to be increasing. Although problems associated with collecting accurate data make it difficult to determine precisely how many people suffer from malaria, in 2002 an external evaluation of RBM set up by the WHO said:

"Anecdotal evidence and the strong consensus among experts suggests that, at the very least, the malaria burden has not decreased. What is more likely, and believed to be the case by most of those involved, is that malaria has got somewhat worse during this period" (Malaria Consortium, 2002).

The authors of chapter six, "Cost effective means of reducing the diseases of poverty," examine some of these UN-sponsored programmes and ask why they have to date been less than successful. In the cases of HIV/AIDS and malaria, the root of the failure lies in serious strategic errors on the part of the planners in control of the programmes. With HIV/AIDS, the leaders at UNAIDS and the World Health Organization have consistently prioritised palliative treatment of people already infected over the prevention of new infections, leading to the depressingly predictable increases in HIV incidence rates.

Turning to malaria: the UN's Roll Back Malaria consortium has until recently underpinned its prevention strategy with the promotion of insecticide-treated bednets, while refusing to endorse demonstrably more effective methods, such as spraying the interiors of dwellings with pesticides. The WHO compounded this error for several years by recommending the use of ineffective antimalarial drugs (against the advice of some of its own advisors).

The trouble with these grand plans, as the authors of chapter six show, is that bureaucrats often have little idea about the realities faced by people on the ground, and are sometimes pressured into making questionable strategic decisions by outside political and NGO pressure. The damaging UN policy of prioritising HIV/AIDS treatment, for instance, arose partly as a response to a long and vocal campaign by activists and NGOs. The goal of rolling out ARV treatment to everyone in need seemed feasible according to the spreadsheet calculations done in Geneva, but it failed to take into account the terrible paucity of health infrastructure in the most affected countries. More egregiously, the outside pressure from NGOs and activists distracted the planners from making decisions which would have been politically unpopular, but more effective at reducing the incidence of HIV/AIDS (such as investing a greater proportion of available resources in prevention).

This politicisation of disease is counterproductive: it directs energy and resources towards the causes championed by the most effective and charismatic pressure groups, and away from other approaches that do not attract the same level of cheerleading. UNAIDS has estimated that treating HIV/AIDS will require $22.1bn in 2008, or approximately 30 per cent of all Overseas Development Assistance (ODA) from OECD countries. As more patients become drug resistant and are moved onto second-line therapies, the cost of achieving the UN's goal of putting 10 million on treatment could easily rise to $44bn by 2010 – not including the costs of corruption, recurrent costs, or the lavish running costs of international organisations (and their consultants), which could easily boost this figure to over $62 billion. At around 65 per cent of all ODA spending globally (Adelman *et al.*, 2005), this would leave precious little to tackle the myriad other diseases which afflict people in less developed countries.

Prioritisation

The politicisation of diseases such as HIV/AIDS has warped global health priorities to the extent that the relatively simple and inexpensive are often neglected in favour of the complex and expensive. Donors often lose sight of the fact, for instance, that HIV/AIDS is only one of many health problems faced by less developed countries: the biggest killer of children is chest disorders caused by burning biomass fuels in poorly ventilated homes, followed by diarrhoeal diseases. As the chapter on the "10/90 gap" observed, these diseases are easy and inexpensive to prevent, but have received relatively little attention from the international community.

Another area which delivers extremely cost-effective and quick results is vaccination. Because of vaccination programmes, preventable childhood diseases such as polio, measles and pertussis only account for 0.2 per cent of DALYs in high-income countries. A lack of such programmes in other parts of the world, however, means that these diseases account for an intolerable 5.2 per cent of DALYs in high mortality lower income countries (WHO, 2002). Roughly 3 million people die from vaccine-preventable diseases every year (Center for Global Development, 2005).

Part of the reason why vaccination programmes have been relatively under-resourced by the donor community, as David Bloom and his colleagues argue in their chapter on 'The value of vaccination', is that policymakers have tended to look at the narrow benefits of averted medical costs, instead of looking at the broader economic advantages of the healthier population that universal vaccination would create. As a result, the steady progress made towards achieving universal vaccination coverage in the 1970s and 1980s has stalled in recent years as other health problems have risen up the international agenda.

Who's Health Organisation?

This kind of activity should be a priority of transnational health bureaucracies such as the World Health Organization, argues Richard Wagner in his provocative final chapter. Wagner associates the images of smallpox and Mother Theresa with the WHO: the former because of the WHO's role in eradicating this deadly communicable disease, and the latter because of the body's commitment to improving the lives of the poor. But how far does this vision reflect reality?

Wagner's examination of the WHO's budget for 2006–7 shows that less than half is spent on communicable diseases, suggesting the image of smallpox is misrepresentative. In fact, the greatest proportion of the WHO's resources are spent on issues that are neither trans-boundary nor of primary concern to the poor, such as road safety and obesity. These activities, Wagner argues, are seemingly intended to satisfy the political demands of the WHO's funders – predominantly wealthy countries – and to ensure a steady flow of the funds required to sustain its own bureaucracy. Mother Theresa would not have been proud of the large proportion of the WHO's budget (far in excess of 25 per cent) which is devoted to that bureaucracy. One way to refocus the WHO onto the issues that matter would be to relocate its headquarters from comfortable Geneva closer to the coalface in a less developed country.

Conclusion

In these opening years of the 21st century, we should reflect on and be thankful for how far humanity has travelled in a few short centuries. Vast swathes of people have effectively escaped from hunger and premature death, to paraphrase the work of the Nobel Laureate Robert Fogel. For those countries that have stayed on the margins of the global economy, there now exists an unprecedented number of international and national bureaucracies, NGOs and philanthropic organisations that are dedicated to improving the health of their citizens.

The danger is that often these well-intentioned organisations will continue to advocate and pursue the same interventionist policies that have historically undermined wealth and health in so many parts of the world. In the end, the poorest countries of the world need self-sustaining, efficient health-care systems that allow effective distribution of life saving medicines, as well as the propagation of vital health education. Poverty and weak health infrastructure have the same root causes: corruption and poor governance. Solve the latter and you solve the former. The reform of governance structures must therefore be a priority; that means strengthening property rights, improving legal systems and entrenching the rule of law. This is the only way to achieve the economic growth required to tackle ill-health on a sustainable basis. In the interim, I hope that this book points to a more constructive way forward, which may make the Declaration of Alma-Ata of "health for all" a reality instead of a utopian fantasy.

1 Wealth, health and the cycle of progress

Indur Goklany

"If present trends continue, the world in 2000 will be more crowded, more polluted, less stable ecologically, and more vulnerable to disruption than the world we live in now. Serious stresses involving population, resources, and environment are clearly visible ahead. Despite greater material output, the world's people will be poorer in many ways than they are today."

Global 2000 Report to the President

Introduction

With this Neo-Malthusian vision of the future, the *Global 2000 Report to the President* (Wrigley & Schofield, 1981) began a chilling description of the problems that lay ahead for the world unless radical changes were made. Fifteen years later, Julian Simon (Simon, 1995) quoted these words in his introduction to the monumental collection of essays, *The State of Humanity*. The point of that book, which Simon also edited, was to determine whether trends in human well-being and environmental quality were in accord with a Neo-Malthusian world view.

The State of Humanity, in fifty-eight chapters by more than fifty scholars, documented the tremendous strides in human well-being over the centuries, as well as trends in natural resource use and environmental quality. Based on these discussions, Simon wrote: "Our species is better off in just about every measurable material way" (Simon, 1995).

Figure 1 **Global economic development, AD 1–2003**

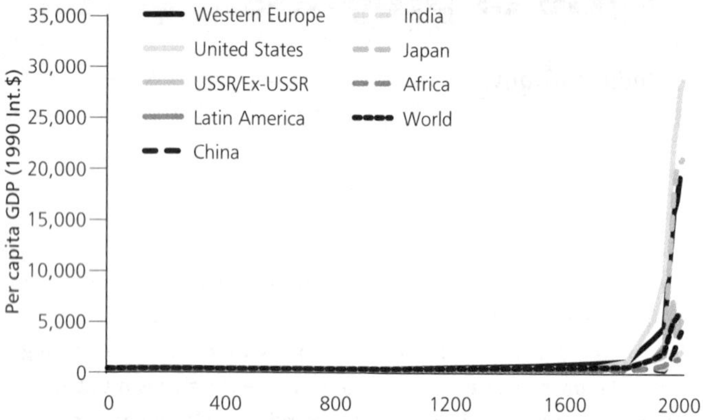

Source: Maddison (2005a); GGDC&CB (2005)

Yet today anxiety about the future continues. Calls to restructure our economy to avoid the pending insurmountable problems are typical. "The challenge facing the entire world is to design an economy that can satisfy the basic needs of people everywhere without self-destructing," said Lester Brown, president of World Watch Institute, in 1998 (Brown, 1998).

This chapter is a conscious effort to emulate, build upon, and update the work of Julian Simon and to provide empirical data to help evaluate the heated rhetoric of Lester Brown and other Neo-Malthusian alarmists. While no one can confidently predict the future, it is possible to scrutinize the past and present to determine the current state of humanity and identify which factors have helped, and which hindered progress.

Thus, the goal of this much smaller chapter is to collect in a convenient and portable volume the historical trends for indicators that are widely used to illustrate human welfare. These trends are presented not only across time, but, where data are available, across countries with different levels of economic development. In some cases, the data go back to when modern economic growth began – around 1800 or even earlier (see Figure 1) (Maddison, 1999a; 2005a; GGDG 1981).[1]

This chapter will address whether and to what extent modern economic growth has improved humanity's lot, using the following indicators.

- *Available food supplies per capita.* Having sufficient food is the first step to a healthy society. It enables the average person to live a productive life, while hunger and undernourishment retard education and the development of human capital, slowing down technological change and economic growth.
- *Life expectancy.* To most people, this is the single most valuable indicator of human well-being. Longer life expectancy is also generally accompanied by an increase in disability-free years.
- *Infant mortality.* Throughout history, high levels of death in early childhood have produced enormous sorrow, reduced population growth, and lengthened the time spent by women in child-bearing.
- *Economic development.* Gross domestic product (GDP) per capita is a measure of people's income. Thus, it measures the wealth or level of economic development of a country. While wealth is not an end in itself, it indicates how well a nation can achieve the ends its people desire, from greater availability of food, safe water, and sanitation to higher levels of education and health care.
- *Education.* While education is an end in itself, it also adds to human capital and can accelerate the creation and diffusion of technology. Education (particularly of women) helps to spread knowledge about nutrition and public health practices.
- *Political rights and economic freedom.* The ability to conduct one's life creatively and productively usually depends on having political rights and economic freedom. They are critical

to maintaining liberty and the pursuit of happiness, which are among the inalienable rights of human beings.

♦ *A composite human development index.* Using an approach similar to that employed in the United Nations Development Program (UNDP), this index combines indicators for life expectancy, education, and per capita income (UNDP, 2000).[2]

After examining trends in the above indicators, this chapter will address whether differences in human well-being have widened between developed and developing countries and whether urban residents fare worse than rural residents. Finally, it will discuss the factors that appear to be responsible for the remarkable cycle of progress that has accompanied modern economic growth.

Hunger and undernourishment

Concerns about the world's ability to feed its burgeoning population have been around at least since Thomas Malthus's "Essay on the Principle of Population" two hundred years ago. Several Neo-Malthusians of the twentieth century confidently predicted apocalyptic famines in the latter part of the century in the developing countries (Ehrlich, 1968; Paddock & Paddock, 1967). But even though the world's population is the largest it has ever been, the average person has never been better fed.

Since 1950, the global population has increased by 150 per cent (FAO, 2005), increasing the demand for food, but at the same time the real price of food commodities has declined 75 per cent (Mitchell & Ingco, 1995; World Resource Institute, 1998; World Bank, 2005). Greater agricultural productivity and international trade have made this possible (Goklany, 1998). As a result, average daily food supplies per person increased 24 per cent globally from 1961 to 2002, as indicated by Table 1. The increase for developing countries was even larger, 38 per cent. The decline in real prices, moreover, increased the availability of food for people in the lower rungs of the economic ladder.

Table 1 **Daily food supplies (Kcal/capita/day), c. 1800-2002**

Year(s)	Pre- or early-industrial phase[ab]	1961	1975	1989	2002
France	1,753 (1790)	3,194	3,247	3,563	3,654
Developed countries		1,928	3,147	3,308	3,314
Eastern Europe		3,118	3,412	3,436	3,194
India	1,635 (1950–51)	2,072	1,942	2,417	2,459
China	2,115 (1947–48)[c]	1,641	2,090	2,642	2,951
Developing countries		1,930	2,144	2,519	2,666
Sub-Saharan Africa		2,055	2,065	2,093	2,207
World		2,254	2,422	2,710	2,804

a Data are for the year(s) shown in brackets.
b Many developing countries, e.g., India and China, barely embarked upon industrialization until after World War II.
c Based upon data for 22 provinces.
Sources: Burnette and Mokyr (1995); Fogel (1995); Goklany (1999a); WRI (2005)

The Food and Agriculture Organization estimates the minimum daily energy requirement for maintaining health and body weight and engaging in light physical activity to be between 1,720 and 1,960 Calories (properly, kilocalories) per person per day (FAO, 1996). Adding to this threshold an allowance for moderate activity results in an estimate of the national average requirement from 2,000 to 2,310 Calories per person per day. (This assumes equal food provisions are likely to be equally available to the population.)

The improvements in the food situation in India and China since the middle of the twentieth century are especially remarkable. By 2002, China's food supplies had gone up 80 per cent from a barely subsistence level of 1,636 Calories per person per day in 1961. India's food supplies went up 50 per cent from 1,635 Calories per person per day in 1950–51. Between 1969–71 and 2000–02 such increases in food supplies helped reduce the number of chronically undernourished people in developing countries from 956 million to 815 million (or from 37 per cent to 17 per cent of their population) despite an 83 per cent growth in population (FAO, 2002; 2004; 2005).

Figure 2, based on cross-country data for 1975 and 2002 from the

Figure 2 **Food supplies per capita vs. income, 1975–2002**

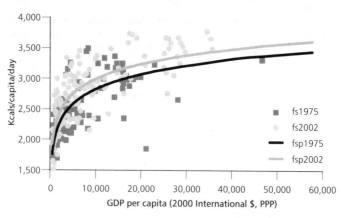

Source: Based on data from World Resources Institute (2005), World Bank (2005b)

World Resources Institute and the World Bank[3] shows that available daily food supplies per capita (FS) increase with both GDP per capita – a surrogate for per capita income (or "income" or "affluence") – and the passage of time.[4] The upward slope for each year probably reflects the fact that the wealthier the country, the greater its ability to afford more productive technologies to increase crop yields or purchase food in the global market through trade. The upward shift of the available food supply curve from 1975 to 2002 is consistent with the fact that for any given level of resources (represented by GDP per capita), over time food production increased largely due to technological change.[5]

According to Figure 2, if a hypothetical country's per capita income were frozen at $1 per day (in 2000 International dollars), available daily food supplies would have increased from 1,652 to 1,818 calories per capita per day from 1975 to 2002, an increase of 10.0 per cent, due to technological change alone. And if income were increased to from $1 to $2 per day in 2002, available daily food supplies would rise a further 13.5 per cent to 2,064 calories per capita. Thus, if a country had doubled its per capita income between 1975 and 2002 (equivalent to an annual economic growth rate of 2.6 per cent), available food supplies per capita would have increased by 25 per cent.

Life expectancy

Life expectancy at birth is probably the single most important indicator of human well-being. For much of human history, life expectancy was between 20 to 30 years (Preston, 1995). By 2000–2005 it had increased to 66.8 years worldwide, as Table 2 indicates (World Bank, 200?). For the wealthiest group of nations, the Organization for Economic and Cooperative Development (OECD), life expectancy at birth was 78.5 years in 2003 (World Bank, 2005b). Life expectancy in the countries that are developed today fluctuated in the early nineteenth century, followed by small declines in the middle two quarters of the nineteenth century. Then, with a few notable exceptions and some minor fluctuations, it began a sustained improvement that continues to this day.

In England and Wales, life expectancy was 35.9 years in 1801. After some ups and downs, it increased to 40.8 years in 1831 but then declined to 39.5 in 1851. After further fluctuations in the range of 40.2 to 41.2 years, it has been climbing since 1871 (Floud & Harris, 1997). The same broad pattern seems to fit the United States from the 1850s to the present, with steady improvements from 1880 onwards (Haines, 1994). The nineteenth century fluctuations were probably due to a combination of factors. Urbanization, ignorance of germs, and poor sanitation helped spread infectious and parasitic diseases such as cholera, smallpox, malaria, tuberculosis and typhoid.

Once solutions to these diseases were identified – in some cases before understanding their causes – nations cleaned up their water supplies and instituted basic public health measures, such as sanitation, pasteurization, and vaccination. Mortality rates dropped rapidly in the late nineteenth and early twentieth century.

Table 2 **Life expectancy at birth (in years) from the Middle Ages to 2003**

Year(s)	Middle ages	Pre- or early-industrial phase[ab]	1900[d]	1950–55[e]	1975–80[e]	1985–90[e]	2003[f]
France		~30 (1800)	47	66.5	73.7	76.0	79.4
UK	20–30	35.9 (1799–1803)[c]	50	69.2	72.8	75.0	78.3
Developed countries	20–30			66.1	72.3	74.1	75.6[d]
Eastern Europe				64.2	69.5	70.3	67.9[d]
India		24–25 (1901–11)	24	38.7	53.3	57.2	63.1
China		25–35 (1929–31)		40.8	65.3	67.1	71.5
Sub-Saharan Africa				37.4	47.2	49.4	45.9
Developing countries				41.1	56.9	60.4	63.4[d]
World	20–30	30		46.6	59.9	62.9	65.4

a Data are for the year(s) shown in brackets.

b Many developing countries, e.g., India and China, had barely embarked upon industrialization until after World War II.

c 1799–1803 data are for England and Wales, only. d Maddison (1999b). e UNPD (2004). f World Bank (2005b).

Sources: Wrigley and Schofield (1981); Preston (1995); Lee and Feng (1999); Maddison (1999b); UNPD (2004); World Bank (2005b)

Figure 3 **Access to safe water vs. income, 1990–2002**

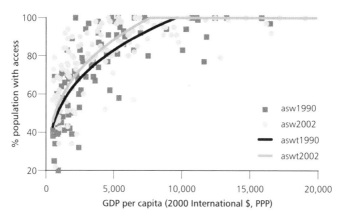

Source: Based on data from World Bank (2005b)

Then, in the first half of the twentieth century, antibiotics, pesticides such as DDT and an array of vaccines were added to the arsenal of weapons against disease. Once the traditional infectious and parasitic diseases were essentially conquered, the developed countries turned to dealing with so-called diseases of affluence: cancer, heart diseases and strokes (plus HIV/AIDS, a nontraditional infectious disease).

During the second half of the twentieth century, the diffusion of technology from the developed to developing countries, as well as greater wealth in the developing countries, increased access to safe water and sanitation services in developing countries. Figure 3 shows the increase in access to safe water (ASW) between 1990 and 2002.[6] It indicates that if a country were to go from a per capita income of $1 a day to $2 a day that would have increased access to safe water from 39.1 per cent of the population to 47.7 per cent in 1990, and from 41.7 to 50.9 per cent in 2002.

Such access, coupled with increases in per capita food supplies,[7]

Figure 4 **Life expectancy vs. income, 1977–2003**

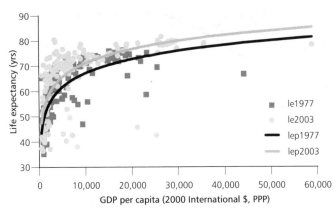

Source: Based on data from World Bank (2005b)

basic public health services, greater knowledge of basic hygiene, and newer weapons (such as antibiotics and tests for early diagnosis) reduced mortality rates.[8] As a result of such advances, life expectancies lengthened worldwide, not just in the richest nations. Average global life expectancy increased from 46.6 in 1950–1955 to 66.8 years between 1950–1955 and 2003, as technology, including knowledge, was diffused around the world (World Bank, 2005b).

Figure 4 shows, using data for 1977 and 2003, that life expectancy increases as GDP per capita increases.[9] Like the previous figures, it also shows the gains from technological change with the passage of time. A hypothetical doubling of GDP per capita from a dollar to two dollars a day would increase life expectancy from 40.7 to 46.2 years in 1977, and from 44.6 to 50.2 years in 2003. Thus, at these levels of affluence the gain from technological change between 1975 and 2003 is 3.9–4.0 years.

Figure 4 also suggests that because of technological change today's developing countries may have higher life expectancies than did the developed countries at equivalent levels of income. This, indeed, is the case for China and India, countries once synonymous with poverty and wretchedness. In 1913 when the United States had a GDP per capita of $5,301 (in 1990 International, PPP-adjusted dollars) (Maddison, 2005a), its life expectancy at birth was 52.5 years (Bureau of the Census, 1975). In 1977, when China and India had GDP per capita of a mere $895 and $937 respectively (also in 1990 International dollars) (Maddison, 2005a), they had life expectancies of approximately 65.4 and 52.9 years (World Bank, 2005b).

Not only are we living longer; we are also healthier (OECD, 1998; Shalala, 1998). Disability in the older populations of such developed nations as the United States, Canada, and France has been declining (U.S. Department of Health and Human Service, 1997). In the United States, for instance, the disability rate dropped 1.3 per cent per year between 1982 and 1994 for persons aged 65 and over.

Robert W. Fogel, the Nobel Prize-winning economic historian, notes that age-specific prevalence rates of specific chronic diseases and disabilities were much higher in the century preceding World War II than they are today. White males aged 60–64 are two-and-a-half times more likely to be free of chronic diseases today than their counterparts of a century ago. During the course of the twentieth century, the onset of chronic diseases has been significantly delayed – by 9 years for heart diseases, about 11 years for respiratory diseases (despite higher smoking rates), and nearly 8 years for cancers (Fogel, 2003).[10]

According to the World Health Organization, health-adjusted life expectancy (HALE) for the U.S., China and India, were 69.3, 64.1 and 53.5 years, respectively, in 2002 (WHO, 2004).[11] This is substantially more than these countries' corresponding *total* life expectancies before industrialization (see Table 2).

Figure 5 shows trends in life expectancies from the years 1950–55 to 2003 for various income groups and other entities.[12] Although life expectancy has on average increased worldwide since the 1950s, more recently there have been dramatic declines in many

Figure 5 **Life expectancy 1950–2003**

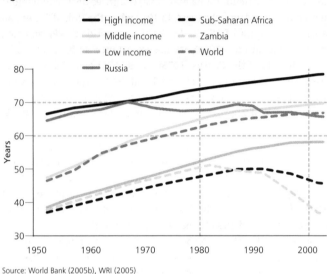

Source: World Bank (2005b), WRI (2005)

areas of Sub-Saharan Africa as well as less pronounced declines in Russia (Becker & Bloom, 1998) (which is somewhat representative of the former Soviet Union.

Russia's decline since the late 1980s in large part reflects economic deterioration concurrent with , and following, the fall of the communist government. Between 1989 and 1998, GDP per capita (in 1990 International dollars) declined 44 per cent before it rebounded (GGDC&CB, 2005). However, in 2003 it was still 21 per cent below its 1989 level. Yields of cereal, which represent 50 per cent of all crops, fell, and food supplies per capita, nutritional levels, and public health services all declined (Goklany, 1998). Alcoholism increased, as did accidental deaths, homicides, hypertension and suicides (Becker & Bloom, 1998). Life expectancies similarly declined in other countries in Eastern Europe and the former Soviet Union.

Table 3 **Infant mortality (<1 year of age, per 1,000 live births) from the Middle Ages to 2003**

Year(s)	Middle Ages	Pre- or early-industrial phase[ab]	1950 –55[c]	1970 –75[c]	1985 –90[c]	2003[d]
Sweden		240 (1800)	19.7	10.2	6.0	2.8
France		182 (1830)	45	15.9	7.8	4.4[e]
Developed countries	>200		59.1	21.4	12.7	7.1[c]
Russia			97.5	27.7	23.7	16.0
China			195.0	61.1	50.0	33.0
India			190.0	132	94.5	63.0
Developing countries			179.8	104.7	77.9	62.4[c]
Sub-Saharan Africa			177.0	134.2	112.4	101.0
World	>200		156.9	93.2	70.4	56.8

a Data are for the year(s) shown in brackets.
b Many developing countries, e.g., India and China, had barely embarked upon industrialization until after World War II.
c Based on UNPD (2004).
d Based on World Bank (2005b).
Sources: Mitchell (1992); Hill (1995); UNPD (2004); World Bank (2005b)

However, they have rebounded in the former region, as well as in many countries in the former Soviet Union (World Bank, 2005b).

Life expectancies have dropped much more dramatically since the late 1980s in a number of Sub-Saharan countries, due to a vicious cycle involving new and resurgent diseases, particularly, malaria, HIV/AIDS and tuberculosis, and a drop in economic output (UNDP, 2000). No country for which data are readily available has had a steeper decline than Zambia.

Infant mortality

Before industrialization, at least one out of every five children died before reaching his or her first birthday. As Table 3 shows, infant mortality, measured as the number of children dying before reaching

Figure 6   **Infant mortality vs. income, 1980–2003**

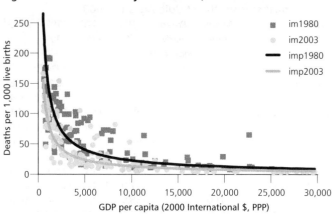

Source: Based on data from World Bank (2005b)

one year, typically exceeded 200 per 1,000 live births (Hill, 1995). The rate fell to 57 worldwide in 2003 (World Bank, 2005b). This is roughly the same level that more developed countries had reached in the 1950–55 period (World Research Institute, 1998; UN 2000). In the United States, as late as 1900, infant mortality was about 160; in 2004, it was about 6.6 (Bureau of the Census, 1975; NCHS, 2005a).

In the developing countries, the declines started later but may be occurring more rapidly in some areas. For instance, between 1950–55 and 2003, India's infant mortality fell from 190 to 63, and China's from 195 to 30 (UNPD, 2004a; World Bank, 2005b).

These declines were most likely due to a combination of greater economic development and technological factors, including wider knowledge about the factors that contribute to infant mortality and how to reduce them.[13] Figure 6, which uses data for 1980 and 2003 from World Bank (2005b), shows that infant mortality drops with greater affluence and with time.[14] According to this figure, if a hypothetical country doubled its GDP per capita from a dollar to two dollars a day it would have decreased infant mortality from 355 deaths per 1,000 live births to 199 in 1980, and from 207 to 116 in 2003.

The declines in infant mortality were accompanied by declines in maternal mortality that were equally, if not more, spectacular. In the United States, for instance, while infant mortality rates declined from around 100 per 1,000 live births in 1915 to 6.8 in 2001, maternal mortality rates declined from 220 per 100,000 live births to 9.9 (Bureau of the Census, 1975; 2004).

Economic development

Long term trends in economic growth, based on data from Maddison, are shown in Table 4 for various countries and regions including the United States, India, China, Japan, Europe, Latin America, Africa, the former Soviet Union and the world (Maddison, 2005; GGDCECB, 200?). While these estimates are less than precise, they do indicate that for most of this millennium, GDP per capita worldwide was below $600, measured in 1990 international dollars. Acceleration of economic growth began around 1800 and has been dramatic in recent years (see Figure 1). Today, it is more than ten times that (see Figure 5).

At the same time, the cost of basic necessities such as food has declined substantially in the last few decades in real (constant dollar) terms. More importantly, they have declined relative to income levels. For instance, between the years 1897 to 1901 and 2001 to 2003, U.S. retail prices of flour, bacon, and potatoes relative to per capita income dropped by 92 per cent, 85 per cent, and 82 per cent, respectively (Bureau of the Census, 1975; 2004).

Not only are basic necessities cheaper and the average person's annual income higher, but workers spend fewer hours on the job. Between 1820 and 2001, average hours worked per person employed declined 39, 20, and 45 per cent for the U.K., U.S., and Japan, respectively (Maddison, 2005). Ausubel and Grübler estimate that for the average British worker, total life hours worked declined

Table 4 Gross domestic product per capita (in 1990 International $, PPP-adjusted), A.D. 0–2003

Year	1	1000	1500	1700	1820	1913	1950	1989	1996	2001	2003c
Western Europe	450	400	771	998	1,204	3,458	4,579	15,856	17,097	19,256	28,797
United States	400A	400a	400	527	1,257	5,301	9,561	23,059	25,066	27,948	
USSR/Ex-USSR	400	400	499	610	688	1,488	2,841	7,098	3,854	4,626	5,267
Latin America	400	400	413B	441b	692	1,481	2,506	5,123	5,556	5,811	
China	450	450	600	600	600	552	439	1,827	2,820	3,583	4,185
India	450	450	550	550	533	673	619	1,270	1,630	1,957	2,194
Japan	400	425	500	570	669	1,387	1,921	17,942	20,494	20,683	21,104
Africa	430	425	414	421	420	637	894	1,463	1,403	1,489	
World	445	436	566	615	667	1,525	2,111	5,140	5,517	6,049	

a Based on Maddison (1999a) estimate for "North America."
b Based on the arithmetical average for Brazil and Mexico.
c Based on GGDC (2005), adjusted per Maddison (2005a).
Source: Maddison (2005a); GGDC (2005)

Figure 7 **Global economic development, AD 1950–2003**

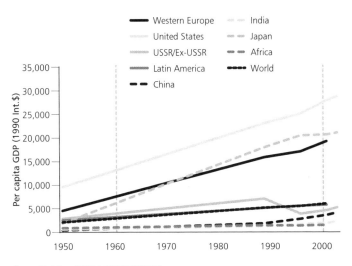

Source: Maddison (2005a); GGDC&CB (2005)

from 124,000 in 1856 to 69,000 in 1981 (Ausubel & Grübler, 1995). Because the average Briton lives longer and works fewer hours each year, the life hours worked by the average British worker has declined from 50 per cent to 20 per cent of his or her disposable life hours. In other words, the average person has more disposable time for leisure, hobbies, and personal development.

Thus, trends in real wages measured in dollars per hour would show an even more dramatic improvement than the income growth shown in Figure 7. Between 1820 and 2001 GDP per man-hour for the U.K., U.S., and Japan increased 19-, 28- and 56-fold, respectively (Maddison, 2005b). However, even these trends substantially underestimate the true improvements in economic well-being because methods to convert current dollars in one year to real dollars in another year are not robust when there has been a

Figure 8 **Post-secondary schooling vs. income, 1990–2002**

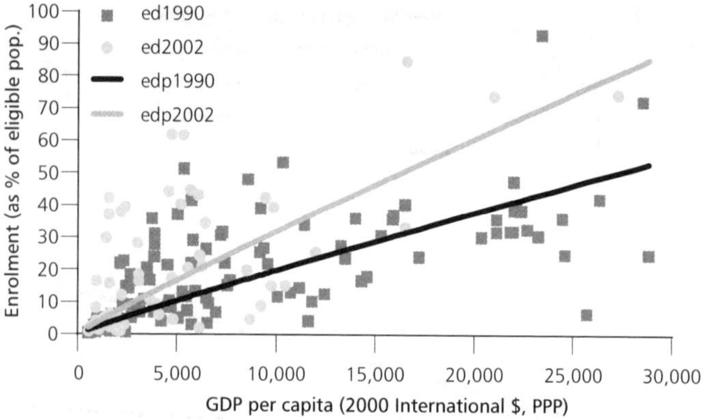

Source: Based on data from World Bank (2005b)

vast technological change between the two years. Goods and services available in the year 1950, for instance, were vastly different from those available in 1995. Personal computers, cell phones, VCRs, and instant access to the Library of Congress's electronic catalogue, to mention a few, simply were not available in 1950. Today, for a few hundred dollars people can buy goods and services they could not imagine, let alone buy for all the money in the world even a generation or two ago.

Education and child labor

Figure 8 shows that the per cent of the eligible population enrolled in postsecondary education increased with time and with affluence across a range of countries (World Bank 1999).[15] Table 5 shows long-term improvements in the levels of education for the United States, France, China, and India based on data from Maddison (Maddison, 1995; 1998). Globally, postsecondary enrolment increased from 6.8

Table 5 **Education (average number of years per person aged 15–64), c. 1820–2001**

	1820	1870	1913	1950	1973	1992	2001
France			6.99	9.58	11.69	15.96	
UK	2.00	4.44	8.82	10.60	11.66	14.09	15.45
USA	1.75	3.92	7.86	11.27	14.58	18.04	20.21
Japan	1.50	1.50	5.36	9.11	12.09	14.87	16.61
India				1.35	2.60	5.55	
China				1.60	4.09	8.93	

Sources: Maddison (1995, 1998, 2005b).

Figure 9 **Average income vs. economic freedom index, 2002**

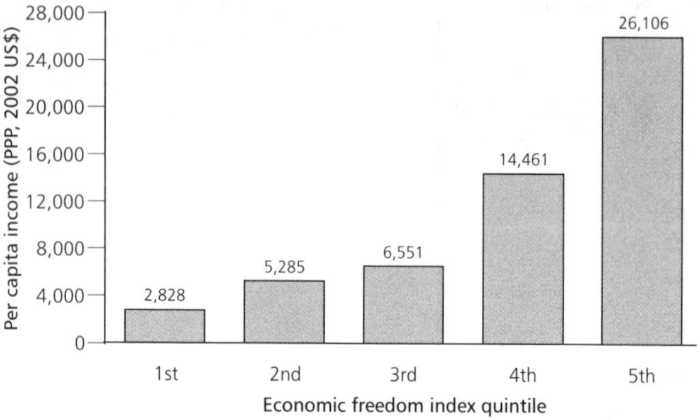

Source: Gwartney & Lawson (2004)

---

per cent in 1965 (World Bank 1999) to 25.6 per cent in 2001 (World Bank 2005a).

Literacy has increased worldwide as well. Between 1970 and the early 2000s, global illiteracy rates dropped from 46 per cent to 18 per cent (World Bank, 2005b; UNESCO, 2005). Complementing these increases are declines in the portion of the population aged 10 to 14 years who are working. Worldwide child labor measured this way has declined from 24.9 per cent in 1960 to 10.5 per cent in 2003 (World Bank, 2005b).

Political and economic freedom

In 1900, no country had universal adult suffrage; and only 12.4 per cent of the world's population enjoyed even limited democracy (Freedom House, 2002). Today 44.1 per cent of the world's population is deemed free by Freedom House, while another 18.6 per cent is considered partly free (Freedom House, 2005). Multiparty electoral systems were introduced in 113 countries in the quarter century following 1974 (UNDP, 2000).

Economic freedom is also ascendant around the world. Gwartney and his coworkers have constructed an index of economic freedom that takes into consideration personal choice, protection of private property, and freedom to use, exchange, or give property to another. According to this index, economic freedom increased from 1990 to 2002 in 102 of the 113 countries for which they had data for both years (Gwartney & Lawson, 2004; Gwartney, 1998). Their analysis indicates that the more economically free a country's population, the higher its economic growth (see Figure 9).

Human development index

While the above indicators make a strong case for a steady increase in many aspects of human well-being, it is possible to create a single indicator that incorporates a number of key measurements of well-being. The United Nations Development Program (UNDP) has popularized this approach with its Human Development Index. This index is based on life expectancy, education, and GDP per capita.[16]

According to the UNDP's latest *Human Development Report*, the Human Development Index (HDI) has been going up for most countries (UNDP, 2004). This index is somewhat arbitrary. It probably understates improvements for the majority of the world's population because it omits measurements of hunger and infant mortality, both of which have improved for the majority of the world's population. Nevertheless, the data show that:

◆ All but three of the 102 countries for which data are available showed improvement in the human development index between 1975 and 2002. The exceptions – Zambia, Zimbabwe, the Democratic Republic of Congo – were all in Sub-Saharan Africa. Each had increased its HDI between 1975 and 1985 (due to longer life expectancy and higher literacy rates despite a decline in GDP per capita).[17] However, these gains have been more than erased since then due to continuing economic declines in affluence, lower life expectancy due to HIV/AIDS and the resurgence of malaria, and the conflict in the Democratic Republic of Congo (which Zimbabwe chose to involve itself in, and which created refugee problems in neighboring countries, including Zambia) (*Daily Mail* and *Guardian*, 1998; UN High Commission on Refugees, 1998; 1999a; 1999b). Intermittent droughts and their effects, exacerbated by poor governance, also contributed to declines in Zambia and, to a greater extent, in Zimbabwe.

♦ Twenty of the 138 countries with available data showed a decline in HDI between 1990 and 2002. The majority of these countries (thirteen) were in Sub-Saharan Africa. For this set of countries too, the declines could be attributed to HIV/AIDS, resurgent malaria, and, in some areas, declining affluence as well as the direct or indirect effects of conflict within – or in nearby – countries.

♦ Of the 20 countries that had lower HDIs in 2002 than in 1990 (based on UNDP data), five were in the former Soviet Union; none were in Eastern Europe. Following the collapse of the communist regimes in Eastern Europe and the former Soviet Union, the drop in affluence in those areas accompanied by the deterioration in health status led to a decline in their HDIs. However, by the mid- to late-1990s, the economic situation in these countries had bottomed out. As a result, despite drops in the early-1990s, a number of these countries had higher HDIs in 2002 than in 1990.

♦ The remaining two countries with HDIs known to be lower in 2002 than 1990 were the Bahamas and Belize. Their declines, which were relatively minor, had nevertheless been reversed by the mid- to late-1990s.

In summary, the data indicate that human well-being has improved and continues to improve for the majority of the world's population. Over the past 15 to 20 years, however, well-being has been reduced in many Sub-Saharan, and continues to deteriorate. On the other hand, while matters had also regressed in Eastern European and the former Soviet Union nations, they now seem to be rebounding. These broad regional trends can be grasped when one considers that between the mid-1970s and the early-2000s:

♦ Affluence broadly advanced around the world for most income and regional groups with some exceptions – major oil exporting countries,[18] Sub-Saharan Africa, the former Soviet Union and a handful of Latin American countries (e.g., Nicaragua, Honduras, Peru, Bolivia and Argentina) (GGDC&CB 2005; World Bank 2005b; see also Figure 7). A common thread for the last three groups was that they all suffered from internal conflicts and/or failed economic policies.
♦ Life expectancy also increased generally around the world except in Sub-Saharan Africa and some areas in the former Soviet Union (see Figure 5).

The critical factor underlying declines in HDI is the lethal combination of deteriorating wealth exacerbated by serious public health problems (e.g., deadly new diseases such as HIV/AIDS or resurgent diseases such as malaria and tuberculosis), and vice versa. This is most painfully illustrated by the experience of Sub-Saharan countries.

When AIDS first appeared, it resulted in almost certain death. Developed countries, particularly the United States, launched a massive assault on the disease. U.S. deaths due to HIV/AIDS dropped from a high of approximately 52,000 in 1995 to 19,000 in 1998 (Centers for Disease Control and Prevention, 2002; 2003, 2005; Martin et al., 1999). Since then fatalities have leveled off at around 18,000 per year. In 1996, HIV/AIDS was the eighth leading cause of death in the U.S.; by 1998 it had dropped off the worst-fifteen list. But similar improvement is unlikely to occur soon in Sub-Saharan countries because they cannot afford the cost of treatment unless

Figure 10   **Human development index, US, 1850–2002**

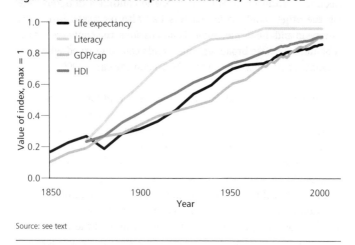

Source: see text

it's subsidized by the governments, charities, or industry from the richer nations.

For the United States, I have constructed an index similar to the HDI. Instead of education per se, I use literacy data, which are more readily available.[19] The minimum value for each of the three components corresponds roughly to what it was around 1820, approximately the start of industrialization. These are: 30 years for life expectancy, 73.7 per cent for literacy, and $1,257 (in 1990 International dollars) for GDP per capita (Costa & Stecker, 1997; Maddison, 2005a). For the maximum values, I assume 85 years, 100 per cent, and $40,000, respectively, similar to what UNDP assumes in its Human Development Reports (UNDP, 2000). My index assumes that literacy stays at 99 per cent after 1970. This actually understates the level of improvement since it does not account for long-term increases in the educational level of the average American. Based on these assumptions, Figure 10 shows trends in the composite HDI and its individual components for the United States from

1870–2002. Despite minor fluctuations in the components, there has been a general improvement in overall human well-being in the United States during the twentieth century. Each component improved throughout the century except for literacy, which reached saturation around 1970.

Have gaps in human well-being widened?

While human well-being has improved continually over the past two centuries, it is often claimed that inequalities continue to widen between the developed and developing nations. A typical observation is the following from the United Nations Development Program's 1999 Human Development Report:

Nearly 30 years ago the Pearson Commission began its report with the recognition that, "the widening gap between the developed and developing countries has become the central problem of our times.' But over the past three decades the income gap between the richest fifth and the poorest fifth has more than doubled. Narrowing the gaps between rich and poor … should become explicit global goals …" (UNDP, 1999).

As Figure 7 showed, there are wide – and, in many cases, growing – disparities in income between the richer and poorer countries. The gaps in per capita income between Western Europe and the United States and other regions have ballooned since the start of modern economic growth about two centuries ago, and many people remain terribly poor (Maddison, 1998; 1999a). However, the increasing gap in incomes between the richer and poorer countries does not mean that income gaps between all human beings in the world, regardless of where they live, is necessarily widening (Economist, 2004). More importantly, it does not follow that the well-being of the relatively poor groups is declining.

In 2001, according to the World Bank, 1.1 billion people, mainly in the developing world, lived in "absolute poverty" (defined as subsisting on less than one U.S. dollar per day based on 1993 purchasing power parity) (Ravallion, 2004). Nevertheless, contrary to conventional wisdom (Goklany, 2002), this was an improvement over matters in 1981 when 1.5 billion people fell into that category. In the intervening twenty years the world poverty rate declined from 33 to 18 per cent mainly because of robust economic growth in Asia, especially China and, to a lesser extent, India (Ravallion, 2004). On the other hand, the numbers and proportion of the population living in absolute poverty has increased in Africa, because of its generally dismal economic performance and its inability to cope not only with new diseases such as AIDS/HIV but also the more familiar diseases of malaria and TB. Other analyses also affirm that the number and proportion of people living in absolute poverty has declined worldwide, but not in Sub-Saharan Africa (Sala-i-Martin, 2002; Bhalla, 2002). However, they estimate fewer people live in absolute poverty worldwide than does the World Bank (Economist, 2004; Sala-i-Martin, 2002; Bhalla, 2002).

Measurements that describe human well-being more directly than income show the same general pattern. Yes, gaps in life expectancy and infant mortality between the more and less developed countries are substantial. But, these gaps have narrowed by 50 per cent since the 1950s. The gap in life expectancy was 25.0 years in the 1950–1955 but fell to 12.3 years in the 1995–2000, while the gap in infant mortality fell from 121 to 59 deaths per 1,000 live births (UNPD, 2004a). For these indicators, the gaps between Sub-Saharan Africa and the developed countries also shrank from the 1950s through the late 1980s, but since then, for reasons already articulated, the life expectancy gap has grown substantially (see Table 2 and Figure 5) while the infant mortality gap continued to shrink, but at a much reduced rate. Similarly, hunger is less prevalent worldwide than it was thirty years ago, and except for Sub-Saharan Africa the number of people suffering from chronic under-nourishment has declined in both absolute and relative terms (FAO, 2002; 2004). And with respect to child labor, another critical indicator of human well-being, the gap between richer and poorer nations has shrunk since at least 1960. Here, too, the shrinkage has been least for the gap between Sub-Saharan Africa and other income groups (Goklany, 2002).

Figure 11 **Rural (R) vs. Urban (U) divide access to safe water and sanitation, 2000**

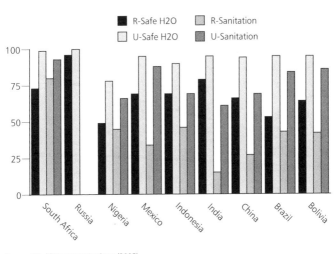

Source: World Resources Institute (2005)

Thus, while income inequalities might have widened between countries, they seem to have shrunk between people. More importantly, in the aspects of human well-being that are truly critical – life expectancy, infant mortality, hunger – the world is far more equal today than it was a half century ago, notwithstanding relapses in Sub-Saharan Africa and, to a lesser extent, some countries in the former Soviet Union.

Are rural residents better off?

Historically, as the currently developed countries embarked on modern economic growth, the welfare of urban dwellers generally lagged behind that of their rural compatriots (Easterlin, 1996; Fogel, 2000; Lerner & Anderson, 1965). Fogel notes that U.S. cities with

Figure 12   **Cereal yield vs. income, 1975–2003**

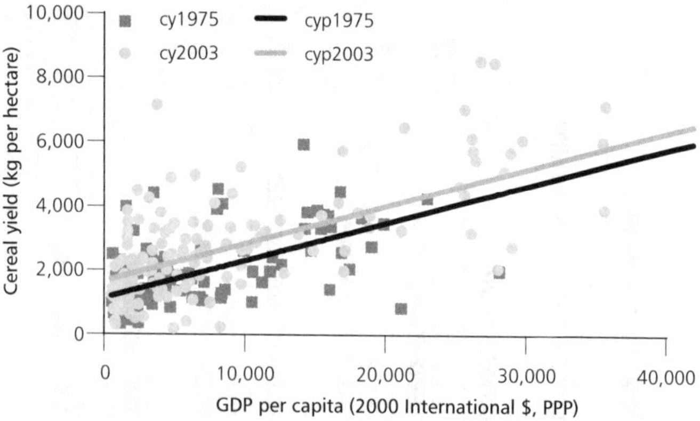

Source: Based on data from World Bank (2005b)

populations above 50,000 had twice the death rates of rural areas in the 1830s (Fogel, 2000). Evidently, overcrowding, lack of knowledge about hygiene, and the lack of safe water and sanitation made urban populations more susceptible to contagious diseases such as cholera, typhoid and tuberculosis. The image of urban suffering compared to a healthier rural life is reinforced in the mind of anyone who visits the over-crowded and polluted urban areas of the developing world, which give the impression that life in developing countries is worsening as cities grow.

In fact, however, urban residents are better off in most developing countries. When measured by the United Nations' Human Development Index and its related Human Poverty Index, there is more progress and less deprivation in urban areas (UNDP, 2000). For instance, in Swaziland, the rural HDI was 35 per cent below the urban level in 1999, reflecting less access to safe water, sanitation and public health services; lower rates of literacy; and higher rates of undernourishment. Figure 11 shows the urban–rural divide for access to safe water and access to sanitation for 2000 in some of today's more populous developing nations. In each case, rural residents have lower access.

The cycle of progress

We have seen that human welfare advanced more in the past century than it did in all the rest of mankind's tenure on earth. I contend that this progress in human well-being was sustained, and perhaps even initiated, by a cycle composed of the mutually reinforcing, co-evolving forces of economic growth, technological change and free trade.

Technology increases food production through various mechanisms. It boosts yields through special seeds, mechanization, judicious application of inputs such as fertilizers and lime, and reductions of losses to pests, spoilage and wastage. Use of this technology is closely linked to economic development because not everyone can afford it. One reason why poorer countries have lower cereal yields is that farmers cannot afford sufficient fertilizer and other yield-enhancing technologies (Goklany, 1998; 2000). Thus we see in Figure 12 that yields increase over time and with wealth.[20] Higher crop yields translate into more food. And if food deficits exist despite increases in domestic production, with greater wealth they can augment food supplies by purchasing food and agricultural products through trade on the open market (see Figure 2). Thus, global trade in conjunction with improved technology increases food security (Goklany, 1995; 1998). The infrastructure – ships, refrigerated trucks, roads, and rails – that trade depends on, as well as financial mechanisms that transfer money and hedge risks, are products of technology, capital, and human resources.

More food also means more healthy people who are less likely to succumb to infectious and parasitic diseases. That – along with capital and human resources targeted on improvements in medicine and public health (see Figure 2) – has reduced mortality and increased life expectancy worldwide (Fogel, 1995; World Health

Organisation, 1999). Hence, as populations become more affluent, mortality decreases, as shown in Figure 6 for infant mortality, and life expectancy increases, as shown in Figure 4 (Goklany, 1999b; Pritchett & Summers, 1996; World Bank 1993). Thus, a wealthier population is healthier.

A healthier population is also wealthier because it is more productive (Barro, 1997; Bloom, 1999; Fogel, 1995; World Bank, 1993; World Health Organisation, 1999). Fogel estimates that the level of food supplies in eighteenth century France were so low that the bottom 10 per cent of the labor force could not generate the energy needed for regular work, and the next 10 per cent had enough energy for about half an hour of heavy work (or less than 3 hours of light work) (Fogel, 1995).

Citing a United Nations study, Easterlin notes that when malaria was eradicated in Mymensingh (now in Bangladesh), crop yields increased 15 per cent because farmers could spend more time and effort on cultivation (Easterlin, 1996). In other areas elimination of seasonal malaria enabled farmers to plant a second crop. According to the World Bank, the near-eradication of malaria in Sri Lanka between 1947 and 1977 raised its national income by an estimated 9 per cent (World Bank, 199?). A joint study by the Harvard University Center for International Development and the London School of Hygiene and Tropical Medicine estimated that if malaria had been eradicated in 1965, Africa's GDP would have been 32 per cent higher by 2000 (Malaria Foundation International, 2000; *Guardian*, 2000).

A healthier and longer-lived population is also likely to invest more time and effort in developing its human capital which contributes to the creation and diffusion of technology. It is not surprising that levels of education have gone up with life expectancy or that researchers today spend what at one period was literally a lifetime to acquire skills and expertise necessary for careers in research.

In addition, several measures undertaken to improve public health provided a bonus in economic productivity. Draining swamps not only reduced malaria but also added to the agricultural land base (Easterlin, 1996). The World Bank reported that an international program to curtail river blindness, the Onchocersiasis Control Program, a mixture of drug therapy and insecticide spraying, had protected 30 million people (including 9 million children) from the disease (World Bank, 1993), and would free up 25 million hectares (60 million acres) of land for cultivation and settlement. Similarly, improved food supplies and nutrition by themselves may aid learning. This is one of the premises behind school meals programs (Watkins, 1997).

Improvements specific to health, food, and agriculture also benefit from a larger, more general cycle in which broad technological change, economic growth and global trade reinforce each other. Other technologies – invented for other reasons – have led to medical advances and improved productivity or reduced the environmental impacts of the food and agricultural sector. For example, computers, lasers, and global positioning systems permit precision agriculture to optimize the timing and quantities of fertilizers, water, and pesticides, increasing productivity while reducing environmental impacts. Plastics – essential for food packaging and preservation – also increase productivity of the food and agricultural sector. Transportation of every kind increases the ability to move inputs and outputs from farms to markets, and vice versa. Broad advances in physics and engineering have led to new or improved medical technologies, including electricity (without which virtually no present day hospital or operating room could function), x-rays, nuclear magnetic resonance, lasers and refrigeration.

These specific impacts do not exhaust the benefits of broad economic growth, technological change and global trade. Technological change in general reinforces economic growth (Barro, 1997; Goklany, 1998), giving countries more resources to research and develop technological improvements and to increase education (Goklany, 1995).

As Figure 8 showed, the proportion of the eligible population enrolled in postsecondary schools increases with wealth. Anecdotal evidence reinforces the importance of wealth in developing human capital. Wealthy countries have the best education. An informal survey of fellow immigrants suggests that many of the most talented people from poorer countries end up in the universities and research establishments of the richer nations not only because they expect a higher quality of education but because they anticipate job opportunities that will better use their education and talents. In 1993, for instance, ten of the richest (and most well-educated) countries accounted for 84 per cent of global research and development and controlled more than 80 per cent of the patents acquired in the United States and in developing countries (UNDP, 1999).

Freer trade contributes directly to greater economic growth, helps disseminate new technologies, and creates competitive pressures to invent and innovate (Goklany, 1995). As an example, trade accelerated the cleanup of automobile emissions in the United States because the threat of cleaner cars from imports advanced the introduction of catalytic converters in the 1970s (Barbour, 1980; Seskin, 1978).

By expanding competition, trade helps contain the costs of basic infrastructure, including water supply and sanitation systems. A vivid example of the importance of trade in improving human well-being comes from Iraq. Because of trade sanctions, it was unable to properly operate and maintain its water, sanitation, and electricity systems, resulting in significant public health problems (United Nations, 200?).

Trade also helps augment food supplies. In fact, between 2000 and 2002, international trade allowed developing countries to enhance their grain supplies by 11.6 per cent (FAO, 2005).[21] The corresponding figure for Sub-Saharan Africa was 23.5 per cent. Thus, in the absence of trade, food prices would have been higher (which would have priced more poor people out of the market), and hunger and malnutrition would have been more prevalent in developing countries. Also, cultivation of marginal lands would probably have increased to narrow the shortfall between food supply and demand.

In terms of income alone, trade raises incomes for both the poor and the rich (Dollar & Kraay, 2000; Frankel & Romer, 1999). Dollar and Kraay (Dollar & Kraay, 2000) also find that economic growth favors rich and poor equally, confirming analyses by Ravallion and Chen (Ravallion & Chen, 1997) and Easterly and Rebelo (Easterly & Rebelo, 1993). Similarly, increased protection of property rights and fiscal discipline (defined as low government consumption) raise overall incomes without increasing inequality.[112]

Thus, each link in the cycle – higher yields, increased food supplies, lower mortalities and higher life expectancies – is strengthened by the general forces of economic growth, technological change and trade. Qualitatively, at least, this explains why all the figures for cereal yields (Figure 12), food supplies per capita (Figure 2), safe water (Figure 3), life expectancy (Figure 4) and post-secondary education (Figure 8) when plotted against per capita income look similar, and all look like mirror images of Figure 6 for infant mortality rates.

However, the experience of Sub-Saharan Africa warns us that a cycle that moves forward can also go into reverse if a deteriorating public health and a declining economy undermine each other.

Conclusion

Since 1800, global population has increased over six-fold (FAO, 2003; McEvedy & Jones, 1978). Manufacturing industries have increased over seventy-five times in value (Bairoch, 1982) and carbon dioxide emissions from fossil fuel combustion has increased 600 times (Marland et al., 2005). Overall, global economic product has multiplied more than sixty-fold.[22] Despite the environmental disruption which might have been caused by all this activity, the state of humanity has never been better. Specifically:

♦ In the last two centuries, the average person's life expectancy at birth has doubled, infant mortality is less than a third of what it used to be, and real income has grown sevenfold. Food is more affordable. A child is less likely to go to bed hungry and a woman is far less likely to die in child birth.

◆ Children are more likely to be in school than at work. People are more educated and freer to choose their rulers and express their views. They are more likely to live under the rule of law and are less fearful of being arbitrarily deprived of life or limb, freedom, property, wealth and other basic human rights. Not only is work less physically demanding, but people work fewer hours and have more leisure time and money to devote to optional pursuits.

◆ Although gaps between richer and poorer nations may be expanding in terms of per capita income, gaps in the critical aspects of human well-being (particularly life expectancy, infant mortality, hunger and malnourishment and literacy) have for the most part shrunk over the past half-century, despite regression in Sub-Saharan Africa and in the countries of the former Soviet Union.

◆ Developing nations on the whole have benefited from knowledge and technology generated in developed countries. With respect to the most critical indicators of human well-being – life expectancy, infant mortality and hunger – developing countries are better off than were developed countries at equivalent levels of income. These improvements have come from reducing death and disease due to inadequate food supplies and infectious and parasitic diseases such as cholera, malaria, typhoid, diarrhea, dysentery and other water-related illnesses.

◆ The reductions in water-related diseases and diseases caused or aggravated by inadequate food and nutrition have not yet run their full course. Thus, improvements in infant mortality and life expectancy in developing countries may continue, shrinking the gap between developing and developed countries for these indicators.

However, once the easy and relatively cheap improvements in health and life expectancy have been captured, the gap may widen again. Further improvements will come only through dealing with nontraditional diseases such as AIDs and the diseases of affluence. While the United States has reduced deaths from HIV/AIDS by almost 65 per cent between 1995 and 2003, treatment is expensive and unaffordable to most in the developing world. This illustrates not only the need for improved technology but also the importance of economic growth as well as trade in ideas and products.

It must be noted, however, that like other cycles, the Cycle of Progress can also go in reverse. Whatever gains the last half-century brought to Sub-Saharan Africa, they could be more than erased unless countries in that region undertake the policy and institutional reforms necessary to break the vicious cycle of falling incomes and poorer health that currently grips many parts of that area.

Economic growth, technological change and trade become even more crucial for the continued improvement in the state of humanity when one considers that global population may grow anywhere between 15 and 120 per cent during this century, according to the United Nations' latest projections (United Nations Population Division, 2004a; 2004b).

2 South Africa's healthcare under threat

Johan Biermann

Introduction

South Africa's health care is provided by the government (public) health sector, funded by taxpayers, and a private sector that is financed in various ways. The government sector provides care to those who cannot afford private care and are not beneficiaries of private philanthropy. The private sector provides services to members of medical aid funds, those who choose to pay out of pocket for health care, employees of companies in company-owned and funded facilities, government contract patients, and those who benefit from private philanthropy.

Under South Africa's apartheid system, health services were racially segregated. The demise of apartheid combined with rapid urbanisation resulted in an ever-increasing mismatch between the location of government hospitals and clinics and the geographical distribution of the population. Large centrally situated government hospitals in the cities, previously reserved for use by the white population, now serve everyone and are struggling to cope with the demand for health care.

The government health sector is under strain, suffering from shortages of medicines, poor and unclean facilities, poor service delivery, rude personnel and a shortage of doctors and staff (National Dept of Health, 2002). In 2002, of the 197,898 provincial staff positions across the various health professions 84,205 (42 per cent) posts were vacant (Health Systems Trust, 2002).

Large numbers of medical personnel have left, and are leaving the country for Australia, New Zealand, Canada, the United Kingdom and the United States. There are 600 South African doctors registered to practise in New Zealand while 10 per cent of Canada's hospital-based physicians and 6 per cent of the total health workforce in Britain is South African (Health Systems Trust, 2004).

Associated with staff shortages, there is a severe lack of skills across the entire spectrum of health services provision, with the government sector lacking highly trained personnel, sophisticated technology and managerial skills (Health Systems Trust, 2003).

By contrast, South Africa's private health-care sector is one of the best in the world. It provides health-care services to a large cross-section of the population and attracts foreigners as health tourists because it offers an excellent service at internationally competitive prices. South African private hospital groups have won tenders to provide health services in the United Kingdom. Medical schemes are innovative and are exporting some of their ideas to other countries. The world's leading pharmaceutical companies are represented in the country and many have manufacturing plants and carry out clinical trials in South Africa. Most governments of developing countries would welcome a private health-care sector of the high quality that exists in South Africa and to see such substantial investments in health care in their own countries since a relatively large private health-care sector allows a government to utilise its scarce tax resources to provide better health care for the poor. Counter-intuitively, the South African National Health Department does not seem to recognise either the value of the private health-care sector to the people and the economy of South Africa, nor the benefit to poor South Africans. This must be puzzling to an impartial observer.

The government is disturbed by the rapid growth of what it regards as an expensive private health sector, which it believes is providing superior health care to the affluent few while the under-resourced and under-staffed government health sector is stagnant and struggles to provide care to the many. In response, it has adopted legislation that aims to establish a unified national health system in which the government's health department will tightly regulate, plan and manage public and private health-care provision.

This paper examines the threat to health-care delivery posed by South Africa's recent health legislation, particularly the National Health Act 2003, and offers suggestions for an alternative health-care dispensation in which all patients, rich and poor, would receive high-quality private care.

South Africa's health-care challenge

One of the basic assumptions that characterises the debate about South Africa's health care is the respective proportions of the population that are served by the government and private sectors. The government's policy documents claim that 84 per cent of the South African population depend on the government health sector (National Treasury, 2001; Ornell et al., 2001). This figure is apparently based on the assumption that the approximate 16 per cent of the population who are members of private medical schemes, are the only patients treated in the private health sector.

However, as explained below, the fact that approximately 16 per cent of the population are members of private medical schemes does not necessarily mean that the remaining 84 per cent are treated in the government health sector. This automatic but incorrect assumption is perpetuated in the Draft Charter of the Health Sector of the Republic of South Africa, published in 2005, which claims that there is a small minority of South Africans (between 15 and 20 per cent of the population), who have a high degree of access to health services and a large majority (between 75 and 80 per cent of the population), who have either limited access to health services or no access at all (National Department of Health, 2005). The "high degree of access" refers to that proportion of the population who can afford private health care and the "large majority" to those who, if they needed it, would obtain health care in the government health sector.

Accurately determining the percentage of the population that is dependent on the government health sector is of vital importance.

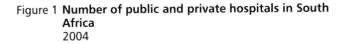

Figure 1 **Number of public and private hospitals in South Africa** 2004

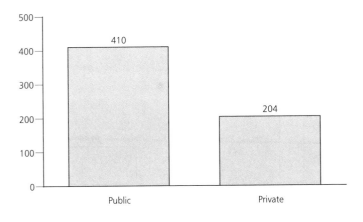

It is even more important to determine how many people actually use government health services, the frequency of that use, and nature of the services they utilise. The possibility that some people may, or are entitled to, use a particular service does not mean that they will do so. If future policies are to be based on incorrect figures for the respective quantities of services provided by the government and private health services, it will have serious consequences for future health policies. It is thus essential that an effort be made to obtain a better understanding of the existing situation.

A cursory glance at the available hospital and hospital bed statistics would appear to support the government's claim that the government sector supplies health-care services to all but a small proportion of the population. In 2004 there were 410 public hospitals with 105 665 beds (79.6 per cent), and 204 private hospitals with 26 593 beds (20.4 per cent)[1] (Figures 1 and 2)

Despite the fact that only about 20 per cent of the hospital beds

Figure 2 **Number of public and private hospital beds in South Africa**
2004

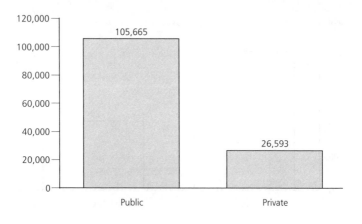

are private, there are indications that close to half the population may use private health services. This can be shown by building a picture of the South African health market, bearing in mind that accurate numbers are not available and wide variations are found in population and poverty statistics.

According to official figures, South Africa had a population of 44.8 million people in October 2001 (Statistics South Africa, 2003). Poverty estimates range from 40 per cent (Government Communication & Information System 2002) to as high as 60 per cent (Department of Provincial & Local Government, 2001) of the population. Based on a poverty datum line of R800 per month for a household, 52 per cent of households lived in poverty in 1996 (Health Systems Trust, 2003). It would thus be safe to conclude that at least half the population, or 22.4 million people in 2001, could not afford comprehensive formal health care.

Research shows that in 1999 about 20 per cent of the population

Table 1 **Comparison of sectors used by medical aid and non-medical aid members (Doherty et al. 2002)**

Place of consultation	1995		1998	
	Without medical scheme	Medical scheme members	Without medical scheme	Medical scheme members
	%	%	%	%
Government sector	71.2	32.6	68.5	20.5
Private sector	28.8	67.4	31.4	79.5

had private medical insurance cover, consisting of medical scheme membership (which covered an estimated 16 per cent of the population), other forms of health insurance, and workplace health services provided by private firms (National Treasury, 2001; National Treasury, 2003; Cornell et al., 2001). At that time it was estimated that potentially 30 per cent of non-scheme members (nearly 25 per cent of the total population) used private health services on a direct payment basis (National Treasury, 2001; National Treasury, 2003; Cornell et al., 2001). Furthermore, those who paid out of pocket used either private or government care, while some used both, as did members of medical schemes. This was confirmed by surveys conducted in 1995 and 1998 (Doherty et al., 2002), summarised in Table 1.

These figures reflect a slight trend towards greater use of private health-care services.

An important consideration too is that many South Africans consult traditional healers and use traditional remedies. According to the Minister of Health traditional healers are the first to be consulted in as many of 80 per cent of all consultations.[2] Also, there are many people who make little or no use of the services of health-care providers.

Based on the available evidence, a range of between 16 per cent and 45 per cent of the population use private health care, and potentially between 55 per cent and 84 per cent use the government health sector.

Table 2 **Estimate of South African Medical Scheme Market 2001**

	% of RSA population	Persons
Member of medical scheme	16	7,272,640
Not a member but potential member of medical scheme	30	13,636,200
Poor (unable to afford medical scheme membership)	54	23,891,160
Total	100	44,800,000

This can be compared to a study of the market potential for medical schemes, undertaken by a private medical insurer, which estimated that 16 per cent of the population was covered by medical insurance in 2001, that a further 30 per cent could afford medical insurance but was not insured, and that 54 per cent of the population was unable to afford medical insurance (Gore, 2002). Among this last group are some who purchase private health care on an irregular basis and would not automatically become government health-service patients.

As the estimates quoted in the above study are in broad agreement with medical scheme membership and poverty estimates they are used to construct a broad picture of the South African health-care market in 2001. This is shown in Table 2 above.

If the composition of the health-care market set out in the table is correct, the government health sector spends its money on a potential 54 per cent of the population (24 million people) and not 84 per cent as claimed. However, this makes the challenge of providing health care to the poor no less daunting. It is huge, not only in terms of the number of poor people, but also in terms of difficulty of delivery as 75 per cent (Government Communication & Information System, 2002) of the poor live in rural areas where health services are least developed.

The National Health Act 2003

By the government's own admission its health sector is not coping with the demand for health care. The Minister of Health, Dr Manto Tshabalala-Msimang, has been quoted as stating that the health system was 'in shambles'[3] and Dr Kgosi Letlape, chairman of the South African Medical Association, has described the situation in the government health sector as 'horrendous'.[4]

In response to the situation, the government has embarked on an ongoing programme of expanding and upgrading government health facilities and services, while, on the regulatory level, it has adopted the National Health Act 2003, which seeks to establish a unified national health system over which the National Department of Health will wield enormous power.

The ostensible aim of the new health legislation is to allow the health department to control and manage the entire health system, so that it can reallocate and redistribute private and public health resources in a "more equitable" manner. The unified national health system envisaged in the legislation is to be characterised by (National Health Act, 2003; National Department of Health, 200?):

- Planning interventions in the form of national, provincial and district health plans.
- Economic interventions in the form of price controls, compulsory minimum benefit requirements for medical schemes, limitations on risk rating of patients by medical schemes, prohibitions on re-insurance by medical schemes, and the establishment of a system of social health insurance.
- Licensing in the form of certificates of need (CON) requirements for the establishment or expansion of facilities and the introduction of new technologies, enabling the Minister of Health to control the number of private hospitals and beds, the location of new hospitals, where doctors may practise, and the dispensing of medicines by general practitioners.
- Compulsory public service for medical graduates, prescribed medical education curricula emphasising primary health care

over specialist care, prohibition of insurance policies that cover medical expenses, compulsory acceptance of members by medical aid funds, compulsory membership of medical aid schemes and limitations on medical aid funds and insurers, restricting their ability to introduce innovative and more cost-effective services.

The Act introduces South Africa's own version of a centrally planned, socialised health system, in which the facilities, the equipment, the doctors, nurses and other medical professionals, and services, whether in the public or private sector, have been regulated, licensed, certified, approved and price-controlled by the government.

A critique of the recent legislation

The unified national health system envisaged in the National Health Act 2003 ignores the failures of the country's existing government health sector and the evidence from other countries with government (socialised) health systems which shows that these systems are inefficient, expensive, lack sophisticated medical equipment, have long waiting lists for medical procedures and appointments with specialists, do not provide equal access to and equal treatment for all citizens, provide lower quality health care than private systems, control costs by rationing care and medical technology, and fall far short of attaining their lofty ideals. The experience in the countries that serve as role models for South Africa's health-care plans, such as the United Kingdom and Canada, is particularly relevant (Goodman & Herrick, 2002; Esmail & Walker, 2005; Piper, 2002).

Centrally planned health care

In a fully socialised health system everything is centrally planned, controlled and co-ordinated. The government owns all the hospitals and medical facilities and government health planners determine how many hospitals and beds there should be, where they should be located, the type and quantity of services and medicines that will be available, the salaries health-care professionals may earn, the amount of money that may be spent on particular procedures and technologies, the type of equipment that may be installed at hospitals and clinics, and the prices that will be charged for health-care procedures and medicines.

South Africa's new National Health Act subjects its private health-care providers to the same controls applied in a socialised health system. Private care, from now on, will thus be private only insofar as health establishments will be privately owned. The government will be planning the entire health-care system, with dire consequences for all patients, rich and poor.

A government attempting to plan and/or provide health care to an entire nation is confronted by the insurmountable obstacles faced by centrally planned and co-ordinated systems: the impossibility of knowing everything necessary to ensure effective, efficient and equitable delivery of goods and services, the ignoring or obliteration of signals provided by prices, the complexity of centralised planning, the difficulty of forecasting the future, and the inefficiency of governments in general.

Centrally prohibited health care

When governments impose plans on their citizens, whatever does not fit in with those plans becomes illegal. This observation lead the economist Murray N Rothbard to remark that a centrally planned economy is a centrally prohibited economy (Rothhard, 2004). Socialised care becomes government-prohibited health care: nothing may be done without prior government approval. So, for example, South African doctors will be prohibited from opening medical practices in areas that government health-care planners believe are adequately served. The planners will somehow know exactly where all doctors should practise and what procedures and equipment they should use in order to meet the needs of all patients.

Government health systems are inefficient
Compared to its private health-care providers, South Africa's government health sector is slow, unwieldy and inefficient because it is not subject to the discipline entailed in making profits, avoiding losses, and earning an adequate return on capital invested. The government sector can always obtain more funds from taxpayers, or, if government health costs and demands for service get really out of hand, ration health care.

The proponents of government health care regard the economic rationing of health care as inequitable, but regard rationing of health care by governments as justifiable, notwithstanding the promises to provide health-care services to all who need them. A health department discussion document makes this admission:

> *Consequently, the achievement of equity within the context of a budget constraint implies the conscious application of a limit on the services that are made available on an equitable basis. In addition, the introduction of new services would have to be on the basis that they lower the costs and improve the outcomes of existing interventions. As the wealth of a country increases, it will become feasible to increase the amount of services provided on an equitable basis.* (National Department of Health, 2002)

In the government health-care sector, therefore, it is said to be for reasons of equity that health services are either limited or not available. However, when economic rationing occurs in the private health sector the proponents of socialised health care describe such rationing as inequitable.

Government health systems, like all government activities world wide, are encumbered by bureaucratic procedures and are consequently unavoidably inefficient. They cannot compete with private providers. The contracts awarded to private health-care providers by the British National Health Service (NHS), which is under severe pressure to speed up the provision of medical care for the more than one million NHS patients who are on waiting lists for surgical procedures, provides an illustration of the greater efficiency of private providers.

South African private hospital groups, Netcare and Life Healthcare are among the companies to whom contracts have been awarded.[5] The contracts require the performance of thousands of medical procedures annually, such as cataract procedures, orthopaedic surgery (including hip and knee replacements), ambulatory surgical procedures (including arthroscopies), general surgical procedures, and ear, nose, throat and oral procedures. Life Healthcare, in a joint venture with Care UK PLC, has been contracted to construct and operate three Diagnostic Treatment Centres in England, which include consulting rooms, radiology (including X-ray, CT scanner, MRI and ultrasound), pathology laboratories, theatres, ICU beds, general beds and a rehabilitation gymnasium.

The contracts awarded confirm the superiority of private care over government care as well as the competency of South African companies in providing world-class medical care. It is unfortunate for government sector patients that these resources are not being used locally to alleviate the pressure on the government sector.

The quality of care and the competitive cost of private health care have made South Africa a destination for medical tourism. Patients come to South Africa from the United Kingdom, where they are entitled to free health care, and pay for medical treatment out of their own resources to avoid the long waiting times for medical care in the British National Health Service (NHS).[6]

The knowledge problem
Proponents of government health systems argue that such systems ensure the optimal and productive utilisation of the country's health-care resources. Their arguments are based on the fallacy that there is someone who actually knows how to allocate health-care resources in an equitable manner and what optimal utilisation of health resources would comprise. However, as explained by Nobel laureate Friedrich Hayek, such a person or organisation cannot exist. Hayek's writings teach us that government planning cannot achieve

the efficiency in the use of resources which market processes make possible because the knowledge required to do so is dispersed among thousands or millions of individuals (Hayek, 1944; 1976). All government enterprises and state-controlled economies fall prey to what has become known as "the knowledge problem" and South Africa is no exception.

To see why it is impossible for government to centrally plan the entire health-care system, let us turn to the National Health Act 2003 to see what the Act requires the health planners to take into account when granting or refusing an application for a certificate of need.

In issuing or renewing a certificate of need for a new hospital, clinic, day-care facility, or expanding an existing one, the introduction of new technologies such as CAT, Sonar and MRI scanners, or employment of more nurses and doctors the Director-General of Health, under **Section 36(3),** must take into account:

- The need to ensure consistency of health services development in terms of national, provincial and municipal planning.
- The need to promote an equitable distribution and rationalisation of health services and health-care resources, and the need to correct inequities based on racial, gender, economic and geographical factors.
- The need to promote an appropriate mix of public and private health services.
- The demographics and epidemiological characteristics of the population to be served.
- The potential advantages and disadvantages for existing public and private health services and for any affected communities.
- The need to protect or advance persons or categories of persons designated in terms of the Employment Equity Act, 1998 (Act No. 55 of 1998), within the emerging small, medium and micro-enterprise sector.
- The potential benefits of research and development with respect to the improvement of health service delivery.

- The need to ensure that ownership of facilities does not create perverse incentives for health service providers and health workers.
- If applicable, the quality of health services rendered by the applicant in the past.
- The probability of the financial sustainability of the health establishment or health agency.
- The need to ensure the availability and appropriate utilisation of human resources and health technology.
- Whether the private health establishment is for profit or not.

Section 36(4) of the Act empowers the Director-General to investigate any issue relating to an application for the issue or renewal of a certificate of need and may call for such further information as may be necessary in order to make a decision upon a particular application. **Section 36(5)** stipulates that the Director-General may issue or renew a certificate of need subject to:

- Compliance by the holder with national operational norms and standards for health establishments and health agencies, as the case may be.

Any condition regarding:
- The nature, type or quantum of services to be provided by the health establishment or health agency.
- Human resources and diagnostic and therapeutic equipment and the deployment of human resources or the use of such equipment.
- Public private partnerships.
- Types of training to be provided by the health establishment or health agency.

Section 37 stipulates that a certificate of need is valid for a prescribed period, but such prescribed period may not exceed 20 years. When an application for a certificate of need is received the health planners in the offices of the Director-General of Health are faced with an impossible task. To properly process an application the health planners have to be all but omniscient, an impossible expectation. They need to know the health needs of everybody in a given geographical area: the number likely to fall ill, the type of illnesses likely to befall them, the existing number of facilities, beds, and equipment, the rates of utilisation of services and facilities, how effective the doctors are, the effectiveness of treatments and medicines, and so on. The equation becomes even more complicated when one considers that people do not necessarily use the health services located closest to them. How does the health planner then determine the trading area for a particular facility?

Let us assume that a gynaecologist applies for a certificate of need to purchase a new sonar scanner. The health planner has to determine the existing number of scanners serving the area, the number of women likely to fall pregnant, the number and utilisation of existing sonar scanners, the number of medical personnel and services available for maternity purposes, the financial sustainability of existing gynaecological practices, and so on. And, once that is done, how does a health planner or the Minister of Health determine for how long a certificate of need should be valid?

Add the policy considerations prescribed in the Act (such as the "appropriate mix" of public and private facilities, compliance with the national, provincial and municipal health plans, correcting inequities based on race, gender, and economic and geographical factors) and a realistic assessment of all the factors becomes impossible. Since there is no objective way to decide on these issues, decisions will ultimately be based on ideological and political expediency.

In view of the complexities, applicants will be required to motivate their applications and provide the information and statistical data necessary to enable the health planners to make decisions. Doctors and service providers will have to pay consultants to prepare applications on their behalf, increasing the cost of providing medical care. However, no matter what information is provided, health-care providers will be at the complete mercy of the health bureaucracy.

Planning and prices

South Africa's health planners are instructed by the new laws and regulations to ignore demand, prices, and the wishes of patients. But, if prices are interfered with, or a market is not allowed to function, there is no way of reconciling supply with consumer demand.

> *The market and prices make the discovery process possible that allows people to utilise more facts than any other known system. By means of prices we constantly discover new facts that improve our adaptation to the ever-changing circumstances of the world in which we live.* (Hayek, 1976)

In the absence of prices determined in a competitive market, economic calculation becomes not merely difficult, but impossible (Von Mises, 1990). To overcome this problem in the former communist countries, economic planners had to copy prices set on world markets. When one considers that central planners in the Soviet Union had to fix 24 million[7] prices, and had to keep adjusting them, relative to all other prices, as conditions changed, one realises that central planning did not just happen to fail, it was impossible for it to succeed.

In a market economy the task of "fixing" prices is undertaken by hundreds of millions of people individually keeping track of the relatively few prices they need to know for their own decision-making.

In a health-care system under political and bureaucratic domination, price controls are invariably introduced, supposedly to make care affordable and to contain costs. This obliterates the very price information system that would allow health-care resources to be utilised most efficiently. By ignoring prices, politicians, health-care planners and policy makers have no means of knowing what the optimal allocation of health resources should be and the fact that they are generally driven by non-economic motives makes matters worse. As a result, health-care delivery becomes a product of political and bureaucratic expediency rather than a response to real health-care needs. Equity, efficiency and effective delivery become the casualties of the absence of market prices to co-ordinate production, supply and delivery of health care to consumers. This is what South Africa's citizens will face if its health department continues on its current course.

Dealing with complexity

The proponents of government health care argue that the market cannot be relied on to allocate health-care resources equitably and efficiently. For example, while in the cities there are a number of private hospitals, most rural towns have none. This leads to the conclusion that urban dwellers are over-serviced due to a duplication of services and as a result rural residents are under-served and deprived of the care they need. Planners then conclude that government should take over the planning and direction of health care in order to resolve what they view as market failure. They ignore the reality that the spatial distribution of economic activities, including private health-care facilities, are the result of a virtually endless number of variables, impossible to be grasped by any individual or planning agency. Modern economic activities are so complex that no government can successfully centrally plan and direct them or any of their components, including health-care delivery.

Evidence of the order achieved by the market surrounds us in South Africa. A patient can make an appointment to see a general practitioner or specialist at a scheduled time, leave the doctor's rooms with a script and present it to his or her pharmacist of choice. The pharmacist, not knowing that a patient would require that particular medicine that day, would in almost all cases be in a position to immediately supply the required product. In the case of a dispensing doctor the patient has the added convenience of purchasing the medicine directly from the doctor. Even in non-emergency cases advanced diagnostic procedures, such as Magnetic Resonance Imaging (MRI) and Computed Tomography (CT) scans are available within hours.[8] Compare this level of availability with that found in socialised health-care systems. Across Canada the median waiting time for CT scans is 5.2 weeks and that for MRI 12.6 weeks.[9] In the United Kingdom patients wait six months or more for MRI scans in 40 per cent of NHS trusts and four months or more for CT scans in almost a third of NHS trusts.[10]

Life for patients in South Africa's centrally planned government health facilities is very different from that in the private health-care sector, with public facilities exhibiting many of the problems common to socialised health systems. Patients wait for hours, and sometimes days, to see a doctor, and medicines may or may not be available. If patients require specialised treatment they are referred to "higher order" facilities, such as district hospitals, where the waiting starts all over again. However, while cross-country comparisons are difficult, waiting times for services in South Africa's government health-care facilities appear to be shorter than those in the national health systems of both the United Kingdom and Canada. In real emergencies patients also have the option of scraping together the cash to utilise private services. The difficulties experienced by patients using South Africa's government health-care facilities do not, however, indicate that the people who work in our government sector have no concern for their patients' welfare. Provide the same people with the same incentives and disincentives they would have in a private facility and there would be a total transformation. The failure of any government health system to deliver adequate and effective health care is inherent in central planning.

No mathematical equation or formula is available to assist our health department to calculate what the health needs of the country's 44.8 million people are at any time, nor what resources to provide, where to provide them and in what quantities. They face the same insurmountable obstacles as all other countries with government provided or controlled health systems and experience the same problems: patients waiting weeks and even months for treatment, a lack of modern equipment and resources, rationing of care, rising costs, budget constraints, and the like.

The private health sector is superior to the government health sector because complexity is reduced through the price system. Private doctors, medical practices and private hospitals make only their own plans, which they constantly adjust and improve to attract and retain patients so as to stay in business. They respond directly to the needs of their patients and have, until recently, not been compelled to fit into any government plan dictating what they may do or not do. The National Health Act 2003 is scheduled to change the situation and as a consequence the convenience and quality of care currently offered to private patients will be in jeopardy.

The problem of introducing new technology

Inventions, innovations and technological developments cannot be predicted in advance and therefore cannot be centrally and bureaucratically planned (Rothhard, 2004). Government health department planners not only do not know what will be invented and when; they also do not know who will do the inventing. Medical advances make a mockery of health plans produced under a national health system and the planners are therefore likely to oppose the introduction of new techniques and equipment.

New technologies are expensive and as a government health system cannot make them available to the whole population at once, it either finds a way to severely limit their use or does not introduce them at all. The higher the cost of the new technologies, the more difficult it becomes for a national health system to make quality health care available to everyone. The only exception is when a new technology reduces the cost of treatment and improves the outcomes of existing treatments (National Department of Health, 2002). If there are no private health-care providers to demonstrate to government planners that new technology improves outcomes and lowers costs, they will have no way of knowing, and will have to make political rather than economic decisions in introducing new technology.

Inequitable distribution of resources

The South African government is concerned by what it views as an inequitable distribution of health-care funding and resources between the private and government sectors. Officials claim that the private health sector consumes more than half the total health expenditure yet provides care for less than 20 per cent of the population. The validity of these generally quoted numbers for the split between government and private health-care provision was earlier shown to be questionable yet, disturbingly, the figures are persistently quoted in government policy statements. According to the Minister of Health, the private health sector spent R43-billion on 6.9 million people in the 2003/2004 financial year while public spending was R33.2-billion for 37.9 million people.[11] Anyone who is not a member of a medical scheme is by this logic automatically considered to be dependent on public sector health care, whether or not they use the services. Basing policy proposals on this flawed logic is intended to justify government intervention. The implication is that, to obtain an equitable distribution of resources, money spent on private patients must be redirected to the government health system.

There are several grounds for questioning both the logic behind the "imbalance of resources argument" and any proposals for "rectification." If we analyse the argument carefully, we see that the officials are saying that some members of the population spend a lot more of their own money on their own health care than the government, utilising taxpayers' money, spends on people who are unable to purchase health care. Compare this to a statement that "some members of the population spend a lot more of their own money on their own food and clothing than the government, utilising taxpayers' money, spends on people who are unable to purchase clothes and food". There is an undoubted food and clothing "imbalance of resources," but the government does not feel compelled to increase the regulation of private-sector providers of these essential commodities, limit the expansion of their production facilities, and require them to obtain official consent before purchasing new equipment for use in their businesses. If government interfered in the same way in food and clothing production it would reduce rather than increase the quantity of food and clothing available to the poor. The economic rules for the supply of health care are the same as those for food and clothing. Reduce investment, increase costs, and the supply will diminish.

The imbalance of resources argument creates the impression that huge amounts of money are floating around in the private health sector, just waiting for someone to use it. In fact, the R43 billion spent annually on private health care is money spent by people paying out-of-pocket for care, and by medical schemes paying for the medical expenses of their members and the cost of providing for government-imposed reserve requirements, administration, and the like. The medical schemes are funded entirely by their members who contribute either directly or through their employers. There is no surplus for government to plunder and spend in the government health sector.

Private health-scheme members, by and large, also pay most of the taxes that government collects to fund its health system. Thus, what the imbalance of resources argument actually says is that members of medical schemes must be denied the quality and quantity of services they currently purchase with their own money so that government can take even more of their money to spend on government-provided health care for others.

Everyone pays when government forecasters get it wrong
When private health-care providers make mistakes in their predictions, they bear the costs of those mistakes. For example, when a private provider over-invests in hospital facilities, when medical equipment remains unused, or when the provider overestimates the quantity of medicines needed over a given period, it loses money. To continue operating, a private provider has to remain profitable, or at least break even financially, and therefore has every incentive to make accurate forecasts and reduce mistakes.

When government health planners make similar mistakes, the monetary costs are inflicted on the taxpayers. The responsible planners are seldom held accountable since they are "hidden" behind a veil of bureaucracy.

Poor patients depend on wealthy patients
Not surprisingly, most new medicines and medical technologies are produced in the USA because there are enough affluent American patients who can afford to pay the high prices manufacturers charge to recover the costs of research and development. Once the sales volumes increase, the prices come down and the medicines and technologies become more widely accessible. Without the wealthy countries to pioneer technology and drug production, poorer countries, such as those in Africa, would never gain access to them because they would not be produced.

South Africa's wealthier patients perform the same function for the poor that wealthy Americans perform for poorer countries: they pay to maintain the highly skilled professionals who carry out high-quality, high-cost procedures, using expensive equipment. In South Africa, without a pool of wealthy patients, skilled professionals would leave for greener pastures and would no longer be here to pass their skills on to others, and expensive equipment would no longer be available. The notion that the wealthy deprive the poor of health services is wrong. Wealthy South Africans "ensure" that poor South Africans have access to better health care.

The "certificate of need," introduced to control the purchase of new equipment by private health-care firms, is ostensibly aimed at controlling costs and the alleged "over-servicing" of patients by rationally allocating scarce resources. However, new technologies that begin as luxuries available only to the wealthy quickly become standard procedures in a rapidly evolving field such as medicine. The National Health Act will have the effect of delaying the introduction of new medical technologies and, therefore, will ultimately have a detrimental effect on health care for all South Africans.

Politicisation of health care

As the government health sector is under political control, the views of key government officials on a particular medical issue directly affect the manner in which the government health sector deals with it. The views of the South African President and Minister of Health on HIV/Aids are considered to have been the main reason[12] for the country's slow response in dealing with the HIV/Aids problem despite the government's commitment[13] to decreasing the incidence of infection.

In a government planned and controlled health system, patients are at the mercy of politicians and those appointed by them to control the system.

The "free health care" myth

Government health policy entitles certain categories of patients, including pregnant women and children younger than six years of age, to receive "free" general care, while "free" primary health care is available to every citizen (Health Systems Trust, 2004). However, the health care is not free. It is provided to patients at the expense of the taxpayer.

The day after Nelson Mandela, during his presidency, announced that "all pregnant women and children under the age of 6 years" would be entitled to "free" health care; some public hospitals could not cope with the large number of women and children who arrived on their doorstep seeking medical care. The event dramatically demonstrated that if the cost is reduced, especially if it is reduced to zero, the demand increases exponentially. To cope with this demand, government health-care providers have no option but to reduce availability or deny health care to patients.

However, the difficulties that arise as a result of the introduction of so-called "free" care are not limited to rationing – it also means less efficient and more expensive health care (Reisman, 1996). A large bureaucracy is needed to administer a socialised health system, which together with the built-in bureaucratic inefficiencies, add even more to the costs of so-called "free" health care. To control costs, officials oppose the introduction of advances in medical technology. Advanced technologies and procedures such as MRI scanners and the implantation of artificial hearts, are a major threat to their budgets.[14]

"Free" health care is therefore not only, not free, it is expensive, it inevitably denies patients access to the latest medical procedures and technologies, and it is not freely accessible..

Quality health care for all

There are two very different approaches to the problem of ensuring that people have adequate access to health care. One approach is for the government to attempt to gradually nationalise all health-care services, ultimately ending with fully taxpayer-funded state-owned health services. This is the apparent aim of the National Health Act of 2003 and also of the recently proposed "Health Charter." But economics and world experience tell us that nationalised health care does not work, for three major reasons. The first is that national health systems do not respond to the day-to-day decisions of consumers and therefore fail totally to supply their needs. The second is that they invite unlimited demand, which cannot be met with limited resources. The third is that a relatively poor South Africa cannot hope to achieve success at implementing a system that some of the wealthiest countries, such as the United Kingdom and Canada, have for decades been trying vainly to make succeed.

The other approach is to establish a health-care environment in which private health-care funding and provision can grow rapidly, serving an increasing percentage of the population to the point where all health services are privately provided. This option will work, as the quality and efficiency of the existing private health-care providers have ably demonstrated, as long as they are not burdened with government demands that detrimentally affect their efficiency.

Whichever approach is chosen, one aspect will not change, one hundred per cent of the funding will be from private sources, firstly through taxes, and secondly through voluntary medical aid or insurance schemes and voluntary out-of-pocket payments.

Citizens have the right to expect that the taxes they pay to fund the health care of the poor will be used in a cost-effective, efficient and equitable manner. They can rightly demand that government health policy be conducive to the continued growth and development of private health care.

South Africa's health-care challenge will be best met if government exchanges its role in health-care provision for that of funder of health care for the poor, purchasing care from competing private health-care providers. The most effective mechanism to achieve the empowerment of the poor is to provide them with resources to purchase health care directly from service providers of their choice. The implications for health-care reform are that government should:

- Refrain from unnecessarily interfering with and micro-managing private health-care provision and encourage those who can afford to pay for their own health care to do so.
- Direct its resources to ensuring that the poor receive adequate care from providers of their own choice.
- Fund the needy directly through appropriate means such as vouchers, smart cards, or contributions on their behalf to competing medical aid funds, to allow poor patients to purchase quality health care.
- Encourage the development of health-care insurance products for the emerging market.
- Remove controls that increase health-care costs or prevent the provision of care by scrapping all requirements for certificates of need, price controls, compulsory community service, registration requirements for medicines already approved in the European Union, the United States, Canada, Australia and New Zealand, and such other countries that meet certain defined standards.

Implementing the above measures would relieve government of the burden of providing health care and would enable it to put substantial financial resources directly in the hands of those who need them most. The essence of the reform programme would be to maximise the role of the private health sector and for government to relieve itself of the liability of providing health care.

The main beneficiaries of such a reform programme would be the poor, who would be given a wide range of health-care choices. Benefits to the taxpayers would be a more efficient use of taxpayer funds and certainty that tax monies earmarked for funding health care for the poor reaches them directly so that poor South Africans would get more and better health care for the same or less money. State assistance to those who should be self-supporting would be eliminated, allowing greater assistance to those who really need it. A further benefit is that over time, those people who prosper sufficiently to take care of their own health care would be removed from the health-care support list.

The government would have responsibility for a thriving, growing, health-care sector that would be the envy of the developing and the developed world. Health professionals would start returning to South Africa instead of leaving it.

Conclusion

Government's policy and discussion documents do not explain how South Africa, a relatively poor country, will succeed in providing equitable health care to all through the envisaged national health system, when wealthy countries have failed in their attempts to do this.

If government's health-care plans continue in the direction of nationalisation, which appears to be the ultimate goal, South Africans will lose their world-class private health-care firms. Patients will lose the freedom to choose their own health care, which is such a vital and personal service, and bureaucratic health-care planners will be making decisions for them. This happens in

Canada, the United Kingdom and other countries that have national health systems. The whole national health system will function badly, just as it does in those countries.

The health of the whole South African nation is threatened by the centrally planned health system envisaged in the National Health Act 2003.

3 Corruption in public health

Maureen Lewis

Institutions and governance have emerged as the back bone of development, and are increasingly being shown as critical to income levels (Rigobon and Rodrik, 2004; Rodrik, Subramanian and Trebbi, 2004; Kaufman and Kraay, 2002), fostering overall development (Kaufmann, Kraay and Mastruzzi, 2005), ensuring sound macroeconomic policies (IMF, 1997; Berg, 2005) and per capita income growth (World Bank, 2003b). The World Bank's 2006 *World Development Report* looks again at the determinants of poverty and argues for an emphasis on equal opportunity and the institutional infrastructure (World Bank, 2006). The recent UK government's *Report on the Commission for Africa* places a premium on governance and institutions as complementary to other actions in bolstering development prospects in the region, and the US government's Millennium Challenge Corporation expects to spend billions of dollars on countries that demonstrate good governance. Thus both theory and empirical evidence is accumulating to place governance at the center of development thinking, spending and action.

At the same time the international community has pledged their support in helping countries reach a set of ambitious Millennium Development Goals (MDGs) that would sharply reduce poverty, raise educational levels and reduce mortality, among other achievements. The combination of the two threads suggests the need to ensure that institutional development is fostered in conjunction with efforts to accelerate progress on economic and social fronts.

Improving human capital in reaching the MDGs and raising

living standards has led to a focus on investments in the social sectors, particularly education and health. These sectors received increasing attention and support from the multi-lateral and bi-lateral institutions over the past decade (IMF and World Bank, 2005). Reaching the MDGs in health will require adequate funding (United Nations Millennium Project, 2005; Commission on Macroeconomics and Health, 2001). However, it is equally important to ensure that health systems function so services can be delivered and health professionals be accountable to the public, government and, where they are providing funds, donors. The strategy to date emphasizes funding and need, with much less concern for effectiveness or, surprisingly, impact, and has largely neglected institutions and governance issues.

The problem with the lack of concern for basic governance principles in health care delivery is that well-intentioned spending may have no impact. Priorities cannot be met if institutions don't function and scarce resources are wasted. Bribes, corrupt officials and mis-procurement undermine health care delivery in much the same way they do for police services, law courts and customs whose functions become compromised by the culture of poor governance and corruption.

This paper examines health systems from the perspective of governance, drawing on the knowledge and experience garnered over the past decade at the national and firm levels and supplementing that with health-specific evidence. It therefore examines the effectiveness of government and specifically the efficiency of its role in producing health care services.

The next section outlines the health care markets, the role of government and the definition and measurement of governance. The evidence from developing countries on various elements of governance and corruption in health care delivery is then reviewed, and the last two sections lay out policy possibilities and implications for the sector.

Health care markets, public health care systems and governance

The growth, governance and corruption literature (Elliott, 1997; Transparency International, 2005; World Bank, 1997; Commission for Africa, 2005) largely ignores governance when it comes to public policies in the social sectors. Implicit in that neglect is that good intentions surrounding these investments are such that governance is secondary, if it has any importance at all. Efficiency in resource use would suggest the need to consider such themes, however.

Characteristics of health care markets

Unlike other goods and services health care services embody some unique characteristics stemming from inherent market failures. First is the asymmetry of information and agency challenge of physicians acting as agents for patients. Patients are aware they don't feel well but they rely on health professionals, often physicians, to act as their agents in diagnosing and treating ailments. Patients are ill-equipped to assess the adequacy and quality of physician decisions and actions, and therefore focus on the environmental and interpersonal aspects of clinical services, the elements they are best able to evaluate.

Second, adverse selection practices by private health insurers lead to an uninsured population disproportionately made up of those most in need of health care: the chronically ill, the poor and those having experienced a catastrophic illness. In settings without health insurance ability to pay limits the same groups from obtaining care so the same constraints apply. Government intervention compensates for the market's reluctance to insure the most vulnerable. And because of the random nature of illness or injury, government subsidies protect the population against financial demands of illness.

Finally, the moral hazard of over-consumption by the insured who do not face the true cost of health care requires active cost containment, the key issue for OECD countries and relevant for development countries as well. A second form of moral hazard is the over production of care by physicians when third parties cover costs. Physician induced demand drives costs in much the same way that consumer behavior does, with similar implications for payers.

In most countries market failures translate into publicly financed and delivered care, and/or regulation from public and private bodies. Most developing countries depend heavily on public intervention rather than regulation, hence the predominance of public health care systems in those countries.

A limitation in assessing existing health care systems is the lack of any single measure of what constitutes a functioning system. Every OECD country has its own, unique health care arrangements with a mix of public and private financing, delivery and regulations. OECD comparisons of system performance tend to be limited to gross measures such as spending levels or mortality statistics. The more meaningful comparisons are those based on specific diseases where costs, treatment options and outcomes can be compared, though countries don't necessarily collect comparable data limiting the extent of meaningful comparisons. For developing countries systems differ and information on comparable indicators simply do not yet exist.

These characteristics explain why government's role is so critical to examine, and why the indicators used in this paper for health care delivery are so different from those used in other studies of governance or health care delivery. This effort documents "government failure" to live up to the objectives of public policy, looking specifically at efficiency enhancement and redistribution, and focusing on incentives as a means to improve performance without compromising equity objectives (Jack and Lewis, 2004).

Producing public health care: a framework

The production function represents the core of public health care systems embodying capital and labor and governance. A simple representation is the following:

Health Outcomes = (L, K, G)

where governance represents some measure of institutional quality or governance. Increases in labor and capital can improve outcomes, but G may dampen or enhance these effects.

Labor encompasses management, physicians, nurses, other medical staff. Capital is made up of infrastructure, equipment and other fixed assets, as well as financing: government transfers for local purchase, in-kind provision of drugs and supplies, and third party and consumer payments. The functioning of the public system is determined by the incentives facing the actors in the system, the manner in which inputs are managed and the accountability imbedded in the incentive structure.

While straightforward in concept, the production function itself is far from simple and the market failures identified above plague both private and public systems (i.e., principal agent and information asymmetry problems), which undermine incentives and limit the extent of accountability. Accountability can be to a central government, local government, communities or patients, or some combination of these.

Measures to assess performance of public systems are lacking. Infant mortality, a readily available and commonly used measure of outcome, better reflects more aggregate measures of well being (such as income and education) rather than the health system, although once the IMR drops below 25–30 per 1000 it better captures the quality and extent of medical interventions. Monitoring basic functions such as hiring, existence of appropriate policies, purchase of drugs, building of clinics and procurement practices, can be easily accomplished but only represents the identification of inputs.

The more complex and important measures of health system performance are such things as staff output, drug and medical supply availability, regularity of funding transfers, state of physical infrastructure, inventory and functionality of equipment, and existence of patient records, factors which reflect whether health systems are meeting minimal efficiency and quality standards. Utilization data and patient satisfaction offer complementary metrics of health system effectiveness since under-utilized public facilities or their by-passing by target groups suggest implementation problems. Despite their relevance, such data rarely if ever are collected on a routine basis in developing countries. Indeed such information only exists for a subset of countries and often for only a segment of the health system. In the absence of comparable monitorable indicators this kind of information can inform policy makers about performance and the pressure points of health systems development before large scale data collection is in place.

Governance and corruption in health care delivery

Health care provision depends on efficiently combining financial resources, human resources, and supplies, and delivering services in a timely fashion distributed spatially throughout a country. This requires a "system" that mobilizes and distributes resources, processes information and acts upon it, and motivates providers' appropriate behavior by individuals, health care workers, and administrators. Good governance is a critical factor in making such a system function.

In health care, good governance implies that health care systems function effectively and with some level of efficiency. Though many governance indicators have been developed for countries in the aggregate, governance indicators for specific sectors, such as health, are not readily available. Consequently, it is necessary to look for proxies that reflect the quality of health sector governance. This paper will focus on one such proxy, evidence of corruption, that results when governance is poor. This section reviews the definition of corruption and its application to the health sector.

Sound institutions and good governance go hand-in-hand. Kaufman and Kraay (2003) define good governance as "the traditions and institutions by which authority in a country is exercised". More specifically it encompasses:

♦ capacity of government to formulate and implement sound policies, manage resources and provide services efficiently;

◆ the process that allows citizens to select, hold accountable, monitor and replace government; and,

◆ the respect of government and citizens for the institutions that govern economic and social interaction.

Multiple institutions collect indicators of governance. Kaufman, Kraay and Mastruzzi (2005) have boiled them down to six dimensions of governance: voice and accountability; political stability and lack of violence; government effectiveness; regulatory quality; rule of law; and, control of corruption – all of which affect the environment within which health care services function. The robustness of the private sector in health will be affected by factors such as poor regulation or an ineffective court system, the elements of particular relevance to service delivery are voice and accountability, government effectiveness and control of corruption.

Voice and accountability reflect external accountability, the effectiveness of citizen and institutional influences on government action. While much of the broader concerns are with human rights, in health factors such as the viability of the political system, media independence and trust in government reflect the degree to which citizens can influence government decisions that affect them. For example, where local leaders are not elected, localities cannot hold public servants accountable for their decisions or actions, and public bodies have little incentive to effectively serve the community. The lack of voice leaves localities at the mercy of public sector whims. Voice and accountability permit communities to be involved in decisions and oversight of health care services.

Government effectiveness encompasses efficiency of the bureaucracy and public servants, roles and responsibilities of local and regional governments, including the administrative and technical skills of government, effectiveness of policy and program formulation, governing capacity, and effective use of resources. Extending the example above, decentralization that comes without funding or local authority undermines potential effectiveness of local jurisdictions as they have no power to affect resource allocations or decision-making and can be the victim of "provider capture" where centrally deployed staff determine service, organization and delivery.

Control of corruption is straightforward. It captures the extent and nature of corruption among public officials, including tracking the incidence of nepotism, cronyism and bribes among civil servants, irregularities in public purchasing and oversight, and the nature and extent to which government manages corruption.

Corruption can be defined as "use of public office for private gains" (Bardhan, 1997) or "the sale by government officials of government property for personal gain" (Shleifer and Vishny, 1993). With either definition good government hinges on the incentives for and accountability of public servants.

Forms of corruption vary. Sparrow (1996) describes the extent of fraud in the US Medicare program, which is exacerbated by heavy reliance on electronic payments in compensating providers. Disinterest on the part of law enforcement officials reflects a belief that costs appear to outweigh the benefits of investigation and prosecution. Large scale fraud discussed in Sparrow suggests the scope of the possible in developed countries where significant resources are devoted to health care; there is heavy reliance on automated payment arrangements most of which are never checked by humans; and inadequate controls are in place to prevent fraud and abuse. Similar types of fraud exist in some middle income countries, but there are far less sophisticated means employed with ample benefit in developing countries.

Governance indicators are built on perceptions of in-country and outside observers, and their application has emphasized cross-country comparisons. On the first point, perceptions are powerful factors in shaping behavior. If investors perceive corruption or patients perceive poor quality, it discourages private investment or health demand, respectively. But perceptions are only part of what is of interest in assessing governance issues in health

Less corrupt and politically stable countries the more attractive they are for private investors and donors (Kaufmann, Kraay and Mastruzzi, 2005). Good governance has been shown to correlate with property rights and civil liberties, and greater foreign investment (Hellman et al., 2000), and to "grease" the wheels of government (Kaufmann and Wei, 1999). Aid effectiveness also rises in countries with good governance. These clearly have relevance to health care.

Capturing the effectiveness of public health care services, the extent of corruption and the degree of accountability pose serious challenges, which contribute to the lagging effort to address governance in the sector. Using national level indicators such as access to health services provides limited guidance on how well the sector is performing. At the same time, performance indicators are scarce, and difficult to aggregate where they exist. The heterogeneous nature of health care and the large number of *sui generis* events; the highly variable and unpredictable nature of health care demand; the multiple actors involved in ensuring effective service delivery; and, the limited choice of instruments for monitoring all contribute to the challenge of defining and measuring governance in the health sector.

Correlates of poor governance and public health care across countries

The evidence on the link between institutions and health has largely relied on analyzing the cross-country relationships between corruption and health outcome measures. With evidence for 89 countries for 1985 and 1997 Gupta, Davoodi and Tiongson (2000) show corruption indicators (using Kaufman, Kraay and Zoido-Lobatón, 1999) negatively associated with child and infant mortality, the likelihood of an attended birth, immunization coverage and low-birthweight. The correlation of corruption in explaining the same health outcomes is reduced once factors such as mother's education, public health and education spending and urbanization are controlled for, but remains significant.

In measuring the impact of corruption on the effectiveness of health spending Rajkumar and Swaroop (2002) analyze data for 1990 and 1997 controlling for GDP per capita, female educational attainment, ethno-linguistic fractionalization, urbanization among other factors, and find that the effectiveness of public health spending in reducing child mortality hinges on the integrity rating (1–5 range based on level of perceived corruption), with higher integrity associated with reduced mortality. Poor governance may help to explain the inconclusive findings of Filmer and Pritchett (1999) on the lack of association between public health expenditures and infant and child mortality.

Wagstaff and Claeson (2005) extend these analyses further and use more recent data. They find that spending reduces under 5 mortality, but only where governance, as measured by the World Bank's CPIA score (Country Policy and Institutional Assessment measure that is scored between 1–5 depending on performance, part of which regards corruption and governance), is sound (a CPIA above 3.25). This study specifically explores the implications of additional spending for reaching the MDGs, and concludes that more spending in medium and low CPIA countries would not be expected to reduce child mortality, and that per capita income growth offers a better investment if mortality declines are the objective.

Because child mortality rates are measured with substantial error, especially in the poorest countries, these results need to be taken with caution. The uncertainty of the direction of causality introduces further limitations in the interpretations of the results. Cross-country regressions are hard to interpret in any event, but as an aggregate assessment they provide general guidance on the relevance of corruption and other factors in affecting health outcomes in developing countries. The inability of country level analysis to elucidate specific country problems leads to the subsequent section that addresses these issues, complementing this introductory look at the correlates of health outcomes.

Figure 1 demonstrates the relationship between governance indices and measures of health performance and outcomes. Measles immunization coverage provides a robust measure of public service performance as it reflects government's ability to perform a critical and basic health service. Measles immunization by itself is particularly important since when administered in infancy it sharply reduces all causes of mortality in childhood (Koenig et al., 1991; Aaby 1995). It is also easily measured. Child mortality is a standard variable for measuring health outcomes, is influenced by a wide range of factors beyond the quality and extent of health care services, but has the advantage that it is available for a large number of countries.

The six panels in Figure 1 show the scatter plots for both indicators and each of the three components of the KKM governance index: government effectiveness, control of corruption, and voice and accountability. Of the three measures, and compared to the aggregate governance indicator (not shown), government effectiveness best correlates with poor outcomes and performance in health care based on the smaller variation conveyed in the adjust R2.[1] Voice has the least explanatory power and it is especially limited for immunization coverage. The panel on voice and accountability suggests why. The highly variable relationship especially among the countries with the lowest governance scores makes any effort to explain variation unconvincing. In higher performing countries more convergence occurs for government effectiveness and control of corruption but much less so for voice. Immunization programs are typically the responsibility of central governments because it is a preventive measure for which demand tends to be low among all but the most educated.[2] The dispersion in the voice and accountability panel is consistent with that fact.

Table 1 provides OLS results showing the strength of governance measures on measles immunization coverage controlling for other relevant factors. Of the various governance indices, government effectiveness explains more of the differences in measles immunization and has a slightly stronger effect than the overall

Figure 1 **Relationship between corruption indices and health outcomes**

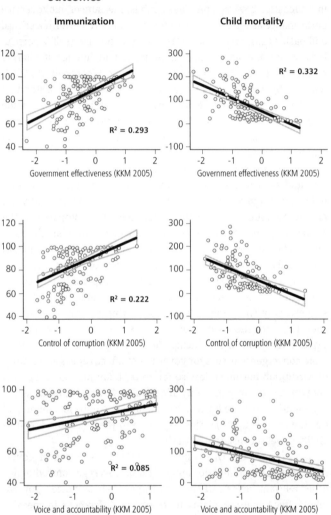

Table 1 **OLS results for measles immunization coverage (% of children ages 12–23 months)**

	(1)	(2)	(3)	(4)	(5)
Log of GDP per capita, PPP (const 2000 int'l $)	2.351 (3.489)	0.808 (3.561)	0.487 (2.451)	−0.136 (2.609)	−1.378 (4.212)
Aggregate governance		6.152 (3.124)*		5.201 (2.442)†	
Government effectiveness	7.026 (3.218)†		6.812 (2.345)‡		8.221 (3.607)†
Average years of schooling of adults, female	1.888 (0.981)*	1.763 (1.008)*			2.337 (1.071)†
Primary completion rate, female			0.293 (0.067)‡	0.309 (0.073)	
Ethnolinguistic and religious fractionalization		−6.021 (2.271)†		−4.059 (2.263)*	−6.671 (2.284)
Road density				−0.037 (0.015)†	
Constant	56.180 (25.664)†	77.120 (27.959)‡	57.689 (17.318)‡	66.128 (19.704)	94.809 (33.118)
Observations	71	68	119	112	68
R-squared	0.434	0.473	0.444	0.470	0.497

Robust standard errors in parentheses
Sources: Kaufmann, Kraay and Mastruzzi (2005); Barro and Lee (2000); Alesina, et al. (2003); *World Bank World Development Indicators 2005*; World Bank EdStats.
*significant at 10%; † significant at 5%; ‡ significant at 1%

corruption index, which would be expected since immunization is a relatively simple technology and requires basic government capacity to do it well. Government effectiveness is consistent in its effect on immunization coverage. Controlling corruption (not shown) is significant but less robust than the other two measures, and voice has no effect at all on the per cent of children immunized. Road density would also be expected to impede immunization coverage, which it does, and it is significant. GDP per capita strongly affects immunizations, but not when other controls are added. Reaching children appears to be more of an impediment due to dispersed population or inadequate infrastructure. Per capita income may not be as important to increasing immunization given the generosity of donor funds, particularly for vertical programs like immunizations. The variable for women's education, a key input in whether children get immunized, is best captured by average years of schooling for females over age 15. However, the sample size declines by 40 countries when this variable is used, so the completion rate of females, the proportion of girls who are currently finishing school, is used as a proxy because girls' current achievements are a reflection of their mothers' support for education and their ability to make household decisions about their children's education.

Table 2 shows the OLS results for child mortality. The R2s are almost 50 per cent higher than those for measles immunization coverage, with income per capita and ethno-linguistic fractionalization explaining most of the variation. Average years of female schooling doesn't have an effect, although girls' completion rates do. Average years of female education becomes significant, however, when ethno-linguistic fragmentation is left out, suggesting either some substitution between these factors, or when the loss for so many observations affects the relationship. Governance is not significant, but it matters when the education variable is female education rather than completion. Road density and urbanization (not shown) have no effect, and that pattern persists with other models. The established inverse relationship between income and child mortality makes these results unsurprising, but the lack of importance of female education is odd given the strength of the relationship in country level studies. These results provide the point of departure for a more narrow focus on both the country level issues and the factors that directly influence health care delivery.

The next section summarizes accumulated evidence on specific components of governance and corruption, including: perceptions of corruption and performance; management challenges in public

Table 2 **OLS results for under-5 mortality rate**

	(1)	(2)	(3)	(4)	(5)
Log of GDP per capita, PPP (const 2000 int'l $)	-66.447	-55.263	-29.148	-24.932	-55.649
	(7.853)‡	(9.847)‡	(8.403)‡	(8.390)‡	(9.856)‡
Aggregate governance	18.747	16.828		-3.069	18.644
	(9.167)†	(9.426)*		(7.588)	(9.866)*
Government effectiveness			-4.773		
			(8.576)		
Average years of schooling of adults, female	-3.819	-3.893			-3.563
	(2.483)	(2.551)			(2.504)
Primary completion rate, female			-1.261	-1.197	
			(0.194)‡	(0.213)	
Ethnolinguistic and religious fractionalization		19.222		20.169	18.934
		(8.220)†		(5.525)	(8.155)
Road density					-0.054
					(0.073)
Constant	639.747	521.888	408.635	342.705	526.372
	(60.938)‡	(85.021)‡	(60.448)‡	(62.343)‡	(85.128)‡
Observations	71	68	119	112	68
R-squared	0.748	0.764	0.745	0.769	0.766

Robust standard errors in parentheses
Sources: Kaufmann, Kraay and Mastruzzi (2005); Barro and Lee (2000); Alesina, et. al. (2003); *World Bank World Development Indicators* 2005; World Bank EdStats.
*significant at 10%; † significant at 5%; ‡ significant at 1%

systems; staff absenteeism; under-the-table or informal payments for health services; corrupt practices including misuse of public funds, irregularities in contracting and purchasing supplies, petty theft and the selling of positions and promotions. As symptoms of poor performance, they provide an empirical base for exploring priority areas for attention and intervention.

Government effectiveness, corruption and accountability in health care delivery

Separating three components of governance – government effectiveness, corruption and accountability – allows targeting policies to specific shortcomings. However, the information base is thin and the elements so intertwined that a separate analysis of each yields little benefit. For example, evidence from provider and other surveys in Mozambique, Nigeria and Uganda suggest that the level of mismanagement,

vague and poorly understood performance expectations and the singular lack of accountability to anyone or any institution makes haphazard and corrupt practices difficult to identify, separate or control (Lindelow, Ward and Zorzi, 2004; Lindelow, Reinikka and Svensson, 2003; Das Gupta, Gauri and Khemani, 2003; McPake et. al., 1999).

There is a fine line between inefficiency and corruption in many instances. Is poor service a function of corruption or simply mismanagement? Better accountability can address both, so should the approach be combined or separated? In the interests of clarity, this section will discuss governance, corruption and accountability jointly reviewing the evidence and offering an interpretation of those findings as they relate to each of these criteria.

This discussion begins with an assessment of perceptions of corruption in select countries to provide that context. It then addresses the production function elements in reviewing country level evidence. The analysis tracks productivity of labor, and capital inputs: drugs, supplies and national transfers, complementing these with a brief assessment of management, a central component for correcting many of the problems identified.

Perceptions of corruption in public health care systems

While not strictly part of the production function, perceptions about corruption reflect how stakeholders view health systems and their effectiveness in producing acceptable health outcomes. Perceptions provide the basis for assessing governance at a national level, and similar estimates have been collected for the health sector in a subset of countries. Extensive, cross-country surveys of public officials, the business community and the general public gauge perceptions of corruption in public service. At a sectoral level a number of recent perception surveys of medical personnel in Latin American public hospitals provide a sense of the kinds and frequency of corruption in facilities as well as the likely perpetrators by profession (Di Tella and Savedoff, 2001). Both types of surveys indicate corrupt practices, which by their nature are not typically visible. Perceptions may be the only alternative in instances where hard data are either unobtainable or unreliable, and corruption in general does not lend itself to straightforward data collection.

Figure 2 summarizes the perceptions of the general population toward corruption in health in a selection of countries for which data are available. Data come from various sources all largely based on perceptions and they are not strictly comparable though they suggest general levels of corruption in the included countries. Coverage is uneven with a bias towards the countries of Eastern Europe and Central Asia (ECA) and South Asia where data are more plentiful. Of those at or above 60 per cent of the population perceiving corruption in the health sector half are ECA countries, results partly due to the disproportionate number of ECA countries.

In corruption surveys interviewing public officials, business executives and the general public in 23 countries, health ranked first as the most corrupt sector in Moldova, Slovakia and Tajikistan, second in Bangladesh, India and Sri Lanka, and in the top four in Kazakhstan, Kyrgyz Republic, Madagascar and Morocco. For the most part these countries also ranked highly on the per cent of the population perceiving high levels of corruption in health – going as high as 95 per cent in Pakistan, 92 per cent in Sri Lanka, 85 per cent in Tajikistan, 82 per cent in Moldova and 80 per cent in Morocco.[3] Expectations on paying for public care correspond to the perceptions of corruption, which in turn are closely related to the need for informal payments, as will be discussed below.

A related 2001 perceptions survey conducted by USAID on corruption among public officials in Bosnia and Herzegovina, Bulgaria, Macedonia, Romania, Croatia, and Montenegro showed that 45–55 per cent of respondents felt that corruption among doctors was widespread. Albania and Serbia showed much higher levels – 61–71 per cent range. Albania's perception score for doctors was an outlier relative to its score for other public officials, but Serbia exhibited levels above those of other countries for most categories of officials, suggesting a relatively more corrupt environment (Vitosha/USAID, 2002).

Business Environment and Enterprise Performance Surveys of administrative corruption in ECA capture business managers' perceptions of health service quality. Across 20 countries only Slovenia and Czech Republic had positive assessments from 60 per cent or more of respondents, indicating management and governance problems in the other 18 systems (Ryterman, Hellman, Jones et al., 2000).

In Bolivia a local survey of patients considered the Health Ministry and public hospitals less corrupt than customs or police, but ranked corruption 2.7 on a scale of 1–4, noting the nepotism, clientelism and higher charges for the unconnected as some key indicators of corruption (Gatti, Gray-Molina and Klugman, 2004), evidence that has been corroborated in other studies as discussed below. Surveys from South Asia suggest similar perceptions of the health sector (Thampi, 2002).

A comparison of corruption perceptions among households in the Philippines and Uganda found 34 and 71 per cent, respectively, reported that corruption is common or very common in government generally. And among local officials, 25 per cent in the Philippines and 61 per cent in Uganda acknowledged some kind of corruption in public services within the municipalities (Azfar and Gurgur, 2001).

Explanations from the surveyed on why corruption is so evident in the health sector emphasize the lack of accountability and transparency in health care operations, and in some the "power of monopoly" where other public or private alternatives simply do not

Figure 2 **Percent perceiving corruption in the health sector**

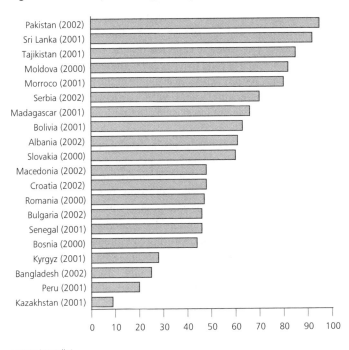

Source: Appendix I

exist (Thampi, 2002; McPake et. al 1999; Lewis, 2000, 2002; Narayan, 2000). While not definitive, perceptions highlight where abuses are assumed and widespread and they have become reliable indicators of corruption. Only a few countries have sector specific data on perceptions. Greater efforts to track such information can guide both policymakers and donors providing a benchmark for individual countries.

Staffing health care delivery

Staffing is arguably the single most important element of health care delivery as little can be achieved without it. Training of the staff, their competencies and ability to function all determine whether labor can drive the expected results. Training typically is adequate if not well beyond that needed in the lowest income countries, especially for physicians. Availability of the full range of competencies, however, often lags with particular inattention to management needs, and lower paid staff with minimal skills can proliferate.

Among the most serious issues in developing countries is the high rate of absenteeism, which undermines service delivery and leads to closed public clinics that compromise the equity and health objectives of publicly financed health care. Two other commonly observed constraints include low productivity of public medical staff, and the outright corruption that underlies the buying and selling of official positions. Capturing low productivity and poor service poses greater difficulties; absenteeism already reflects reduced output, and underperformance. Patient satisfaction provides an additional window into adequacy of staff services.

Absenteeism

Absenteeism poses a chronic, but often unmeasured, problem in publicly financed health care, and can severely limit patient access to services (McPake et. al., 1999; Lewis, Eskeland and Traa-Valarezo, 2004; Narayan, 2000), reduce quality (McPake et. al., 1999; Lewis, La Forgia and Sulvetta, 1996), and suggest corruption (DiTella and Savedoff, 2001).

Absenteeism occurs for various reasons, many of them legitimate or necessary. For example, rural health workers often need to travel to larger towns to receive their paycheck, fetch supplies or drugs or are delayed by poor infrastructure or weather. All lead to absences but are necessitated by inadequate management or other shortcoming of the country context. On the other hand, some staff have other commitments or preferences and don't show up. In effect they

Figure 3 **Absence rates among health workers in selected countries**

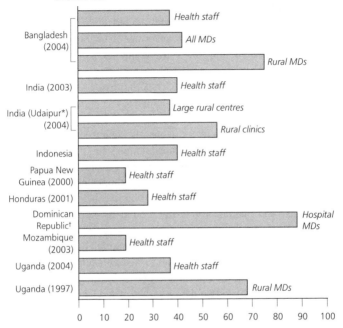

*Udaipur district, Rajasthan, India. †Santo Dominigo hospital, Dominican Republic.
Source: Chaudhury and Hammer (2005); Chaudhury et al. (2004); Banerjee and Duflo (2005); Kushnarova (2005); McPake et al. (1999); Lewis, La Forgia and Sulvetta (1996)

receive a salary but provide minimal if any services. This is effectively theft, a form of "public office for private gain."

Capturing the extent of absenteeism among public service staff is made difficult by the lack of or incomplete nature of staff attendance records. Various alternatives have been applied to examine the issue including perceptions of other providers (DiTella and Savedoff, 2001).

Figure 3 compares absenteeism rates for studies that report such data, and measurements vary, as do level of provider, number of observations within each provider unit and location. Chaudhury, et al., (2004) use a single surprise visit to a nationally representative sample of rural clinics in 5 countries; Banerjee, Deaton and Duflo (2004) tracked absences in 143 government facilities in Udaipar district in Rajasthan, India based on weekly visits over 18 months; Lewis, LaForgia and Sulvetta (1996) used time and motion studies during a two weeks period to track health provider attendance in a single hospital in Santo Domingo, Dominican Republic; and, McPake et al. (1999) directly observed clinics in 10 rural districts in Uganda over the course of one week. Thus the reported absences are captured using different time frames, samples and providers.

Absenteeism rates, measured in these particular studies, range from a low in Mozambique and Papua New Guinea of 19 per cent to over 60 per cent among physicians in a Dominican hospital, in rural Bangladesh and Uganda, but cluster around 35–40 per cent for the others. These results suggest a serious gap in health service coverage due to absent staff, levels considerably above those from similar studies in the same countries for teachers (Chaudhury et al., 2004). As in Figure 2, these results rely on different types of surveys over varying time periods and for a variety of services. What is noteworthy are the range of methods, the lack of consistency and the need to establish acceptable and regular means for tracking staff absenteeism. Otherwise it will remain an ad hoc approach.

Lewis, La Forgia and Sulvetta's (1992; 1996) time and motion studies in inpatient, outpatient, surgery and emergency found that not only did physicians only provide 12 per cent of contracted time, nurses provided virtually no care outside of inpatient services, and staff physicians, residents and interns provided only 7, 4, and 8 per cent of their contracted time, respectively. As found in Uganda (see below), absenteeism was lowest during the early morning hours and in the outpatient department. In the DR, surgery was only conducted before noon during the availability of surgeons, leaving the facility idle for the remainder of the 24 hour day. Interns, residents and auxiliary nurses received virtually no supervision from staff physicians and nurses. The resulting services were under-staffed and reliant on untrained providers with virtually no supervision. The abuses translated into high costs for the public sector with little output, and undermined the quality of health care across the board by relying on ill-trained providers for care and under investing in the quality of future providers.

Residents and auxiliary nurses received virtually no supervision from staff physicians and nurses. The resulting services were under-staffed and reliant on untrained providers with virtually no supervision. The abuses translated into high costs for the public sector with little output, and undermined the quality of health care across the board by relying on ill-trained providers for care and under investing in the quality of future providers.

McPake et al., (1999) recorded attendance and clinic openings. Clinics only remained open for 2–3 hours in the morning with partial coverage by health staff, often on a rotating basis. Doctors, medical assistance, midwives and nurses were available for an average of 12.9 hours per week while nursing aides, dressers and pharmacy orderlies worked an average of 18.5 hours. The latter group of lower level health workers provided 71 per cent of total available hours of staff at the clinics compromising quality as well as coverage. These estimates ignore the "ghost" workers who never attend the facility, suggesting that the average attendance of contracted staff is even lower than the estimates.

Chaudhury and Hammer's (2004) study of absenteeism in rural health clinics in Bangladesh recorded availability of doctors and paramedics of filled positions.[4] On average 35 per cent of staff and 42 per cent of physicians were absent across the 60 clinics visited. In eamining clinics by location, absenteeism in the most rural areas was 74 per cent for doctors. Subsequent multivariate analysis showed that living outside the service village, being female and poor road access increased the likelihood of absenteeism among physicians. Absenteeism was associated with clinics in disrepair as well as with lower patient demand, suggesting that absenteeism compromises quality and quantity of services.

The studies in Uganda and Rajasthan, India added a search for absent primary health care workers. Over the course of 18 months Indian nurses were only to be found in villages served by the sub-center 12 per cent of the time, and all were assigned to staff the clinic on a regular basis. The pattern of absences, and therefore closure of facilities, followed no pattern meaning that patients' likelihood of finding a provider was unpredictable (Banerjee, Deaton and Duflo, 2004). Health workers were often found at home in Uganda, although some employees simply never attended the facility and were designated as "ghost" workers (McPake et al., 1999). The costs represented by absent staff are not insignificant given the higher levels absenteeism, which are consistently higher than those found in education.

Absenteeism based on perceptions provide some orders of magnitude of nonattendance, but may be less objective than the recorded observations or surprise visits discussed above. Nonetheless they are instructive.

Absenteeism is considered the most serious corruption problem in Colombia, but perception of absenteeism varies across the six Latin American countries for which qualitative survey data are available (Giedion, Morales and Acosta, 2001). Surveys of hospital nurses' perceptions of the frequency of chronic absenteeism among doctors reported rates of 98 per cent in Costa Rica, 30 per cent in Nicaragua, 38 per cent in Colombia (Giedion, Morales and Acosta, 2001) and between 24–31 per cent across public and social security hospitals in Argentina (Schargrodsky, Mera and Weinschelbaum, 2001). In Peru estimates of hours absent from work ranged from 12 to 36 hours (Alcҙzar and Andrade, 2001) across the sampled hospitals.

Shaving off hours is more commonly reported than absent days in all the Latin American country surveys. Late arrival and early departure only represented 2–23 per cent of all absences in a four country study (Uganda, Bangladesh, India and Indonesia) of medical personnel based on surprise visits (Chaudhury, et al., 2004). The Colombia case study above estimated that the cost of the lost time in the public hospitals of Bogotҙ was equivalent to over US$1 million per year.

Focus groups in Ethiopia among health workers revealed common understaffing due to late arrivals, long breaks and a general disregard for the necessity of staffing clinics. Absences are frequently motivated by responsibilities at second jobs. Lack of management and manager's reluctance to confront physicians inspires lower level workers to behave accordingly, leading to high absenteeism and low productivity at all levels. (Lindelow, Serneels and Lemma, 2003)

Where absenteeism is endemic, as was the case in Uganda, Rajasthan India and the Dominican Republic, such explanations are far less compelling. One factor shared by all of the examples above is that absent health workers face almost no consequences. There is no accountability for public servants. Without accountability, abuses are more likely to proliferate and eventually undermine the health care system.

Multivariate evidence for education provides some important insights. The correlates of teacher absences in five countries produced mixed findings but in at least three countries infrastructure quality mattered consistently, and, in some, Ministry of Education inspections were also associated with lower absenteeism. Education of mothers, community oversight, location of schools and the training of teachers, had perverse or insignificant effects on absenteeism. To the extent that inspectors were indeed a tool of accountability, they had some effect in Ecuador, India and Indonesia but no effect at all in Peru and Uganda. The consequences of high absenteeism were not discussed nor were any other forms of accountability (Chaudhury et al., 2004).

Absenteeism is symptomatic of an unaccountable and ineffective government, and leads to contempt for government, its policies and practices, and compromises both access to and quality of health care services. Unproductive or absent workers who do not receive any punishment for substandard performance and whose promotion and pay remain the same as those with better performance, undermine morale and reduce output, which in turn leads to a spiral of overall poor performance. Accountability is meaningless or doesn't exist without sanctions, and institutions suffer accordingly.

Purchasing public positions

The insidious practices of selling public positions and requiring bribes for promotion fundamentally undermine good performance and builds a corruption spiral since the newly hired and promoted must find the resources to ensure their continued employment and advancement. The practice has been documented for much of Eastern Europe and Central Asia where the breakdown of government led to the commercialization of public positions (Kaufman, Pradhan and Ryterman, 1988). Outright purchase of public employment through bribes is often anecdotally accepted, but some recent work has tried to quantify it. Evidence from surveys of public officials in Latvia, Armenia and Georgia showed that the "cost" of public positions was well known among public officials and the general public. Interestingly the higher cost jobs were in the most corrupt enclaves of government (Kaufman, Pradhan and Ryterman, 1988).

In Bosnia and Herzegovina bribes were particularly common in the health sector with surveys of officials and citizens reporting that 75 per cent thought bribes were required for obtaining positions and for promotion (World Bank, 2001e). In Ghana 25 per cent of jobs were allegedly bought in government hospitals. In Uganda 20 per cent of municipal officials acknowledged that the practice occurred in the health sector, and in the Philippines 3 per cent noted it (Azfar, Kahkonen and Meagher, 2001).

In focus groups in Ethiopia health officials complained about unfair hiring practices, nepotism and preferential treatment to well connected individuals. Similarly in the Dominican Republic "patronage propelled personnel rolls" leading to one of the highest rates of health personnel to population in the region. Promotions routinely rely on recommendations from politicians, and military authorities that lead to a mismatch between skills and needs (La Forgia et al., 2004). An earlier study found that most care was already provided by under-trained medical students operating on patients without supervision (Lewis, La Forgia and Sulvetta, 1992).

Staff accountability for misconduct is rare. Its absence in accountability is noted for the Dominican Republic (La Forgia et al., 2004), although Cohen (2002) reports that in Costa Rica 27 per cent of users know of a case where sanctions were imposed or a public employee was terminated for corruption or theft. So there are some countries where at least egregious misconduct is disciplined.

Collusion among public officials has also been identified as perpetuating corruption. In Bosnia and Herzegovina (World Bank, 2001e) 35 per cent of officials said health colleagues who refuse bribes face retribution, and similar views were expressed in focus group discussions among public health staff in Ethiopia.

Supplies: mismanagement and corruption
Availability of drugs and supplies complement health professionals and their absence reflect poor management or corruption.

Drug management and leakage
Virtually all qualitative studies that have probed this issue have emerged with the view that quality and drug availability are virtually synonymous, and lack of drugs has been repeatedly shown to discourage utilization of public facilities (World Bank, 2005a). A recent in depth assessment of the Costa Rican pharmaceutical system's registration, drug selection, procurement, distribution and service delivery revealed both great strengths and glaring weaknesses. The study used a combination of (i) interviews with public officials; (ii) industry interviews with local pharmacies and multinational companies; (iii) focus groups with health care professionals; and, (iv) exit surveys for a representative sample of patients.

Clear publicly available procedures, pharmaceutical lists and criteria; reliance on defined, generic drugs; and distribution audits were deemed excellent. The greatest weaknesses were in procurement, specifically in the lack of performance monitoring, quality monitoring, audits and uncontrolled political interference; and in distribution where inventory management, security and information systems were found particularly deficient. Alleged abuses in service delivery by both health professionals and patients were attributed to lack of controls in prescribing and supplying drugs to patients.

Surprisingly, half of exit survey respondents had not received a prescribed drug due to non-availability, an important indicator of ineffectiveness (Cohen, 2002). Costa Rica's strong record in health care delivery and its relatively higher income, greater health spending and education levels among developing countries suggests the difficulty and challenges inherent in managing health systems and drugs in particular.

Drugs tend to be a commonly "leaked" product given that it can fetch a higher price in the private market. In Ethiopia users and providers explained in focus groups the rampant stealing of public sector drugs, their resale in the private market and the common dealings in contraband medicines. They acknowledge the lack of drugs in the public sector and the ready availability of those drugs in private pharmacies and clinics. A health officer in Addis Ababa noted that "most health workers are involved in such things [theft]" attributing this to "outside temptations" and low pay of public servants (Lindelow, Serneels and Lemma, 2003). Surveys in Nigeria found that 28 PHC facilities had not received drugs from the federal government in two years, and a World Bank study reported that les than half the facilities in Lagos and Kogi states had government supplied drug stock in 2001 (Adeniyi, 2001). In Costa Rica 32 per cent of users indicated that they had prior knowledge of theft in government pharmacies (Cohen, 2002), and in a hospital study in the Dominican Republic comparing patient prescriptions and records of administered drugs a significant proportion of drugs went missing.

The average leakage rate for drugs in Uganda was estimated at 73 per cent, ranging from 40 to 94 per cent across 10 public facilities. High demand drugs, such as those to treat malaria, were the least available to patients because health workers and the Health Unit Management Committee members, the entities meant to provide local oversight, expropriated them (Mcpake et al., 1999). A later facility exit survey in Uganda shows much higher drug availability and distribution, however (Lindelow, Reinikka and Svensson, 2003). In China various studies indicate that on average about 30 per cent of public drug supplies are expired or counterfeit (Hsiao, 2005), suggesting poor logistics management, limited oversight and graft.

More insidious and difficult is drug mishandling from the importation of substandard medications, to the repackaging of drugs, substituting lower cost/quality medications, to the pilfering of drug supplies at points of service (e.g., clinics and hospitals). The health consequences of tampering can be serious, but rarely traced to the source of the problem due to ignorance, lack of regulation and enforcement.

In-kind supplies from patients
Interviews and focus groups from around the world reveal the common need to either bring or purchase basic supplies (e.g., bed sheets, bandages) or drugs (Narayan, 2000; Lewis, 2000, 2002) and in some instances equipment. The concentration of private health services adjacent to public hospitals and clinics in many countries attests to the chronic shortages of basic inputs and malfunctioning equipment. In Kyrgyz Republic in 2001 among hospitalized patients 98 per cent brought food, 73 per cent linens, 80 per cent had family members purchase drugs and 76 per cent supplied medical supplies (Falkingham, 2002). Similarly in Tajikistan in 1999 77 per cent spent on food, 93 per cent on medicines and 51 per cent for medical supplies (Falkingham, 2004). Thus the health care system supplied little of the operating inputs in either country. Patients paid for 50 per cent of drugs in the Dominican Republic hospital (Lewis, LaForgia and Sulvetta, 1996).

In Nigeria 25 per cent of health facilities had about half of the minimum package of equipment, while 40 per cent had less than a quarter of what was needed (World Bank, forthcoming). In Ethiopia two separate surveys revealed that only 21 per cent of public hospitals had autoclaves (sterilizers) and 46 per cent had functioning operating theaters, both serous shortcomings given the spreading AIDS epidemic and the high volume of patients (World Bank, 2005b). A study in Udaipur district in Rajasthan, India found patchy avail- ability of basic equipment in health facilities with only a quarter having sterilizers. A third of sub-centers lacked a stethoscope, ther- mometer or scale (Banerjee and Duflo, 2005).

Corruption in the supply chain

Graft and padding of billings form a commonly identified form of corruption in the public sector, and health care is no exception. The constant need for supplies to complement the skills and infrastruc- ture investments of government offer an opportunity for petty theft.

Siphoning of public funds for private gain can occur in the transfer of funds from public treasuries to ministries of health, from the ministries to their provider units, and within the provider units themselves. All of these levels provide opportunity for theft. Misuse of funds often occurs in the process of tendering and payment, something all countries need to guard against through required pro- cedures and regular audits. Having clearly articulated policies and procedures, adherence to policies and regulations, and consistent enforcement of rules discourage illegal behaviors.

In a 4 province survey across 80 municipalities in the Philippines corruption perceptions of households was negatively associated with providers' knowledge (of required immunizations), which in turn was strongly related to immunization coverage and disease incidence in the survey areas. Although significance is not highly robust in all cases, the analysis illuminates the negative relation- ship between corruption and performance at the local level (Azfar, Kahkonen and Meagher, 2001).

The contracting process for construction and the purchase of supplies offers a traditionally rich source of returns for corrupt offi- cials and suppliers through kickbacks, over-invoicing or outright graft. A recent study of 7 Latin American countries provides insights on overpayment for supplies (DiTella and Savedoff, 2001).

In Argentina, Bolivia, Colombia and Venezuela overpayment for supplies in public hospitals points to corruption. Perceptions of staff, their assessment of the probabilities of getting caught and being punished, and examination of hospital records and comparing these with market prices suggest that irregularities are rife. Figure 4 shows the ratio of highest to lowest purchase price for four commonly stocked medical supplies – saline solution, cotton, dextrose and penicillin – across hospitals in each of the four Latin American countries for which data exist. The poor procurement performance underlying the purchases were attributed to gross mismanagement or corruption (Di Tella and Savedoff, 2001).

In Colombia, it is estimated that about 11 per cent of costs could have been saved if accepted public tendering rules had been followed (Giedion, Morales and Acosta, 2001). Results from surveys of physicians and nurses in Argentina (Schargrodsky, Mera and Weinschelbaum, 2001), Colombia (Giedion, Morales and Acosta, 2001) and Venezuela (Jaîn and Paravisini, 2001) show that corruption within facilities leads to overpayment of suppliers, and that combined with the lack of punishment and the low probability of getting caught make it possible. In short, the lack of enforced rules, procedures and accountability effectively allows irregularities in purchasing practices.

In Argentina a similar finding emerged. When the health system transparency policy was introduced the prices of procured supplies dropped sharply but rose again once the policy was no longer enforced (Schargrodsky, Mera and Weinschelbaum, 2001). In Colombia price variations were statistically significant across purchases of public hospitals, and particularly different where they ignored the price lists negotiated and endorsed by a local NGO under contract to the government (Giedion, Morales and Acosta, 2001).

Direct and specific evidence is harder to come by. However, in Ghana interviews with officials and the public suggest that 21 per cent of procurements in government hospitals are corrupt, and 18 per cent of the value of contracts is required in kickbacks to public officials (World Bank, 2000d). Petty theft in the aggregate can lead

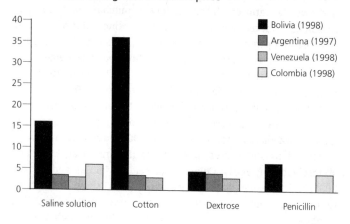

Figure 4 **Comparison of purchase price difference for selected medical supplies across public hospitals in four Latin American countries**
Ratio of highest to lowest price

Bolivia (1998)
Argentina (1997)
Venezuela (1998)
Colombia (1998)

Saline solution   Cotton   Dextrose   Penicillin

Source: Di Tella and Savedoff, 2001

to significant losses, making it not so petty. Anecdotal evidence is abundant, but hard evidence elusive. Qualitative work has unearthed some strong perceptions and knowledge of petty theft providing a sense of its importance, and lending credence to allegations of theft.

Petty theft was considered very common in Costa Rican hospitals where 83 per cent of nurses reported thefts (Di Tella and Savedoff, 2001), and in Venezuela where roughly two-thirds of health personnel were aware of stolen materials, equipment or drugs (Jaîn and Paravisini, 2001). In Peru, theft by both physicians and nurses was viewed as the most common form of corruption, with the highest estimated prevalence in Ministry of Health hospitals – 22 per cent, double that reported for Social Security hospitals (Alc‡zar and Andrade, 2001).

The lack of discipline and oversight makes it easy for corrupt officials to report higher costs for supplies, food and other goods and to pocket the difference. Even in developed countries, pharmaceuticals and supplies tend to be locked and closely inventoried to track supplies and drugs on a continuous basis because theft poses so much of a threat. Most public health systems in developing and transition countries lack the ability to limit access to drug supplies and the infrastructure to control access, although there are some exceptions. The absence of information systems for supplies and drugs, and an inability to sanction (or hold accountable) abusing staff makes control of theft particularly challenging.

Flow of funds

Subsidized health care is meant to rely on public funding and minimally, if at all, on patients. In many places, bureaucratic problems, corruption and mismanagement lead to inadequate public funds at the point of service and the informal charging of patients compensates for inadequate salaries and gaps in discretionary budgets. At the same time informal charging may have serious equity implications undermining the objectives of subsidies.

Leakage of public funds

Whether public resources for staff and other inputs reach the front line – the clinics and hospitals that deliver the services to the population – is critical to a functioning health system. The World Bank has pioneered efforts to measure the extent of leakage, that is, the amount of the line ministries' budgets that reaches the intended communities and the schools, clinics and hospitals funded through national transfers. These public expenditure tracking studies (PETS) simply follow the flow of funds through the labyrinth of government bureaucracy to determine if funds reach each of the designated levels.

First applied in education, PETS identified key problems of effective public management. In Uganda, 87 per cent of funds never reached the schools (Dehn, Reinikka and Svensson, 2003). In Zambia

Table 3 **Leakage rates for health care, selected countries**

Country	Year	Leakage rate	Type of expenditure
Ghana	2000	80%	Non-salary budget
Peru	2001	71	"Glass of Milk" Program
Tanzania	1999	40	Non-salary budget
Uganda	2000	70	Drugs and supplies

Source: Lindelow, Kushnarova, and Kaiser, 2005

it was 60 per cent. Table 3 summarizes available evidence for the health sector in four countries: Ghana, Peru, Tanzania and Uganda where leakage is 70 per cent or higher in all but Tanzania. High leakage means inadequate funding for non-salary spending, which makes the job of service delivery exceedingly difficult and necessarily imposes on patients to finance "free" health care through financial or in-kind contributions. In Nigeria, Papua New Guinea, Rwanda, Senegal, there is evidence of leakage but neither the levels nor the sources of the problem have been determined. Leakages are a reflection of delays and bottlenecks in budget execution and supply management, poor record keeping and underutilization of audits, as well as incompetence and criminal acts. Incomplete and error riddled records complicate efforts to track financial flows, which is why so few countries have comparable data despite the number of country studies undertaken.

In the case of education in Uganda, informing the public of expected school transfers and reporting receipt of funds to the community led to dramatic increases in non-salary budgets. Effectively the community monitored and pressured local officials to make sure that funds were applied as intended (Reinikka and Svensson, 2004).

Informal payments
Informal payments can be defined as "payments to individual and institutional providers, in kind or in cash, that are made outside official payment channels or are purchases meant to be covered by the health care system. This encompasses 'envelope' payments to

physicians and 'contributions' to hospitals as well as the value of medical supplies purchased by patients and drugs obtained from private pharmacies but intended to be part of government-financed health care services." (Lewis, 2000, 2002). More specifically they are under-the-table payments to doctors, nurses and other medical staff for jumping the queue, receiving better or more care, obtaining drugs, or just simply for any care at all.

Informal payments create a parallel market for services within public health care systems, and, like the informal sector, informal payments are typically illegal and unreported. They can be considered a form of corruption, but may just be symptomatic of bad management. While only recently defined and discussed, what emerges from the data is, surprisingly, how widespread informal payments have become.

A major challenge is differentiating informal and gratitude payments given the official co-payment, bribes and gifts that patients pay. Where all fees have been banned any payment by households is clearly unofficial, but in many countries formal fees exist, blurring the dichotomy. It then becomes the level of payment, the nature of the transaction and its timing that become relevant for distinguishing the nature of the payment. For example, in Kyrgyz Republic in 2001 95 per cent of those who paid for services did not receive a receipt while only 3 per cent reported giving a gift to the health personnel and the time of service (Falkingham, 2002). A Bolivia study showed that perception of corruption was associated with the size of informal payment with a significant coefficient of .34 (Gatti, Gray-Molina and Klugman, 2004).

Ex post transactions are particularly problematic because post-service gratitude gestures are common and often expected. Where providers insist on direct pre-payment without involvement of official cash windows, refuse patient care without the fee, receive direct payments for specific tasks, or refuse basic services without a "tip" (e.g., such as moving patients from room to room, or giving injections) informality of payment is likely.

Figure 5 summarizes the frequency of informal payments to

public health care workers among users of health services based on survey data from various sources. The frequency range is enormous from 3 per cent in Peru to 96 per cent in Pakistan. Regionally South Asia stands out for its heavy reliance on informal payments. East Asian experience is split between Thailand and Indonesia with low levels and the former Communist countries, with Cambodia at 55 per cent and a dated estimate for Vietnam at 81 per cent. The proportions for Latin America and Eastern Europe have a wide distribution with low levels in some countries and among the highest in others, making generalizations meaningless. Recent evidence from smaller samples in Africa suggests that informal payments of various kinds are common in Uganda (McPake et al., 1999), Mozambique (Lindelow, Ward and Zorzi, 2004) and Ethiopia (Lindelow, Serneels and Lemma, 2003). In all three, patients pay public providers directly for consultations and drugs over and above any formal charges.

Data sources vary with much of the information coming from either household surveys or governance and corruption studies, although some, like Bolivia (2002), Moldova, Kazakhstan (1999) and Poland used dedicated health facility exit surveys[5], and Albania (2002), Bolivia (2001) and China used province level surveys, and the India data are from a district in Rajastan. Where both large household surveys and smaller studies exist for the same country, the latter always shows higher informal payments. Kazakhstan exhibits dramatically higher payments in the 2002 survey over the 2001 LSMS. Albania's overall LSMS estimate in 1996 was 22 per cent, but jumped to 28 and 60 per cent, respectively, for outpatient and inpatient care in the smaller 2001 survey.

Whether this is due to the greater attention to the issue with dedicated surveys and smaller samples that allow drilling down sufficiently to obtain reliable information on a sensitive subject, or other factors it suggests that some of the broader surveys underestimate the extent of patient payments.

Low levels of informal payments in Peru, Paraguay, Thailand and Kosovo may reflect the existence of and reliance on private

Figure 5 **Proportion who make informal payments among users of health services, selected countries**

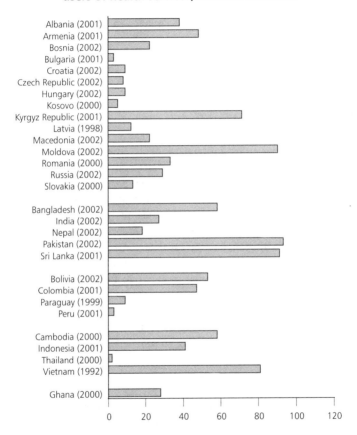

Source: See Source Appendix I

sector alternatives that require significant out-of-pocket payments where consumers tend to have more influence on performance. The Czech Republic appears odd given the rest of ECA but consistent with other findings. Public providers with a monopoly position are in a stronger position to charge patients extra for their services.

Kosovars have not had access to public health care for decades and have financed care out of pocket to private providers. Thais too rely on the private sector for some of their health care. The higher rates reported for Colombia and Bolivia, however, would question that explanation since Colombia has a large private health system not too different from Peru's. The differences may reflect different degrees of oversight in public clinics and hospitals, but more in-depth work would be necessary to reach a firm conclusion since the approach to measuring informal payments varies across countries.

Figure 6 extends the informal payment distribution to encom-pass differences in outpatient and inpatient payments and includes some countries from Figure 5. With the exception of Bulgaria, inpa-tient care is more likely to be financed via informal payments, and often the disparity between the two types of services is dramatic, as is the case with Bangladesh, Tajikistan, Armenia and Albania. Evidence for four Eastern European countries (Czech Republic, Hungary, Poland and Romania) reveals that formal payment are associated with primary and outpatient specialist care and informal payments with surgery and inpatient services (Belli, 2002). House-holds either feel the need to pay for hospitalizations or providers don't give them a choice insisting on payment if services are to be rendered.

Perception surveys of providers or citizens offer additional insights. In Costa Rica 85 per cent of medical staffs indicated that under-the-table payments to physicians were common, and half of patients said they made payments in public facilities roughly equiv-alent to 50 per cent of a private sector consultation. In Bolivia the incidence of informal payments was significantly correlated with perceptions of corruption in specific public hospitals, and 40 per cent of interviewed patients acknowledged making illicit payments for care (Gray-Molina et. al, 2001), this is similar to the results of a household survey in 106 Bolivian municipalities reportedly that 45

Figure 6 **Proportion of patients making informal payments by type of service, selected countries**

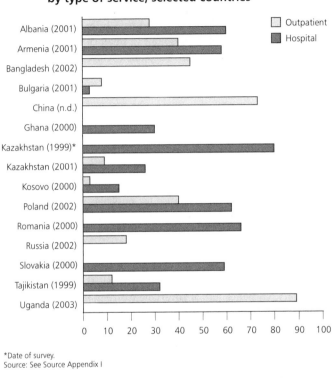

*Date of survey.
Source: See Source Appendix I

per cent of patients paid informally (Chakraborty et al., 2002). Interestingly, national surveys for Bolivia show that over 60 per cent of those interviewed considered health to be corrupt.

A comparative study in five South Asian countries (Bangladesh, India, Nepal, Pakistan and Sri Lanka) found that in all but Sri Lanka most payments were ex ante demands from providers. Bribes are required in all five countries for admission to the hospital, to obtain a bed, and to receive subsidized medications (Thampi,

2002). In Bangalore, India citizen feedback surveys revealed that informal payments were made to ensure proper treatment, but they were typically demanded by providers and 51 per cent of those interviewed indicated they had paid bribes in government hospitals and 89 per cent in hospitals in small cities, but they also paid informally in the private hospitals (24 per cent). More dramatically, bribes were paid to nurses in maternity homes so mothers could see their infants (Gopakumar, 1998). In Albania among the 60 per cent of patients who received care 43 per cent said the gift was requested (World Bank, 2003a). Using focus groups of patients and providers Shahriari, Belli and Lewis (2001) explain the virtual market for publicly provided care in Poland. Informal payments have become the way to obtain the services of specific physicians, with pricing reflecting reputation and demand. It is an implicit form of insurance for possible future needs, and prices are commonly known. Thus the process of negotiation and payment for health services may be informal but it has become a very sophisticated market in Poland.

The motivations of health staff and patients in relying on under the table payments are strong. Physicians argue that low pay, irregular salary payments, lack of government attention and the need to keep services going requires drastic action, and patient contributions offer the only source of funds to fill the gap (Bloom Han and Li, 2001; Belli, Shahriari, Lewis, 2001; Lindelow, Serneels and Lemma, 2003; Kutzin et al., 2003). Patients on the other hand also see low pay as an impetus to contribute, but traditions of gratitude as well as concerns for some future need also play a role.

In Ethiopia feedback from policymakers, experts and health workers revealed that inappropriate payments are rife in the health sector. Patients typically must pay for every service and each item, from registering to paying bribes for changing bed sheets to drugs and supplies (Lindelow, Serneels and Lemma, 2003). Similar reports of itemized charging emerged from qualitative work in Georgia (Belli, Shahriari and Gotzadze, 2004) and Poland (Belli, Shahriari and Lewis, 2001) where there too the public system has become a fee-for service entity. Qualitative studies explore this in some depth. Consumer confusion about the official or unofficial nature of payments is common. Patients pay but they don't always know why and they often do so at multiple locations or for different "services" (Belli, Shahriari and Gotzadze, 2004; Narayan, 2000; Killingsworth et al., 1999).

Multivariate analysis sheds further light on some of the underlying motivations for informal payment as well as whether patient revenues are well spent. In Kazakhstan Thompson's (2004) econometric analysis of patients discharged from three hospitals in Almaty City concluded that informal payments made in the admission department before treatment, and the amount paid subsequently at both admissions and hospital wards shortened admission time for surgery. He found longer lengths of stay associated with payments to both the admission department and directly to individual providers on the wards, and perceived patient quality increased with the amount paid informally. These results confirm the assumption that patients pay to receive more attentive and "higher quality" care as they perceive it. Longer lengths of stay do not necessarily mean better clinical care, but shorter waits, longer hospital stays and better treatment by medical staff tend to be valued by patients. In Kazakhstan paying ensures that health care meets the demands and perceived needs of patients.

Of concern is the relative cost of the services to patients, and numerous studies point out the impact on the poor. Figure 7 summarizes the available data showing the average cost of an outpatient visit or hospital admission as a per cent of half monthly income, roughly equivalent to median income (source). The level of inpatient payments far exceeds the amounts paid out for outpatient services and numerous studies document the extent of hardship some households face in meeting these costs. Inpatient costs can exceed annual family income forcing the sale of assets or the accumulation of debt in order to afford care (Lewis 2000, 2002; Falkingham 2002, 2004; Killingsworth et al., 1999). Selected studies in China of "red packages" paid to providers report that payments

Figure 7 **Average informal payments as percentage of half-monthly per capita income, selected countries (int'l $ PPP)**

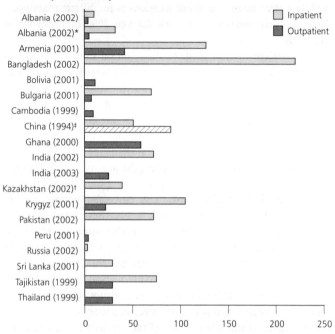

*Survey of 2,000 households in three Albanian provinces.   †Based on hospital exit surveys.
‡Percent calculated as average across various studies. Striped bar indicates referral hospitals.
Sources: World Bank LSMS; Murrugarra 2003; Falkingham 2000 and 2001; Transparency International 2002; World Bank 2000b, 2000d, 2001a; Phongpaichit 2000; Bloom, Han and Li 2001; Banerjee and Duflo (2005)

average between 140–320 yuan per hospital visit (US$16–36), with referral hospitals averaging 400 yuan (US$44), roughly 90 per cent of half monthly income (Bloom, Han and Li, 2001).

Two studies in Albania showed different aspects of the informal payment issue. The analysis of a three province survey showed that rural residents were more likely to pay for services though they paid about the same as those in other income brackets when they did pay, and income had no effect on the probability of having to pay (Hotchkiss et al., 2005). Estimates of the price elasticity of small increases in the price of health services using a national representative survey found almost no effect, indicating that patients are not particularly price sensitive in Albania (World Bank, 2003a).

Exemption for fees offers the potential for husbanding scarce resources for those least able to afford health care. Many systems have instituted such procedures to retain the benefits of co-payments without unduly burdening the poor (World Bank, 2004). Evidence on effectiveness, however, suggests problems with the approach. In Bangladesh data from interviews and observation in a sample of four hospitals showed that 75 per cent of the time the lowest income group paid the least amount both officially and unofficially. In the outlier institution the poor paid more than the wealthiest group but the same as or less than the middle income patients. Payments are also standardized and routinized with specific time periods for charging during inpatient stays rather than at discharge (Killingsworth et al., 1999).

In Rajasthan, India patients regularly pay for "free" outpatient care, though the poorest patients pay 40 per cent less than the highest income patients, though it should be noted that in this part of India everyone is poor it is simply a matter of degree. On average 7.3 per cent of total household spending goes to paying for health care (Banerjee, Deaton and Duflo, 2004). In Uganda exemptions were extended to the politically powerful and those overseeing the local health care program (McPake et al., 1999), a perverse version of exemption meant to ensure equal access but in this case subsidizing the better off. Central Asia's experience has not been encouraging either with minimal exemptions for lower income patients (Falkingham, 2004). Evidence from Kazakhstan showed that for major illnesses the lowest income households spent more than twice their monthly income for health care while the wealthiest households spent the equivalent of half their monthly income reflecting the lack of exemptions for the poor

(Sari, Langenbrunner and Lewis, 2000).

Informal payments are much more widespread than commonly thought. Indeed, donors and governments have urged banning user charges in the interests of equity in access to health services. Sweeping removal of a reliable source of revenue for equity reasons means that those who can and cannot pay receive free care. However the strategy could simply encourage under-the-table payments from both sets of patients since patients already pay and in some cases can afford treatment. While there is some suggestion from Kyrgyz Republic (Kutzin et al., 2003) and Cambodia (Barber, Bonnet and Bekedam, 2004) that instituting formal fees can serve to curtail informal payments, the impact of removing fees has not been assessed. Anecdotal evidence suggests a rise in informal arrangements, but documentation has not confirmed this.

Mismanagement in health care service delivery

Often irregularities and poor governance simply stem from poor management. Where incentives for strong performance either don't exist or are undermined by ineffective management it is not surprising that productivity and performance suffer. For example, if staff advancement caps after a single promotion, a common pattern in many countries, then the incentives to excel are diminished. By the same token the inability to fire public sector staff even in the face of embezzlement or nonattendance erodes managers' authority and the public sector's ability to hold staff accountable. The lack of carrots and sticks dis-empowers public management and thwarts efforts at accountability.

Evidence on mismanagement is spotty. The core issues include human resource management and supervision, basic subsystems function (e.g., procurement, drug logistics), efficiency of fiduciary transfers, input availability, and satisfaction of the target population.

Overall management of health systems, hospitals and clinics typically fall to physicians, few of whom have the training or experience necessary to effectively carry out their jobs. This poses a major problem in Turkey as they move to reform the health system (World Bank, 2003c), and was at the heart of ineffective service delivery in the Dominican Republic (La Forgia et al., 2004). Disincentives to good performance often are due to rigid civil service rules that limit promotion and pay differentials that could be used to reward superior performance. At the same time low productivity or outright abuses can go unnoticed (Lewis, LaForgia and Sulvetta. 1992).

Low wages also lead workers to seek additional employment outside government. In Kogi State, Nigeria, 42 per cent of the staff had not been paid their salaries for more than 6 months in the past year (Das Gupta, Gauri and Khemani, 2003), converting staff into virtual volunteers and eroding the credibility of the health system. In addition to the Nigeria state, reports from Ethiopia, Mozambique and Uganda (Lindelow, Serneels and Lemma, 2003; Lindelow, Ward and Zorzi, 2003; Azfar and Gurgur, 2001) indicated that the need to have additional sources of income effectively compromised providers' ability to carry out their public duties on the scale intended. In qualitative surveys health workers said they missed work or cut short their hours to devote time to other economic activities. Another study in Nigeria showed that the greater the lag in paying salaries the more likely health workers were to engage in pharmaceutical sales and seek other employment in the private sector (Khemani, 2004). Family survival therefore plays a role in absenteeism and low productivity.

Evidence from a number of countries suggests that vague and poorly understood policies, uneven recordkeeping and minimal use of such information contribute to poor management. An assessment in Nigeria found a low level of knowledge among Federal Ministry of Health (FMOH) staff regarding standard procedures and regulations, and current budget allocations. Moreover, current budgets and expenditures did not correspond (World Bank, forthcoming). In Uganda staff records were inadequate. At the facility level only 56 per cent of the staff are to be found in district records, but at the district level there were an additional 109 staff (out of a total of 465) who do not show up on facility rosters (Lindelow, Reinikka and

Svensson, 2003). In Honduras 2.4 per cent of staff were "ghost" workers and 5 per cent of staff had unilaterally moved to other locations (World Bank, 2001f).

Poor recordkeeping capacity and failures to require acceptable reports in Mozambique (Lindelow, Ward and Zorzi, 2004) undermined health care delivery and regular availability of inputs. In Nigeria, existing management information systems were deemed ineffective due to complicated and obscure reporting requirements, incomplete record keeping and low capacity (World Bank, forthcoming). Drug management in Costa Rica, a well run middle income country, exhibits particular weaknesses in logistics and distribution attributed to flawed information systems and inadequate monitoring (Cohen, 2002). Each of these represent deficient aspects of recordkeeping that compromise efforts at management.

Poor management also appears to signal corruption in some instances. In Bolivia multivariate analysis showed a significant association between longer waiting time and corruption indicators (Gatti, Gray-Molina and Klugman, 2003), and in the Philippines perceptions of corruption in public health services discouraged use of public facilities, particularly in poor communities (Azfar and Gurgur, 2001). Corruption no doubt is associated with bad management, the question remains as to whether and how management flaws lead to corruption.

This brief review does not do justice to the complexity of the issue, and more attention to the problem of incentives and management are warranted. Although a chronic weakness of health systems, management is critical to performance and improved effectiveness. Ensuring the availability of funds, hiring and deploying staff, maintaining basic record systems, and tracking facility performance are the basic ingredients for improving management and overall health care delivery.

Policy options for promoting better governance

Improving governance poses an important challenge to governments in transition and developing countries, but there are good examples of things that can be done based on actual experiences. This section is divided by category to summarize the evidence and link these lessons to specific agendas. Accountability and incentives serve as threads across the components because they represent the keys to better policy and outcomes.

Key accountability measures include (i) information on performance and impact, (ii) the ability to audit, (iii) the authority to reward performance, and discipline, transfer and terminate employees who engage in abuses; and (iv) answering to stakeholders on the performance of public services. Accountability tends to be absent due in part to measurement problems but also to minimal management, oversight or evaluation of performance. The high demand from patients for diagnosis and care when they fall ill, and the difficulty in generalizing across medical conditions further complicate oversight and accountability.

Improving government effectiveness

The health system that delivers health care is only as good as its management. This section focuses on government initiatives and management tools that can raise effectiveness and performance.

Adequate incentives for health professionals lie more in the structure of the health care system and its financing than in limited actions that fix existing arrangements. Fundamentally money needs to follow patients at least in terms of tying medical staff time to specific patients. Paying providers whether they see (or are assigned) patients or not, and compensating under and over-performance equally is both unfair and unlikely to build the trust needed in a public health system. How that is accomplished is the challenge, and there are options.

The exception to money following patients may be capitated payments where physicians receive a fixed prospective payment for each patient and extends services as needed. It has been shown to be highly effective at providing the necessary incentives for providers, but typically is combined with clear management and oversight to ensure accountability. Physicians who don't see patients under capitation are managed to assure that they comply with requirements of contracts, so in the end money does follow patients.

Adjustments to pay and benefits, clear criteria for hiring and promotion, defined discipline for misconduct and adequate training to equip workers with needed skills foster a functioning health system. How providers are paid has dramatic effects on performance, as evidence from the OECD countries attests. Payment methods are the cornerstone of incentives for productivity and performance and increasingly developed countries have sought alternatives or at least complementary means to reward performance and productivity.

In most developing countries physician compensation remains salary based. A review of the limited literature on the effect of salary earnings on physician clinical behavior across the OECD concluded that physicians whose earnings are based on salary rather than fee-for-service, bonus payments or capitation showed lower productivity, lower levels of care and higher wound rates from surgery. However, salaried doctors facilitated cost control, a major concern in OECD health systems (Gosden, Pedersen and Torgerson, 1999).

Low wages represent one area of potential temptation for corruption. Where earnings are low individuals have second and third jobs, but they also perceive that low wages entitle them to demand contributions from patients. Civil service reform is often required to address egregious structural problems related to postings, promotion and pay, but the health sector can also serve as a pilot to launch improvements that stimulate better performance. Alternatively experimentation with other payment arrangements may prove more effective.

In Bolivia corruption was lower where management was stronger and some form of **oversight of staff** existed, in this case, frequent written evaluations of performance, key inputs for rewarding and disciplining staff (Gatti, Gray-Molina and Klugman, 2004). In education, **inspectors** were associated with lower absenteeism in some cases, and it may apply in health care. However, business effectiveness studies in the FSU show how inspectors can undermine the system through bribes to certify acceptable performance, so it is important to ensure that such arrangements are working as intended if they are adopted.

In a recent experiment, Leonard (2005) assesses the importance of training and incentives in determining physician performance in Tanzania across a sample of public and private providers. He concludes that while ability is important, **institutional incentives**, particularly the ability to hire and fire staff, are far more powerful than education or experience in explaining the quality of care provided patients, offering an empirical basis for the priority of putting in place incentives to foster improvements in health care.

A fundamental initiative is the establishment of **clear procurement and contracting rules**. Evidence for Argentina and Colombia shows a potential role for effective oversight as discussed. To effectively achieve such results requires existence of clear rules, effective oversight to detect problems, enforcement of rules, and rewards and punishments for good and unacceptable behavior, respectively. The lack of minimal managerial order and oversight are fundamental weaknesses in many public health systems which permit such abuses. In fairness, however, battling these kinds of problems persist in even the wealthiest countries and relentless effort are required to control corrupt practices.

In the Philippines multivariate analysis found that the **frequency of audit by central government and autonomy of local government** increased immunization coverage, suggesting that local governments can benefit from authority, and auditing will further encourage responsible public performance (Azfar and Gurgur, 2001). In Madagascar, sanctions for misuse of funds led to systematic **following of financial procedures**. Most important among sanctions was criticism from supervisors and transfer to less desirable locations. Though the effect of accountability is diluted by the fact that the most common reasons for transfer is displeasing local officials without discussion or vetting of the merits of the transfer, frequent audits of financial records combined with consequences for staff were successful in improving financing management, a cornerstone of government effectiveness (Brinkerhoff, 2005).

The nature of accountability and how to structure incentives is not apparent from the evidence assembled here. Ostensible **community oversight** has been assessed in Bolivia, Madagascar, the Philippines, Uganda. The centralized hiring, promotion and deployment of public health workers in all countries effectively neutralizes the role of local supervision. If the consequences of absenteeism, taking of bribes and stealing of drugs are beyond the authority of local boards or community oversight bodies then those institutions may bring the community together but they will have no influence over the centrally managed health staffs, or service delivery responsiveness and access.

Even where systems exist to promote accountability it does not necessarily mean that they are effective. In Jigawa state in Nigeria hospital management committees meant to oversee and advise hospital managers rarely met, were unclear on their responsibilities, and had little involvement with strategic planning, targeting or budget control (World Bank, forthcoming). In Madagascar, the fact that local committees were powerless beyond moral suasion led providers to ignore their hollow authority and instead respond to supervisors who had a say in their destiny (Brinkerhoff, 2005). To be effective community leaders need authority, and at the same time they need to be accountable to the local citizenry.

Local control where it goes beyond simply oversight holds promise. Under the "Bamako Initiative" that gave communities in selected African countries control over health facilities in exchange for sharing the financing burden showed impressive health status improvements in at least three countries. In Ceara, Brazil the state instituted a health worker outreach program with hired health outreach workers under contract to the state, and handed responsibility for supervision to municipalities. Local control led to better health in the communities covered by the new state program (sources). In Bolivia corruption was lower where local organizing groups were active (Gatti, Gray-Molina and Klugman, 2003). In contrast local control proved ineffective in Nigeria, Madagascar and Uganda (World Bank, forthcoming; Mcpake et al., 1999; Brinkerhoff, 2005) leaving the issue unresolved, but more experimentation and systematic evaluations can help address this.

Strategies to control **informal payments** entail both finding alternative sources of funding and better management. Raising official fees as a substitute for under-the-table payments showed positive effects on patient payment and utilization in two pilot programs: in two regions in the Kyrgyz Republic, and a major referral hospital in Cambodia. In Kyrgyz Republic formal fees reduced informal charges as confirmed by both multivariate analysis and data which showed the proportion of patients making direct payments to providers declined from 60 per cent to 38 per cent while informal payments for the country as a whole rose to 70 per cent. In-kind spending by patients for food and linens in the pilot regions with formal fees remained constant but spending for drugs and medical supplies declined by over 50 per cent though there was no change in the country as a whole. That combined with insurance payments helped to make health care more affordable and quelled under-the-table payments (Kutzin et al., 2003).

In Cambodia reorganization of hospital staffing combined with a transparent official fee policy, clearly designated exemptions, and retained fee revenue that supplemented physician salaries at levels comparable to those earned under the informal arrangements led to more reliable pricing, stable revenue and higher demand. Focus groups identified the deterrent of informal payments to health service use, and the subsequent predictability and equity adjustments improved access without compromising utilization or hospital revenue, the latter a critical component of compensation given salary levels (Barber, Bonnet and Bekedam, 2004). Two instances do not allow sweeping conclusions, but the fact that substituting legal for illegal payments and allowing the points of service to retain revenues proved effective suggests that it is a strategy worth pursuing further

Addressing some of the incentives behind informal payments provide options for reform. Some alternative policies include: standardizing quality and access (e.g., waiting time), allowing and promoting alternative financing mechanisms through the private sector (e.g., private insurance arrangements), and, within the public sector, balancing the number of staff and resources so as to have fewer positions with higher pay. As discussed elsewhere higher pay will not necessarily address corruption by itself, but paying wages that are appropriate to existing labor market conditions, prohibiting side payments and holding providers accountable could together encourage more transparent and fair transactions, and offer incentives for better provider performance. Although it is expensive for countries to raise wages in public health care services, a reform that regularizes and improves pay has the potential to raise productivity. Higher productivity, in turn, would make it possible to provide the same amount of services or more, with fewer workers, thereby offsetting some of the expected increase in the total wage bill. In addition, greater transparency in all fiduciary functions would improve fairness and bolster effectiveness.

In Venezuela, a study of public hospitals found that theft and unjustified absences declined with **greater accountability**, although the rate of approved absences rose, so reforms can be effective but management objectives can sometimes be too narrowly defined (Jaen and Paravinski, 2001). The issue should not be absences per se but performance and both management and accountability mechanism need to focus on these.

Having government contract out services can often improve performance of publicly subsidized services, partly because holding contractors accountable is far easier than doing so with public workers. Often government has few incentives to offer public servants given rigidity in most civil service rules, but retains leverage over contractors. Nonetheless contracting out is far from a panacea as it means developing regulatory capacity which varies from the standard tasks of providers and managers who operate points of service. Experience in Haiti (Eichler, Auzilia and Pollock,

2001), Cambodia (World Bank, 2004) and Central America (La Forgia, 2005) suggest that contracting out can work even in the lowest income environments, the challenge is ensuring continued oversight and accountability of contractors. To date only the four Central American cases have a track record across elections.

Consumer satisfaction surveys help build accountability. Exit surveys, mini-household surveys or focus groups to elicit responses help gauge the strengths and weaknesses of public programs. Including these in annual reporting up the chain of command, and encouraging points of service to use these for management purposes would provide benchmarks for making public services more responsive, and bolstering their impact and effectiveness.

Controlling corruption

This paper has described the wide range of irregularities that characterize health care services in developing countries and suggests that corruption flourishes where there are no standards of performance, oversight, or penalties for unacceptable behaviors. The options discussed here have a track record, but the policy context and actions taken by officials provide the needed detail that explains why certain policies were found effective. Policies themselves are necessary but not sufficient as enforcement is equally important.

Game results from an experiment in Ethiopia used to determine temptation for corruption concluded that higher pay curtails the level of corruption, but only slightly, and that public servants appear to expropriate fewer resources when observability is higher, indicating that better oversight and exposing of inappropriate behavior can have a dampening effect on corruption (Barr, Lindelow and Serneels, 2004). In short, the potential for getting caught offers a strong disincentive for corrupt behavior.

Corruption in the health sector is unlikely to be an isolated public service failure. Addressing irregularities across the functions of the sector – construction, procurement and distribution of drugs and supplies, deployment of underpaid staff, under-the-table payments – requires an **integrated, mutually reinforcing anti-corruption**

strategy with strong political backing and a willingness to take a position and follow through. Indeed, it may well require a government-wide anti-corruption agenda, as Poland has undertaken. Even there it isn't enough to remove informal charges as the studies discussed here indicate. Making clean government a priority allows irregularities to be identified and addressed, which bolsters efforts in the sector to put in place effective oversight and detection, and endorses disciplining corrupt practices once detected. Without the willingness to act on identified corruption countries are unlikely to be able to control such practices.

Higher salaries for public sector workers are frequently proposed as a way to curb corruption, but the evidence is complicated and not straightforward. Moreover, as discussed above, there may be better means of compensating health professionals. In a study of the effect of civil service pay on corruption using cross-country regression and controlling for a wide array of factors, showed that wage levels could affect corruption but must rise dramatically to seriously reduce corrupt behavior (Van Rijkeghem and Weder, 2001). Although challenged on their corruption measures, Rauch and Evans (2000) find no effect on corruption of higher public sector wages, and instead propose that employment security, recruitment and promotion criteria, and management are of greater importance than salary increases. A study in Venezuela found a perverse effect with higher wages correlating with more corruption. Jaen and Paravinski (2001) interpret this as corrupt wage earners capturing wage setting through either influence or bribes. In sum, despite the view that salary adjustments will solve corruption the evidence suggests that while wage levels may play a role in controlling corruption it is not guaranteed and other changes need to accompany higher earnings.

An issue is whether the necessary increases required to eradicate corruption are affordable and realistic for most low income countries. Some increases may be warranted but it would also mean staff reductions to accommodate higher pay. These are considerations that should accompany civil service reform plans meant to raise salaries and curb corruption.

The absence of basic information, regular audits and monitoring evidence define an environment that invites misconduct. As Colombia implemented Law 100 reforming its health care system it unearthed extensive corruption and mismanagement in reporting and record keeping in public programs. In response the Ministry of Health set up a nationwide **database** for data matching and payment controls to identify and correct abuses that were resulting in paying "ghost" workers, among other problems. That combined with a multimedia campaign informing citizens of their rights and obligations under the newly reformed system provided a segue-way into better oversight and involvement of citizens (Soto, 2002).

Drug procurement poses multiple challenges and Chile's experience is instructive in how to institute reforms that serve multiple objectives. Chile's drug and medical supply system run by the government, CENEBAST, was plagued with poor management, frequent stock outs and overstocks of other medicines. The reform was built around a shift from a rules-based system to one grounded in transparency and good incentive structures. Its main components were: (1) introducing electronic bidding for pharmaceuticals; (2) reform of CENEBAST to change its mandate to procurement agent for hospitals and other providers who define drug priorities; and (3) information dissemination that let it be known that pharmaceutical procurement would be under scrutiny. An important element of the institutional reform was allowing other agencies and the private sector to purchase, store and transport drugs, removing CENEBAST's monopoly position.

The reform reduced information asymmetries between providers and the procurers of pharmaceuticals. and produced clear and fair rules resulting in bids from a broader spectrum of companies and lower prices for government hospitals and clinics. Overall in 1997, US$ 4 million was saved just in pharmaceutical purchases (Cohen and Montoya, 2001).

Nigeria has taken an aggressive stance on the issue and has rooted out considerable illegal manufacturing, identified substandard importation, recalled all "repackaged" drugs, and ensured **that drugs meet a basic standard** of potency, labels are clear and correct, distribution is achieved through legal channels and oversight of provision, storing and handling are systematically regulated. Evidence from elsewhere, however, is scarce as this is an area where little action has taken place at the country level and/ or these have not been evaluated. Middle income countries, like Costa Rica, tend to deal with the problem more aggressively (Cohen, 2002), but regulation remains inadequate given the ease and lucrative nature of drug corruption.

More information to citizens about resource flows from central and local governments and clarity on the roles and responsibilities of local authorities. Though it requires better data on performance, tying local outputs and resource allocations from central government (conditional resource transfers) offers a structure to undermine corruption and improve service delivery. Where citizens are informed and empowered to oversee the process, they have both a financial stake and the tools to enforce policies. Without the latter, citizens will be far less likely to view involvement as worthwhile.

Citizen report cards offer another possible means of engaging citizens in oversight to improve the quality and integrity of public services. Pioneered in public services generally, report cards have not yet been assessed as a means of improving health services, but through investigative studies they equip citizens with information on the shortcomings or failures of health services. Use of press reports based on the studies provides both evidence (rather than anecdotes) as well as a public forum for debate, which together help localities identify where change is needed (Gopakumar, 1998; World Bank 2004). Like information more generally, having authority to take action is the *sine qua non* of effectiveness in report card use.

Voice

Although not strongly associated with health outcomes, voice captures citizens' ability to get information, challenge government and ensure that services meet their needs. The record is mixed on the effectiveness of voice in improving service delivery, but some useful lessons emerge.

Information is necessary but not sufficient for citizens' to be empowered. Without the information citizen action can only be random stabs at perceived problems. Information allows concerted action. In Uganda informing citizens of fiscal transfers from the central government by posting budget receipts on school doors and announcing them in the local press led to significantly higher receipts, a more informed public and a better financed school system (Reinikka and Svensson, 2004). Similar initiatives would apply in health since local health districts are financed through central allocations. In Colombia regular press reports on procurement regularities reduced overpayment by almost 200 per cent. Despite the scope of these findings, conclusions are tentative given the small number of cases, but these suggest promising directions.

The evidence on the role of local voting is uneven. It appears to have a minimal if any effect on corruption at the local level, though the number of studies is small and therefore not necessarily representative of the developing world. In Bolivia no association was found between perceived corruption and voter turnout, participation of citizens in cultural and religious associations (a proxy for social capital) or the number of NGOs, the institutions that are meant to represent citizen voice in municipal budget councils (Gatti, Gray-Molina and Klugman, 2003).

In the Philippines and Uganda surveys showed that despite high election turnouts for both local and national elections voter numbers were unrelated to corruption levels, and electoral preferences in both countries were shaped by other factors. A multivariate analysis of the Philippine data showed that low levels of corruption (as measured by an index of household and public official responses) were correlated with voting in local elections and reading national newspapers. Moreover, in both countries civic activities were common, suggesting that citizens remain active in government despite a corrupt environment. That environment may help to explain why voting had little effect on corruption (Azfar, Kahkonen and Meagher, 2001). Other factors clearly have a stronger influence on voter choices.

These results lead to the tentative conclusion that voice can take many forms and none by itself will necessarily lead to the effective control of corruption. However, the expression of voice via the press or direct community involvement appear to be more powerful tools than voting in influencing public performance. Public service delivery does not affect voting patterns or candidate selection sufficiently. Voting may be too blunt of an indicator, one that captures a range of interests of constituents. Health will only predominate if it is the pressing issue of the moment. Otherwise other concerns drive voter preferences. Some of this may be due to entrenched corruption where localities regardless of their oversight simply do not have enough clout to influence public sector behavior. Where hiring and promotion remain centralized, local voice will have less effect in any case. Popularity of candidates, other factors that appeal to voters and insufficient evidence on things like corruption no doubt play a role, but it is difficult to be definitive given the paltry evidence and the complexity of the issue.

Community oversight can work but it doesn't always. In Boliiva corruption is lower where local oversight groups are active "suggesting that bottom-up accountability can be effective in keeping corruption in check" (Gatti, Gray-Molina and Klugman, 2004). In contrast, Uganda's Health Management Committees expropriated drugs and supplies providing virtually no oversight or support to local service delivery (McPake et al., 1999), and in Nigeria village development committees and PHC Management Committees had little impact on health care performance largely due to their lack of authority (World Bank, forthcoming).

Efforts by a local NGO in Kenya attempted to empower communities to monitor teacher attendance using both reports to the school hierarchy on performance and community awarded prizes to the best performing teacher. Neither served to improve attendance, despite the active participation of communities. In contrast, an NGO experiment in India using cameras to record teacher attendance, which are tied to compensation bonuses resulted in a dramatic improvement in delinquent behavior (Banerjee and Duflo, 2004). It may be that voice has less weight in influencing behavior than more remunerative approaches combined with air tight monitoring. As cellular phones become cheaper and more functional in rural areas photos sent electronically offer another possible alternative means of monitoring progress at the local level.

While voice matters in many service delivery instances, its role in health seems to be less straightforward. The specialized nature of medicine, the heterogeneous products of the sector and the status of physicians in most societies complicates oversight by communities, and voting is a relatively blunt instrument for influencing the quality and responsiveness of health services.

Conclusions

The review of country evidence and the examination of the cross-country factors that influence performance (and to some extent outcomes) in health care suggest that governance plays an important role. If the health system is not governed well, health workers are absent, patients pay illegal fees, and basic inputs are stolen without any consequences for those who mismanage or corrupt the system, performance of health services will be poor and population health will suffer.

Many health systems rely on anecdotal evidence to guide policy. What this paper has attempted to do is provide the evidence and outline the major challenges facing health systems, dealing with issues typically ignored or unaddressed. Better country level data can help in diagnosing the problem and some of the experiments here may offer possible solutions.

The second conclusion is that the returns to health investments may be very low where governance is not addressed. Even with a time lag, investments such as those seen in Uganda, Dominican Republic and Ethiopia, countries for which detailed data exist, will be unlikely to see high returns from public health spending. As incomes and education rise a shift to private provision may offer higher returns – something that is already underway in the Dominican Republic and India, and something likely to occur in lower income countries where governance is poor and the private sector steps in to replace public service. There may be individual returns to the shift, but equity objectives are likely to suffer. Even the poor select to pay significant amounts of disposable income to obtain private care, a sad commentary when public services go underutilized.

Third, a countries' health system is the institution that must be engaged and on the front line if governance is to improve government effectiveness and control corruption in the sector. Without bolstering the key institution for the sector it is unlikely that the goals of reducing poverty, mortality and morbidity can be achieved. The evidence here points to serious problems of governance across the globe in developing and transition countries, which thwart the goals.

Finally, achieving the dramatic and permanent declines in mortality envisioned by the Millennium Development Goals is doubtful unless governments shift their attention to the institutional factors that affect performance in the health sector. A dysfunctional environment limits the chances that more funding can have an impact, and much of the discussion above highlights situations that will not necessarily benefit from large increases in funding unless more is done to bolster the capacity of the institutions expected to implement the agenda. Funding without the necessary institutional strengthening could lead to perverse results, and assistance for both governance and financing will be needed in the health sector.

This review demonstrates that as a first attempt to compile evidence, what is striking is the fragmented nature of the evidence is surprisingly fragmented. It also shows the lack of meaningful indicators for cross country comparison, and an absence of critical data at the country level. One issue not discussed but obviously of importance to policy is the variations in government capacity across income levels. Reforms in Chile apply to many countries, but some will have resources too limited to take on similar reforms. Nonetheless, there are elements that can be adopted. For example, the Chilean drug procurement reforms in electronic bidding and institutional reform of drug purchasing agencies are well within the purview and capacity of most countries, even if the shifts are more modest in scale. Reforms in any case are entirely country specific given the political nature of health care. What the examples provide here are possible directions, all of which will necessarily be adapted to country circumstances.

Even without these important inputs simply having benchmark countries with which to compare countries would strengthen the cross country evidence. Acceptable indicators, benchmarks and additional attention to systemic issues would enable more robust indicators of overall performance, which in turn would inform policymakers and donors of challenges and opportunities for improving health institutions.

What needs addressing is the context and framework under which health systems function. First and foremost is better accountability. Greater professionalism among health staff, effective training and supervision of staff at all levels, routine audits of all aspects of fiduciary transactions, improved records and recordkeeping to provide systematic data to managers and the bureaucracy, and procedures that can facilitate service delivery in a more user friendly fashion all need to be addressed. Running hospitals, clinics and other points of service in the manner of a business or of a ministry of finance would be particularly helpful. The discipline implied and the need to be accountable provides the incentives that improve productivity, patient satisfaction and performance. That is where health systems need to move.

Incentives that raise performance – ensuring appropriate, targeted training so health professionals are equipped to do their job; linking pay and performance; reviewing and auditing performance; improving recordkeeping; and upgrading logistics for drugs and supplies – need to be an integral part of health systems. Investments in institutions require these kinds of initiatives, and donors are in a position to foster such improvements with both funding and advice to oil the wheels of progress and support the emergence of strong institutions.

Where public services are free or subsidized, with the intention to promote access and utilization of vital health services, the abuses related to lack of drugs, staff absences and informal payments undermine these objectives as well as the credibility and effectiveness of public services more generally. Without attention to these non-medical issues, clinical care quality and equity in access will be lost, leading to both lower health status and poorly spent public revenues. Addressing these public program failures are critical to effective government to and functioning health care systems. Because good governance promotes economic growth and effective public services, the health sector cannot afford to be sidelined on this agenda.

Source appendix 1: figures 4 and 5

Country	Data year	Source
Albania	2002	Vitosha, 2002
Albania	2002	World Bank LSMS Survey
Armenia	2001	Murrugarra & Cnobloch, 2003
Bangladesh	2002	Transparency International, 2002
Bolivia	2001	World Bank 2001b
Bosnia	2000	World Bank, 2001e
Bosnia	2002	Vitosha, 2002
Bulgaria	2001	LSMS Survey
Bulgaria	2002	Vitosha, 2002
Cambodia	1999	World Bank, 2000b
China	n.d.	Bloom, Han and Li, 2001
Colombia	n.d.	Corruption Survey
Croatia	2002	Vitosha, 2002
Czech Republic	2002	Horthava, Maly', 2002
Georgia	2000	Chawla, 2001
Ghana	1998	Worldbank LSMS Survey

Ghana	2000	World Bank, 2000d
Hungary	2002	Gaal, 2002
India	2002	Transparency International, 2002
Indonesia	2001	Partnership for Governance Reform, 2002
Khazakhstan	2001	World Bank, 2001c
Kosovo	2000	LSMS Survey
Krygyz	2001	Falkingham, 2002
Kyrgyz	2001	LSMS Survey
Latvia	1998	Anderson, 1998
Macedonia	2002	Vitosha, 2002
Madagascar	2001	Tranparency International, 2003
Moldova	2000	Carasciuc, 2001
Moldova	2002	Stempovscaia, 2002
Morroco	2001	Tranparency International, 2003
Nepal	2002	Transparency International, 2002
Pakistan	2002	Transparency International, 2002
Paraguay	1999	World Bank, 2000c
Peru	2001	World Bank, 2001
Poland	1998	Chawla, Berman & Kawiorska, 2001
Romania	2000	World Bank, 2001d
Romania	2002	FBS
Russia	2002	Shishkin (2003)
Senegal	2001	Tranparency International, 2003
Serbia	2002	Vitosha, 2002
Slovakia	2000	Anderson, 2000
Sri Lanka	2001	Transparency International, 2002
Tajikistan	1999	Falkingham, 2000
Tajikistan	2001	Carasciuc, 2001
Thailand	1999	Phongpaichit, Treerat, Chaiyapong & Baker, 2000
Vietnam	1998	LSMS Survey
Uzkbekistan	2001	FBS

4 **Diseases of poverty and the 10/90 Gap**

Philip Stevens

Introduction: What is the 10/90 Gap?

Activists claim that only 10 per cent of global health research is devoted to conditions that account for 90 per cent of the global disease burden – the so-called '10/90 Gap' (Medecins Sans Frontiers, 2001). They argue that virtually all diseases prevalent in low income countries are 'neglected' and that the pharmaceutical industry has invested almost nothing in research and development (R&D) for these diseases.

Citing this alleged imbalance as justification, activists have for some years been calling for a complete redesign of the current R&D paradigm in order to ensure that more attention is paid to these 'neglected diseases' (Love & Hubbard, 2003). This could include measures such as an 'essential research obligation' that would require companies to reinvest a percentage of pharmaceutical sales into R&D for neglected diseases, either directly or through public R&D programs (Medecins Sans Frontiers, 2001), or the creation of a new public entity to direct R&D. This topic is now under discussion by a World Health Organisation working group following the report of its Commission on Intellectual Property, Innovation and Public Health.[1]

But does such an imbalance really exist and what would be the effect of redesigning the R&D system? This chapter investigates the realities of the 10/90 gap and its relation to the diseases of poverty.

Neglected diseases

Many scholars and activists have suggested that because there is little market for treatments for tropical infectious diseases such as leishmaniasis, lymphatic filariasis, Chagas' disease, leprosy, Guinea worm, onchocerciasis and schistosomiasis, there is a consequent lack of suitable drugs. These so-called 'neglected' diseases predominantly effect poor populations in low income countries (Murray *et al.*, 2001), and pose particular social and economic problems for those affected.

Patrick Trouiller, for example, has pointed out that of the 1,393 total new drugs approved between 1975 and 1999, only 1 per cent (13 drugs) were specifically indicated for a tropical disease (Trouiller et al., 2002). Research conducted by the DND Working Group and the Harvard School of Public Health in 2001 revealed that of the 20 global pharmaceutical companies surveyed, only two had research projects underway for the 'neglected' diseases of Chagas and leishmaniasis (Wirth, 2001)

Neglected diseases are a tiny fraction of total mortality

However, these bare statistics serve to mislead people into thinking that the poor are suffering at the expense of the rich. The reality is that 'neglected' diseases often do not represent the most pressing public health priorities in low income countries. They constitute a small fraction of their total disease burden (Figure 1). According to the 2002 World Health Organisation's (WHO) World Health Report, tropical diseases accounted for only 0.5 per cent of deaths in high-mortality poor countries, and only 0.3 per cent of deaths in low-mortality poor countries.

Moreover, treatments already exist for many of these diseases. Schistostomiasis (bilharzia), which predominantly affects children in Africa, can be treated with praziquantel at a cost of just 8 cents per 600mg tablet (Fenwick, 2006). Onchocerciasis (river blindness) is controllable with ivermectin. A range of treatments exist for lymphatic filariasis (elephantiasis). In fact, the WHO acknowledges that there are

Figure 1   **Number of daily deaths from diseases[7]**

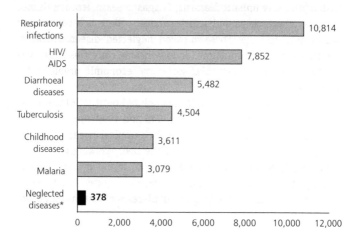

*Neglected diseases are defined as African trypanosomiasis, Chagas disease and leishmaniasis

only three diseases that are genuinely 'neglected': African trypanoso-miasis, leishmaniasis and Chagas disease (WHO/IFPMA, 2001).

This notwithstanding, research and development into the diseases of poverty is far from moribund. Several public-private partnerships exist that specifically focus on diseases of poverty. In particular, the Medicines for Malaria Venture (MMV), the Global TB Vaccine Foundation (Aeras),[2] the International Aids Vaccine Initia-tive (IAVI), and the Infectious Disease Research Institute (IDRI)[3] coor-dinate publicly-funded R&D projects with private companies. Due in part to these arrangements, there are at least 63 drugs in the R&D pipeline targeting HIV/AIDS, including 15 vaccines (Moran et al., 2005). There are at least 30 more drugs in the R&D pipeline for malaria, and 22 for tuberculosis.[4]

In addition, there are now PPPs that focus on developing drugs for African Trypanosomiasis, Chagas Disease, Leishmaniasis, and Dengue Fever, which have bolstered the number of potential treatments in the R&D pipeline for diseases that disproportionately affect people in poor countries. There are currently at least eight potential treatments in varying stages of clinical trials, and a further 16 in preclinical development.[5]

Research at the London School of Economics shows that the PPP approach has outperformed stand-alone industry efforts in producing drugs that are particularly suited for conditions in less developed countries. PPPs have often proved to be a quicker way to get drugs to market, generally equalling or exceeding industry standards. Finally, it appears that PPPs are more cost-effective than other approaches. For example, the Medicine for Malaria Venture's synthetic peroxide project has moved to Phase I clinical trials for a total cost of US \$11.5 million – lower than the industry norm for developing a New Chemical Entity for western markets (Moran et al., 2005).

Most disease in lower-income countries is caused by poverty

Despite this increased activity, it is worth pointing out that a large proportion of illnesses in low-income countries are entirely avoidable or treatable with existing medicines or interventions. Most of the disease burden in low-income countries finds its roots in the consequences of poverty, such as poor nutrition, indoor air pollution and lack of access to proper sanitation and health education. The WHO estimates that diseases associated with poverty account for 45 per cent of the disease burden in the poorest countries (WHO, 2002). They include:

♦ **Tuberculosis**, **malaria** and **HIV/AIDS**, which account for nearly 18 per cent of the disease burden in the poorest countries (WHO, 2004).

- **Respiratory infections** caused by burning biomass fuels and low-grade coal in poorly ventilated areas also constitute a significant health burden for poor people. According to the WHO, exposure to biomass smoke increases the risk of acute lower respiratory infections (ALRI) in childhood, particularly pneumonia. Globally, ALRI represent the single most important cause of death in children under 5 years and account for at least two million deaths annually in this age group (Bruce et al., 2002).
- **Diarrhoeal diseases**, caused by the poor sanitation which is endemic in economically deprived areas, may be easily and cheaply treated through oral re-hydration therapy. However, diarrhoeal diseases still claim 1.8 million lives each year, (WHO, 1999) and are the second biggest killer of children worldwide, after respiratory infections.
- **Malaria** can be prevented through a combination of indoor residual spraying of dwellings with insecticides, the use of insecticide treated bed nets and the use of prophylactic medicines. Malaria infections can be cured with drugs such as quinine, mefloquine or artemisinin combination therapy (Muheki, et al., 2004; PAHO, 2006).
- **Yellow fever** – a vector-borne, viral disease with high mortality rates – can be prevented by using prophylactic vaccination. An affordable and effective vaccine is available, but nearly all countries in which the disease is enzootic prefer to wait until an epidemic is evident before mass-treatment of the affected population is undertaken (Monath & Nasidi, 1993; Monath 2005). Education can also play an important role in reducing the incidence of insect-borne diseases, for example by encouraging people to remove sources of stagnant water (insect breeding sites) from near their dwellings.
- **Tuberculosis** can be prevented by improving nutrition, and can be treated with DOTS therapy. This method can detect and cure disease in up to 95 per cent of infectious patients, even in the poorest countries (WHO, 1999).

- Education is vital for the prevention of **HIV/AIDS** – and this entails the full engagement of civil society. A combination of anti-retrovirals (ARVs) and good nutrition can help to control the viral load and suppress the symptoms of HIV/AIDS.
- Treatable **childhood diseases** such as polio, measles and pertussis, account for only 0.2 per cent of Disability Adjusted Life Years (DALYs) in high-income countries, while they account for 5.2 per cent of DALYs in high mortality lower income countries (WHO, 2002). Vaccines for these diseases have existed for at least 50 years, yet only 53 per cent of children in sub-Saharan Africa were immunised with the diphtheria-tetanus pertussis (DTP) jab in 2000 (WHO, 2002a).
- **Malnutrition** particularly affects people in poor countries. In particular, micronutrient deficiencies contribute to illness and poor health. For example, as a result of Vitamin A deficiency, 500,000 children become blind each year (WHO, 1995) and many of them die, despite the fact that such outcomes can be avoided by inexpensive, easy-to-administer food supplements (WHO, 1997). Vitamin A deficiency also weakens the immune system, leaving children vulnerable to other illnesses such as diarrhoea and measles. Estimates suggest that Vitamin A deficiency contributes to or causes approximately 800,000 childhood deaths each year (Rice et al., 2004).
- **Dengue** is a mosquito-borne viral infection prevalent in over 100 countries. According to the WHO, two-fifths of the world's population is at risk from dengue, and there are around 50 million infections every year.[6] Dengue can be prevented with a range of techniques to control insects. These include covering water containers and applying insecticides to larval habitats. During the 1950s the principal vector, *Aedes aegypti*, was eradicated from 22 countries in the Americas by the application of DDT.
- **Pertussis** (whooping cough) is a particular threat to infants. Somewhere in the range of 20 to 40 million cases occur every year, mostly in less developed countries, and as a result,

Table 1   **Deaths caused by 'developed country' diseases**[21]

% of deaths caused by/in	High mortality developing countries	Low mortality developing countries	Developed countries
Malignant neoplasms (cancers)	6.3	9.9	21.2
Diabetes	0.6	1.5	1.7
Neuropsychiatric disorders	1.3	1.4	2.9
Cardiovascular diseases	18.9	23.4	47.8
Respiratory diseases (asthma)	4.0	6.7	5.0
Digestive diseases	2.7	3.4	3.7
Total 'developed-countries' diseases	33.8	46.4	82.3

between 200,000 and 400,000 die every year.[7] An effective vaccine against pertussis has existed for some years, but currently 20 per cent of children worldwide do not receive it.
+ **Leprosy** was for many centuries an incurable and widespread disease. However, the development and adoption, in the early 1980s, of multidrug therapy (dapsone, rifampicin and clofazimine) has led to a 90 per cent decline in its prevalence.[8]

Poverty-related diseases cause far higher levels of mortality in low-income than high-income countries (Table 1). Most of these diseases and deaths can be prevented with pre-existing treatments and prevention programmes. Diseases for which there is no treatment currently available, such as dengue fever, contribute towards a far smaller proportion of low-income country mortality rates than diseases which are easily preventable or treatable. It is estimated that 88 per cent of child diarrhoeas, 91 per cent of malaria and up to 100 per cent of childhood illness such as measles and tetanus can be prevented among children using existing treatments (Jones et al., 2004). This means that up to 3 million child lives could be saved each year if these medicines could be distributed effectively to all areas of need.

Figure 2 **Projected global deaths by cause**
2005 (all ages), millions

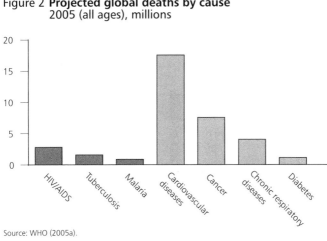

Source: WHO (2005a).

Illnesses of low and high-income countries are converging

Exponents of the 10/90 Gap are also inaccurate when they claim that low-income countries, which constitute the majority of the world's population and disease burden, suffer from completely different diseases than high-income countries. The premise that only 10 per cent of the global health research budget, both private and public, is used for research into 90 per cent of the world's health problems is factually incorrect.

In reality, the nature and spread of diseases suffered in both rich and poor countries is converging rapidly. According to the WHO, ailments such as cardiovascular disease, cancer and diabetes now account for 45 per cent of the global disease burden. Around 80 per cent of this burden now occurs in low and middle-income countries (WHO, 2005a). Chronic diseases cause four out of five deaths in lower-income countries. In absolute terms, more people in the lower-income countries (compared to higher-income countries) die

Figure 3 **Projected death rates by specific causes for selected countries**
2005 (all ages), thousands

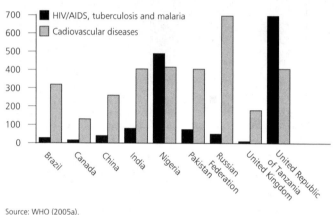

Source: WHO (2005a).

as a result of non-communicable diseases. Cardiovascular diseases are one of the most significant causes of death in lower-income countries (Figures 2 and 3).

The WHO argues that much of this disease burden is attributable to less healthy diets and increasing physical inactivity. This may be so, yet the global rise of chronic diseases is also partly the result of more people living beyond middle age, thanks to greater global economic growth and prosperity. The prevalence of chronic disease, however, does challenge the myth that the current commercial R&D paradigm is failing to produce drugs that meet the needs of the global disease burden. Significant resources currently are being deployed towards developing treatments for cancers, cardiovascular diseases, neuropsychiatric diseases and diabetes. In fact, levels of drug development increasingly reflect the global disease burden, so lower-income countries therefore stand to benefit from drugs that are currently in the R&D pipeline (Figure 4).

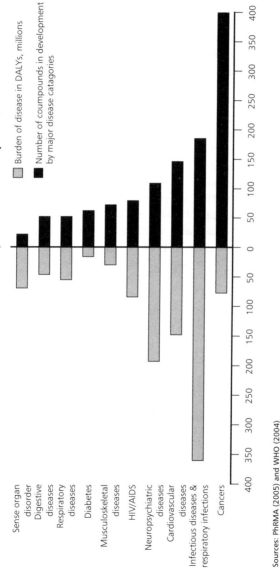

Figure 4 **The global disease burden vs. number of compounds in development**

Sources: PhRMA (2005) and WHO (2004)

Lower-income countries also currently benefit from drugs that were originally developed for wealthier markets. Polio, pertussis (whooping cough) and diphtheria, for example, were once endemic in wealthier countries, but have been practically eradicated from these areas due to simple vaccines that were developed a few decades ago.

Now, three-quarters of the world's children – including millions in low-income countries – are vaccinated against such diseases, saving at least three million lives a year and preventing long term illness and disability in millions more. Tuberculosis treatments were originally devised to combat the disease in wealthier countries, and many populations in lower-income countries now reap the dividends of this advance in medical science in the form of mass vaccination programmes. HIV/AIDS treatments in the form of ARVs were originally developed with wealthy consumers in mind. Those treatments have now spread to poorer countries which are most affected by the disease, but are unable themselves to bear the cost of R&D for such treatments.

Statins are also an increasingly important tool in the fight against cardiovascular diseases in lower-income countries, with many of these powerful drugs now off-patent and open to generic competition. Again, these treatments originated – and are still being developed – in wealthier countries under the current commercial R&D paradigm.

Access is the real problem – not innovation

If treatments exist for the majority of poor countries' health problems, why then do mortality rates remain so high? Any discussion of this question must address the problem of access to essential medicines, which remains an intractable political and economic problem. According to the WHO, an estimated 30 per cent of the world population lacks regular access to existing drugs, with this figure rising to over 50 per cent in the poorest parts of Africa and Asia (Figure 5).

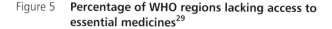

Figure 5   **Percentage of WHO regions lacking access to essential medicines**[29]

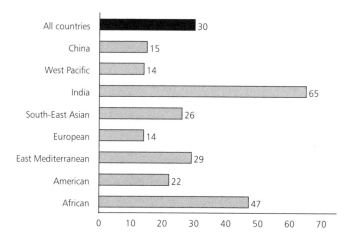

Within these populations, it is the poorest socio-economic groups that disproportionately suffer from a lack of access to existing medicines.[9] The implications of this failure of public health policy on global mortality are profound – according to one study, over 10 million children die unnecessarily each year, almost all in low-income or poor areas of middle income countries, mostly from a short list of preventable diseases such as diarrhoea, measles, malaria and causes related to malnutrition (Black, 2003).

Only one-half (approximately) of sub-Saharan African children are vaccinated against childhood diseases, and in isolated areas that number is as low as one child in 20 (WHO, 2002a). A variety of factors conspire to create this desperate situation, many of them caused by government mismanagement and interference. These

"An estimated one-third of the world population lacks regular access to essential drugs, with this figure rising to over 50 per cent in the poorest parts of Africa and Asia. And even if drugs are available, weak drug regulation may mean that they are substandard or counterfeit."

WHO Medicines Strategy Report 2002–2003

include weak healthcare systems, taxes and tariffs on medicines and inadequate risk pooling mechanisms. These and other barriers to access are discussed in detail in chapter 8.

The 10/90 Gap is a red herring

The evidence presented here suggests that activists who cite the 10/90 gap as justification for the wholesale reform of the R&D paradigm are setting their sights on the wrong target. It is fallacious and misleading to argue that commercial R&D neglects almost entirely the diseases of the poorer parts of the world. Private companies are responsible for developing and producing majority of the drugs that already exist on the WHO's essential medicines list, and hundreds of private research initiatives are currently underway to address the world's biggest killers that impact both rich and poor countries. The so-called 'neglected diseases' rarely constitute a country's most pressing health priorities. The WHO itself has argued that the key factors behind the excessive mortality caused by these diseases include unavailability of health services and failure to use prevention and treatment strategies, rather than the unavailability of medicines (WHO, 1999).

The health problems faced by the world's poorest populations are not caused by the non-existence of drugs specifically related to their problems and diseases. The real problem is ensuring that these populations can actually access vital medicines. Many governments fail their populations in this respect by imposing punitive tariffs and taxes on medicines, and by failing to foster healthcare systems or functional risk pooling mechanisms. The governments of poor countries also hinder the creation of wealth, imposing obstacles in the way of owning and transferring property, imposing unnecessary regulatory barriers on entrepreneurs and businesses, and restricting trade through extortionate tariffs. It is these and other political failures that have left poor populations without the necessary resources to access the medicines that could so easily transform their quality of life.

Campaigners who cite the 10/90 Gap as the prime mover behind the health problems of the poor are in fact betraying the very people they are attempting to help. In seeking to radically alter the current R&D paradigm, they risk undermining the incentive system that has led to the development of treatments for a great majority of the health problems suffered by both high and low income countries.

Emerging health threats, ranging from drug-resistant strains of AIDS and tuberculosis to avian flu, remind us of the importance of ensuring that the pharmaceutical industry continues to discover and develop new drugs. Innovation is a fragile process, and it can be weakened or thwarted by poor public policies. Heavy taxation, regulation or public vilification of pharmaceutical companies will reduce their incentives to invest in researching these vital drugs, because shareholders will be uncertain of generating a return. If commercial companies are no longer able to prioritise and manage their own R&D spending unmolested by government, the consequences for global health will be tragic.

Furthermore, the public sector offers no panacea for activists who seek to wrest the ability to conduct R&D away from commercial enterprises and towards the public sector. The public sector's trophy cupboard of health R&D successes is almost empty, because governments lack both the technical skills and the ability to pick winners that have rendered many pharmaceutical companies so commercially successful.

In the 1980s, the US Agency for International Development funded research into a vaccine for malaria, which absorbed $60 million and failed to achieve any of its goals. This failure is a neat illustration of the drawbacks to the public procurement of R&D. Because the researchers were operating to the demands of a public sector employer rather than the market, they gave out wildly optimistic statements about the progress of their work in order to ensure a continued supply of funds. Government-funded project directors also have an incentive to fund unpromising work – illustrated by the project leader's demand for further funds, despite the unpromising nature of his early work. Finally, because the recipients of government subsidies are paid before delivery, they remove incentives to properly conclude the research.

By seeking to derail the R&D capabilities of the pharmaceutical industry, exponents of the '10/90 gap' are in danger of creating a self-fulfilling prophesy. A global R&D treaty, in which the profits of pharmaceutical companies are heavily taxed and their intellectual property rights undermined, would be almost certain to have the unintended consequence of effectively turning off the tap of innovation that is essential to dealing with the world's changing health problems.

5 Increasing access to medicines

Prof Khalil Ahmed,[1] Franklin Cudjoe,[2] Eustace Davie,[3] Dr John Kilama,[4] Prof Martín Krause,[5] Andrés Mejia,[6] Barun Mitra,[7] Nonoy Oplas,[8] Martín Simonetta,[9] Philip Stevens,[10] Jose Luis Tapia,[11] Margaret Tse,[12] Jasson Urbach[13]

As has been demonstrated in the previous chapter, access to medicines in many less developed countries is extremely low. According to the WHO, an estimated 30 per cent of the world population lacks regular access to existing drugs, with this figure rising to over 50 per cent in the poorest parts of Africa and Asia (WHO, 2003). As chapter 4 has also shown, there is some concern that certain diseases unique to less developed countries do not represent a viable commercial prospect for would-be innovators of new medicines, resulting in a shortage of appropriate treatments. Citing this alleged 'market-failure' as justification, some have proposed alternative mechanisms to the commercial R&D paradigm in order to stimulate research into these areas.

This chapter examines some of the factors that prevent existing medicines from being distributed in the most effective manner, as well as those elements of governance which actively undermine the supply of new medicines.

We begin with a description of the major barriers to access, which include weak healthcare systems, taxes on imported medicines, and poorly functioning insurance markets. We then examine several related issues, including the impact of poor government policy on the supply of medicine and the impact of pre-market regulations and price controls.

Weak healthcare systems

Healthcare systems and associated infrastructure are vital for the effective distribution of medicines. If healthcare systems are starved of resources, it is unlikely that they will be able either to procure necessary drugs or be able to employ sufficient numbers of doctors and other trained personnel necessary to prescribe and administer medicines.

The majority of low-income countries lack the basic infrastructure required to distribute medicine successfully. Road networks are often unreliable or non-existent, making it difficult to ensure a constant supply of medicines to remote areas (Saleh & Ibrahim, 2005). Electricity is often unavailable, especially in rural areas; where it is available, it is often supplied in an erratic fashion. This increases the cost and difficulty of running refrigeration systems in clinics and hospitals. As a result, vaccines are often not maintained at sufficiently low temperatures to ensure product stability. Protease inhibitors (used in second-line ARV treatments) are one example of a drug that needs to be refrigerated (Kumarasamy, 2004), yet due to erratic power supplies and other issues, it is impossible to ensure constant refrigeration in the world's poorest countries.

In this situation, it is extremely difficult to ensure the distribution of the safe and effective medicines that have already been developed to tackle the diseases of poverty. For example, a relatively effective treatment for tuberculosis is Directly Observed Therapy Short Course (DOTS), which requires between 6 to 8 months with close patient monitoring to ensure compliance. ARV treatment for AIDS sufferers also requires close supervision over the lifetime of the patient. Even in the relatively efficient health care systems of high-income countries, maintaining adherence to HAART (Highly Active Anti-Retroviral Therapy) treatment during clinical trials is fraught with complexity (Kumarasamy, 2004). Achieving such adherence in poor countries with weak health care systems is practically impossible.

Intervention by global public health authorities and the provision of public funds is not a guarantee that existing medicines will be effectively distributed. Consider the example of malaria, discussed in the next chapter: despite the establishment of the Roll Back Malaria initiative and the injection of specific funds, the most modern and potent anti-malarial drugs were still not being correctly used six years after the initiative began (Attaran, 2004).

Weak healthcare systems do not simply result in a failure to distribute existing treatments. They also have a knock-on effect for the demand for new drugs, and can act as a serious disincentive to would-be innovators of new medicines. If a product is unlikely to reach its intended market, what is the point of developing it in the first place? Well-equipped and properly staffed modern medical facilities are adept at disseminating the latest medical tools and drugs (Dussault & Dubois, 2003). Conversely, inefficient distribution and communications channels have an adverse effect on the speed with which new medicines reach patients, if they reach them at all (Gambardella et al., 2000).

Frequently, public spending and foreign aid injections into national health systems do not translate into the delivery of services and medicines to the poor. A multi-country study by Filmer and Pritchett (1999) showed that public spending on health in lower-income countries has only a minute impact on mortality. The authors showed that a significant proportion of deaths of children below five years could be averted for as little as US $10 each, yet even in the poorest countries, the average amount spent by governments per child death averted is a staggering US $50,000–$100,000.

There are many reasons for this low level of performance. First, public health agencies tend to be woefully inefficient and corrupt, especially in lower-income countries. As a result, the proportion of a donor's contribution that actually results in delivery of healthcare services (whether they are vaccines or nurses' salaries) is often very low. Health officials may sell aid-financed drugs on the black market. Studies in Guinea, Cameroon, Uganda, and Tanzania estimated that 30 to 70 per cent of government drugs disappeared before reaching the intended patients (Filmer, Hammer & Pritchett, 2000).

Second, social programs nominally targeted at low-income groups are frequently captured by the articulate and influential rich (Deolalikar, 1995; Castro-Leal et al., 1999; Barat et al., 2003).

Third, public funding and provision can crowd out private funding and provision of healthcare. If a government starts to provide a good or service for 'free', this is a clear signal to private providers to exit the market. The net amount of healthcare provided may remain constant – but where there was once diversity of provision, there is now an effective monopoly, which has its own efficiency problems. As a result, public funding and provision typically has little to no impact on actual health outcomes (Filmer, Hammer & Pritchett, 2000).

Case study: How the South African health system hinders access to medicines

Jasson Urbach, Free Market Foundation, South Africa

The experience of the South African public health system offers some insights as to why 20 per cent of the country's population is unable to access essential medicines (UN, 1999).

At the outset it should be made clear that there are two distinct and separate health sectors in South Africa. The dichotomy is largely a hangover from past policies formulated under the apartheid regime. On the one hand the private health sector provides a world-class health service, with excellent facilities, advanced technology, well-remunerated staff and good access to all medicines. On the other hand the public sector is plagued with inefficiency and for the most part South Africa's public health care system struggles to meet the needs of the patients it is supposed to be serving. The result is that patients seldom receive the level of care that they deserve.

The South African government receives medicines at substantially reduced costs from large multinational pharmaceutical companies. However, historic and ongoing lack of infrastructure, personnel and poor logistics means that frequently the medicines do not reach those for whom they were intended. Furthermore, those that do have access to public sector health facilities usually end up queuing for hours, and are often turned away, trying to get even the most basic medicines. Not surprisingly, in 2000 the World Health Organisation (WHO) ranked South Africa's health-care system 175th out of the 191 member countries.

There is also a great deal of theft in public hospitals. For instance, in Mpumalanga province, 46 medical professionals ended up behind bars in the first two months of 2003, charged with the theft and resale of government medicines meant for the rural poor in Mpumalanga. Those arrested included a manager of a rural hospital, doctors, pharmacists and medical technicians as well as a syndicate of 'bag men' who delivered stolen drugs, including birth control pills, pain killers and antibiotics, to private doctors.

The medicine shortages caused by the syndicate's medicine thefts reportedly prevented routine operations from being performed, and complicated the day-to-day treatment of patients at the Rob Ferreira and Themba hospitals in Nelspruit, the capital of Mpumalanga.[14] The extent and nature of theft and corruption in the public health system reinforces the severe shortcomings in hospital management, administration and control systems.

The South African drug regulator, the Medicines Control Council (MCC), is notoriously inefficient and tardy with its approval process. On average, drugs that have already been registered for use in the US, EU and Japan can wait for 39 months to be approved by the South African system. A further barrier to access in South Africa is Value Added Tax (VAT). The SA government continues to charge VAT on pharmaceuticals despite the fact that the tax is highly regressive since it disproportionately affects the poorest members of society.

If the South African government is serious about increasing access to medicines to the poorest of the poor, then they will waive VAT on all medicines. VAT is counter-intuitive in the sense that if one of government's primary objectives is to have a healthy and productive workforce, surely it does not want to tax the sick and vulnerable. The VAT received by government on pharmaceuticals is relatively insignificant. However sick people could use the money that would have been spent on VAT for a number of beneficial alternatives, including food.

According to the latest estimates by the official government statistical agency, Statistics South Africa (SSA), approximately 26 per cent of the South African labour force is unemployed. If discouraged work seekers are also included, this figure jumps to approximately 41 per cent. The consequence of mass unemployment is that there are large numbers of individuals that currently live in extreme poverty. Indeed, it is estimated that there approximately 5 million people in South Africa live on less than a dollar a day. Therefore, it is not unreasonable to assume that many of them simply cannot afford to buy even basic pharmaceutical drugs. While the government claims to take responsibility for the health care of the indigent, it is obviously not capable of meeting unlimited demands.

How do we remedy this situation? In the long run, the only way to increase access to medicines is through increasing the wealth of the citizens of a country and this is only possible through economic growth. In the short term, the government can substantially improve its distribution of drugs by privatising the distribution process and reduce waiting times by simply approving drugs that have already been approved for use in developed countries. Finally, the South African government's preferred policy of price controls will not increase access. On the contrary, it will simply reduce supply by eroding the incentives of potential suppliers.

Jasson Urbach is a research economist with the Free Market Foundation (Southern Africa) and assistant director of the health advocacy group Africa Fighting Malaria.

Taxes and tariffs

Many governments of lower-income countries compound the problem of weak healthcare systems by imposing a range of taxes on medicines, including port charges, central, regional and local taxation, as well as import tariffs and VAT. Other government-imposed measures or regulations may include pre-shipment and inspection costs, and pharmacy board fees. Taken together, these add significantly to a drug's retail price, with negative consequences for access to medicines, especially for the poorest.

In a survey of nine countries, Levison and Laing found that that costs resulting from government policy or regulation added an average of 68.6 per cent to the cost of imported pharmaceuticals (Levison & Laing, 2003).

Why Do Governments Tax Medicines?

Given the massive negative impact of local price inflators on the cost of medicines for the poor, it must be asked why governments choose to implement such policies. There are two main reasons: to protect local industry and to raise revenue.

Protection of local industry. In some cases, policies are designed to protect domestic industry, without little if any regard for how this may affect citizens. Both Levison (2003) and the European Commission (2003) observe that Nigeria, Pakistan, India and China all have significant local industries and are included in the group of countries with the highest import duties. Opponents of tariff removal support this policy, suggesting that reducing or abolishing tariffs could undermine the domestic industry which relies on high import barriers to survive. This argument is somewhat tenuous, as very few low-income countries – other than those listed above – have indigenous pharmaceutical industries of any significance. At any rate, industry protection via tariffs often leads to entrenched inefficiencies and results in expensive, poor quality products.

Income Generation. Taxes and tariffs generate revenue for the government. In some very poor countries, import tariffs in general represent an important source of income for governments where collection of other sorts of taxes is difficult. However, tariffs on medicines are rarely a significant source of revenue.

Taxes and tariffs under the microscope

Tariffs are often a particularly important factor in determining the end-user price of pharmaceuticals in low-income countries (Bate et al., 2005). A 57-country study conducted on behalf of the European Commission in 2003 examined taxes and tariffs on pharmaceutical products used in the treatment of communicable diseases.[15] The study found that the countries that apply the highest tariff rates include Nigeria, Pakistan, India and China (European Commission, 2003). As a result, large sections of the populations of these countries are being priced out of treatment by their own governments.[16]

Another disturbing government levy on pharmaceuticals is value added tax (VAT). VAT is a revenue-raising instrument that can exist at several levels of the political system, and may be applied to different classes of products, or certain sectors (Levison & Laing, 2003). The European Commission (2003) found that VAT was imposed on pharmaceuticals at average rates of over 12 per cent.

Table 2 shows the combined impact of taxes and tariffs (customs duty + VAT + other duties) on the retail price of medicines in selected poor countries. The global average is 18 per cent, with Malaysia having the lowest rate (0.01 per cent) and India the highest (55 per cent).[20]

By driving up the cost of medicines, these taxes and tariffs price the poorest people out of the market for life-saving treatments.

Table 2 **Duties and taxes on retail medicines**

Country	*Combined total duties and taxes*
India	55%
Sierra Leone	40%
Nigeria	34%
Pakistan	33%
Bolivia	32%
Bangladesh	29%
China	28%
Jamaica	27%
Morocco	25%
Georgia	25%
Mexico	24%

Table adapted from European Commission, 2003.

They are regressive because they adversely affect the poor and the sick. Such government policies effectively impose a wedge between the demand for drugs and their supply. In markets where profit margins are already low, drug companies have fewer incentives to supply their existing products, much less to innovate new products specifically aimed at these markets. As Levison (2003) observes: "Economically...tariffs impede the action of a competitive market where the best drug will achieve the best price and [they] protect inefficient [local] producers who charge high drug prices." (Appendix Figure 2 shows how taxes restrict the demand for medicines.)

Non-tariff barriers

Beyond visible barriers such as tariffs, manufacturers wishing to export to overseas markets often face significant hurdles and complexity in registering their products. These tend to emanate from local drug approval agencies, and often appear to be designed to protect local industry rather than achieving better outcomes for patients.

Some examples of such non-tariff barriers are the following:

- *Harmonisation*. Certain countries are guilty of requiring importers to attain standards higher than those required by relevant trade bodies, often without any scientific justification.
- *Transparency*: Many countries fail to provide adequate information regarding the regulations and procedural norms concerning methods of sampling, inspection and testing of drugs. New regulations are often introduced without giving the producers in exporting countries an opportunity to understand and/or comply those regulations. Often the standards are available only in the language of the importing country or are presented in a very complicated manner. As a result, exporters lack clear guidance about the specific requirements, which can lead to rejection at the point of import.
- *Conformity assessment issues*: Importing countries may require testing to occur at a single location which may be at an inconvenient location, adding an additional burden of cost and time. Certificates may have limited validity, requiring frequent re-testing, while on occasion importing countries may not recognise the certificates of international bodies.
- *Marketing restrictions*: Often, importing countries require their own standard of labeling on products, which can be cumbersome to exporters from lower-income countries who are trying to export to a range of different countries, all with different criteria.
- *Restrictions on port of entry*: Several countries allow imports only through designated ports, which increases transit times and transaction costs.

One example is South Africa's Medicines Control Council (MCC), which requires that all new medicines must attain its own regulatory approval before they can be marketed in the country – even if they have already been approved by reputable foreign regulatory bodies such as the US FDA. However, the extreme inefficiency of the MCC means that drugs which have already been registered for use in the US, EU and Japan wait an average 39 months for approval in the South African system.

Another example comes from Namibia, which announced in 2002 that all medicines registered in the country prior to independence (1990) should be re-registered (Bate et al., 2005).

The low purchasing power of the majority of citizens in poor countries means they do not constitute significant markets for foreign manufacturers. In the face of such non-tariff barriers, companies will often forego the regulatory complexity and expense of registering their products in that country (and will instead invest their resources elsewhere). The result is that fewer medicines are approved – even when they are desperately needed – and there is a lower level of local competition in the marketplace which would otherwise drive prices down and increase access.

To make matters worse, many governments now adopt the WHO's list of 'essential medicines' as the basic formulary, denying their citizens access to medicines not on the list (see Box).

WHO Essential medicines list

Dr John Kilama, Director, Global Bioscience Development Institute

If poor people in the U.S. and the EU had access only to the limited range of options on the World Health Organization's Model List of Essential Medicines (EML), most doctors would denounce that situation as unacceptable. So, too, would most healthcare workers in other developed countries around the world. Why then has no one questioned the rationale behind the WHO's List of Essential Medicines – frequently the authority that dictates the drug selection process for many health Ministries in poorer countries?

The WHO EML represents the most comprehensive

international compilation of essential medicines for public health. The list was compiled beginning in 1975, in the wake of World Health Assembly's decision to focus on high quality, reasonably priced essential medicines. Since it was first published in 1977, the WHO EML has ostensibly aimed to provide for the majority of people worldwide affordable, safe and effective medicines for most of their health needs.

The first model list identified 208 individual drugs and since then multiple deletions and insertions have been made. Drugs can be removed from the list if their safety is found to be questionable following the appearance of new data.

Despite this, the concept of the EML is ill-fitted to the myriad health needs of people in lower-income countries. Diseases such as diabetes, hypertension, cancer, cardiovascular disorders, gastrointestinal disorders, dermatological disorders and arthritis are just as common in Africa as in developed countries. Yet the WHO Essential List of Medicines does not provide medical practitioners in Africa with sufficient choice for dealing with these diseases.

Medical practitioners are well aware that each individual responds to medicine in a unique way. An anti-anginal medicine such as Verapamil produces a range of different results in any given population. It may not work in one individual who suffers from anginal disorder yet it may produce good results in another individual who has very similar symptoms. So why recommend only a few products as 'essential' if we know that different people respond differently to the very same drug product?

Unfortunately, in Africa, if your disease cannot be treated with any of the drugs on the WHO List of Essential Medicines, you are simply out of luck. You need to go outside the essential list to get relief, but that may not be possible. Most African health ministries have adopted the

WHO guideline as their approach to healthcare, making it all but impossible to obtain the most appropriate drugs. This approach is irrational, and is not good for public health.

The African healthcare crisis extends beyond the highly publicised problems of HIV/AIDS and malaria. Although the international community has paid little attention, hypertension and diabetes are also widespread in Africa, and the combined number of deaths from those two diseases nearly equals the toll from HIV/AIDS.

When it comes to treating those diseases, however, Africans have limited options. Even those who can afford drugs that are not on the EML do not have the opportunity to do so. That is because most African governments allow the importation of only those drugs that are on the list. When it comes to drugs for hypertension, for example, there are only six drugs on the WHO list. If one of those six listed drugs cannot control an African's hypertension, he or she will die because no other hypertension drugs are registered for sale in that country.

The disease burden in lower-income countries is coming increasingly to resemble that of higher income countries, especially in terms of cardiovascular diseases and cancers. Plenty of new drugs are coming on stream to combat these diseases, but the rationale behind the EML denies patients in poorer countries access to these new drugs. This is because the EML deliberately favours listing generic medicines over patented ones. In this way, the treatments available to patients in poorer countries do not match the contours of the disease burden. This also discourages innovation, as the EML sends confusing and inaccurate signals with regard to which diseases are most prevalent at the local level.

Tensions are mounting. In Kenya, a dispute has broken out between those who import essential medicines and those who want to import brand name drugs, of which generic copies are sold in Kenya. Importers of 'essential' medicines on the WHO list do not want brand name drugs to be imported because importers are afraid of competition. They know there is a vibrant market for these drugs, which poses a threat to their commercial interests.

A more fundamental question must also be considered: Why even define some drugs as essential and not others? All drug products are essential to those people who need them. Each disease requires personalized treatment. Our goal should be to provide doctors with enough options to use exactly the right drug to fit the needs of each patient. Instead, the drug list seems to be designed to suit the needs of various vested-interests and pressure groups. As a result, the EML does not correspond with the actual demand for drugs on the ground.

Inadequate health insurance

Health insurance enables individuals to pool their financial resources and thereby protect themselves against the risk of unexpected and expensive illness. In return for monetary payment, an insurer agrees to compensate the individual in a specified way should defined, uncertain events actually happen.

When health insurance systems function well, demand for healthcare increases because larger numbers of people are covered against the costs of ill health. Several studies have shown the link between greater uptake of therapeutic medicines among poor and vulnerable populations, and the availability of health insurance in the United States (Department of Health and Human Services, 2002; Poisal & Chulis, 2000). However, many low-income countries do not have properly functioning health insurance schemes. In 1998 not one low-income country with a gross national product (GNP) per capita below US $761 had a social health insurance scheme (Carrin,

2002). Those individuals not covered by insurance pay for health-care out of their own resources (or are nominally provided such services by the state). Since these people are already poor, their ability to purchase medicines – especially expensive medicines – is likely to be very low indeed. So the lack of availability of insurance acts as a significant barrier to access to medicines and constraint on demand.

One reason for the low level of insurance coverage in poor countries is the lack of adequate court systems and generally an absence of the rule of law, which makes the enforcement of legal agreements difficult, long-winded and expensive. Health insurance takes the form of a contract in which payment is made in advance of pay-out by the insuring company. In an environment where contracts are difficult to enforce, it is not surprising that many people are unwilling to risk paying into an insurance scheme. This specifically relates to a failure on the part of government to create an adequate rule of law and supporting institutions.

Another reason for low levels of insurance coverage in poor countries relates to the level of regulation placed upon private health insurers. For example, insurance companies may be required to offer certain kinds of insurance, regardless of whether or not consumers want the coverage. This is the case in South Africa, where the government has banned insurers from excluding high risk applicants, and compelled them to include cover that is not necessarily appropriate. The South African government is also working towards establishing a system that will require well-run funds to transfer their surpluses to badly-run funds. This latter intervention will limit the ability of actuaries to balance contributions against risk. Such regulations increase the costs associated with offering insurance, which increases the price at which it is offered. As a result, relatively fewer people are able to afford insurance. Paradoxically, regulations intended to protect consumers ultimately harm them (Soderlund & Hansl, 2000).

Governments also stifle the development of properly functioning insurance markets in less obvious ways. Weak governance structures, including poorly defined property rights, excessively bureaucratic rules for business, and an absence of the rule of law in many middle and low income countries mean that large sections of the population are forced to seek employment in the informal economy. The informal economy tends to be disjointed, which implies that it would be difficult for potential insurance companies to take advantage of economies of scale. At the same time, the diversity and transience of such workers and their dependents means that enrolment is difficult and costly, if not altogether impossible.

The International Labour Organisation estimates, for example, that between 1990 and 2000, 85 per cent of all new jobs in Latin America were created in the informal sector. In Zambia, only 10 per cent of the workforce is employed in the formal sector. Accordingly, in sub-Saharan Africa only around 25 per cent of the work force is enrolled in health insurance schemes and most of those have been civil servants or employees of large multinational companies (Shaw & Ainsworth, 1995).

The size of the informal economy in many lower-income countries is directly attributable to weak governance. As Peruvian economist Hernando de Soto has convincingly argued, a lack of enforceable property rights and contracts, coupled with excessive regulation and bureaucracy, stifles the creation of legitimate employment opportunities (de Soto, 2000). A recent World Bank study found that, on average, it takes a business in a rich nation six procedures, 8 per cent of income per capita, and 27 days to become legally recognized. In poor or lower-middle-income economies, by contrast, it takes an average of 11 procedures, 122 per cent of income per capita, and 59 days. These relatively high costs mean that to a large extent, economic activity in such countries is informal. The same study found that weak property rights and heavy business regulation have an especially adverse effect on the ability of women and the poor to join the formal sector, despite the fact that such regulation is often designed to protect them (Wofford & Shanahan, 2004).

By presiding over such destructive governance, governments not only diminish the ability of their citizens to create wealth, but also hinder the ability of functioning health insurance markets to develop. Without functional insurance markets, it seems unlikely that medicines will ever be available universally.

The lack of insurance has a knock-on effect on the potential market for drugs, acting as a disincentive to pharmaceutical innovation. Properly insured populations provide a stable and predictable market for medicines, reducing the investment risks of innovators. For those concerned about both access to existing medicines and the incentives to innovate new medicines, it is essential to ensure that effective insurance schemes are allowed to flourish. For this to happen, the regulatory environment needs to be as accommodating as possible. This should be a priority for policy makers who share these concerns. (Appendix Figure 3 shows what would happen to the market for medicines in poor countries if these demand-side barriers were lifted).

Barriers to innovation of new medicines

The absence of a functioning market economy not only keeps people poor and undermines access to and demand for medicines and other goods; it also directly affects the supply of medicines. Governments that fail to foster the rule of law discourage companies from supplying medicines in several ways. Slow, expensive and corrupt court systems make it difficult to enforce contracts, which in turn discourage potential suppliers from entering into supply contracts. Also, the risk that trucks carrying medicines will be stopped and the cargo stolen or impounded, or a bribe levied by corrupt law enforcement officers reduces the incentives of companies to supply medicines. In addition, difficulties enforcing trademarks mean that a company which attempts to market its products may find that it faces competition from cheaper – but typically less effective, ineffective, or even harmful – counterfeit products. The evidence suggests that judicial dysfunction impedes economic growth, and restricts the ability of inventors and creators to commercialise their inventions (Sherwood, 2000).

As such, these general institutional failures greatly reduce the incentives to develop new medicines, especially for diseases that primarily affect the poor. In addition, there are several specific issues in the institutions of many poorer countries that negatively affect incentives to develop new medicines.

Weak intellectual property legislation in low and middle-income countries

Some have claimed that patents create a barrier to access to medicines by increasing prices. While this is theoretically plausible, this scenario still does not explain the low rate of access to medicines that are already off patent and thus open to competitive, generic-based production.

It is true that when a state grants a patent, it provides the inventor with temporary exclusivity over the patent product or process. This can incur real costs, including the possibility to keep prices artificially high when, in absence of legal protection, market forces would drive prices down to their marginal cost – the lowest price at which a good can be sold without the producer making a loss. However, as Amir Attaran has shown, more than 98 per cent of drugs on the WHO's 'Essential Medicines' list are not patented in any poor country. As we have also illustrated, there are many factors that conspire against access, but patents on these specific medicines are not one of them (Attaran, 2004). In any case, these criticisms of patent protection must also be weighed against their benefits.

When it comes to creating incentives to encourage the development of new medicines for the diseases of poverty, protection of intellectual property (IP) can play a crucially important role. The high cost of developing a new pharmaceutical product (estimated at upwards of $500 million in the US) (DiMasi et al., 2003), combined with the relatively low cost of copying the same product (typically a few millions of dollars), means that developers must be assured that they 'own' the product before they will commit such substantial sums.

Patents stimulate competition in several important ways that contribute to an environment in which new, better, more effective and efficient medicines replace older, less effective and efficient ones. Importantly, this environment is also one where access to such innovations can be encouraged through mechanisms of markets.

One such mechanism is the provision of information about new medicines, through advertising and other marketing tools. By increasing demand for the medicine, such marketing sends a signal to other pharmaceutical companies that it may be worth investing in a competing product.

More generally, IP protection in countries with incipient or extant knowledge-based industries is likely to spur economic growth, with positive consequences for the demand for medicines.[21] Weak IP laws enable the emergence of copy industries at the expense of innovator industries – with negative consequences for economic growth because the added value of the copy industries is typically lower than that of innovator industries.[22] In addition, innovator companies based in countries with strong IP protection will be less likely to engage in joint knowledge-oriented projects with firms in countries with weak intellectual property protection (Maskus, 2000).

It is perhaps not surprising, then, that between 1997 and 2001, 180 of the 184 new molecular entities were developed in the US, the EU and Japan,[23] where intellectual property protection is the strongest.

In addition to providing incentives to local companies to invest in the development of innovative products, IP protection in poor countries may spur innovation by foreign companies to serve local needs (e.g. developing drugs and vaccines to treat and prevent tropical diseases) (Lanjouw, 1998). By contrast, countries that exploit their weak intellectual property regimes by threatening to issue compulsory licenses for drugs reduce the incentives to invest in such research and development (Rozek, 2000).

The contrasting cases of India and Singapore shed some light on the link between strong intellectual property legislation and innovation.

In India, Indira Gandhi's government passed laws in 1972 that made it impossible to patent pharmaceutical products, with the result that the past 33 years have seen practically no new drugs created within that country to tackle its most pressing diseases. Instead, a large generics industry developed. Yet for all the copies of medicines being produced by India's then 20,000 or more pharmaceutical companies (many of them small-scale 'mom and pop' operations), access to medicines in India remained deplorably low, standing at less than 40 per cent in 1999 (Lanjouw, 1999). In addition, despite being a global centre for the manufacture of generic AIDS drugs, only 12,000 of India's 5 million HIV positive citizens were receiving antiretroviral drugs by the end of 2005 (UNAIDS, 2006).

India's implementation of a TRIPS-compliant patent law has probably in part reduced the number of companies producing copies of drugs but it has had no discernable impact on rates of access to medicines, which almost certainly remain extremely low. Again, the fact is that there are far more serious problems at play which affect access to medicines besides intellectual property rights, such as an entirely inadequate medical infrastructure.

Nevertheless, the recent changes in India's intellectual property law already have stimulated Indian firms to develop drugs for diseases that predominantly affect the local population. For instance, Nicholas Piramal has recently opened a US $20 million research and development centre in Bombay to carry out basic research in a wide range of health problems, ranging from cancer to malaria. Ranbaxy (India's largest pharmaceutical company) and Dr. Reddy's are also pursuing similar R&D projects. India currently has the largest number of FDA approved pharmaceutical manufacturing companies outside the US, and has increased spending on R&D from 4 per cent, five years ago, to 8 per cent today.[24]

The change in patent law is also attracting significant foreign investment. Multi-national pharmaceutical companies such as Merck and Bristol-Meyers Squibb now see India as a prime location for establishing research facilities. India is attractive not only because of its lower basic costs, but also because of the many well-educated researchers that can reliably conduct capital-intensive clinical trials and more complicated forms of later stage drug development. The management consultants McKinsey estimate that by 2010, US and European pharmaceutical companies will spend US $1.5 billion annually in India on clinical trials alone (Padma, 2005).

Many Western firms are also seeking to partner with local expertise. One recent example is collaboration between Danish-based Novo Nordisk and Dr. Reddy's to create a new treatment for diabetes. Japanese firms have also expressed interest in investing substantial sums into Indian R&D projects. Instead of imposing prohibitive barriers, as it once did, the Indian government actively has courted these foreign investments by providing incentives, such as a 10-year tax break to pharmaceutical companies that are involved in research and development.

Such developments mean that an Indian firm may well develop a vaccine for malaria or improve current tuberculosis therapies, resistance to which contributes to the deaths of over 1,000 people each day in India alone. Investments are even going into R&D for a vaccine for HIV/AIDS. Human trials are underway for the second preventative HIV vaccine candidate produced in India.[25]

In a relatively short time, India's new patent law is also hastening collaboration between the information technology sector and the pharmaceutical and biotechnology industries. Until recently, the fledgling research-based biotech and pharmaceutical sectors relied on patenting in the U.S and Europe.

Instead of exporting raw materials and basic active ingredients that are used to manufacture generics, firms in India now have the ability to compete globally, producing high value-added, life-saving medicines. This will also contribute to the country's continuing economic growth and its concomitant increase in life expectancy (which has already risen from 36 years in 1951 to its current estimated level of 61 years.

Singapore likewise illustrates the benefits of improved patent protection. In 2001 it implemented a new patent law which brought the country into compliance with international standards. As a result, US $5 billion in FDI has helped to sustain that country's position as one of Asia's strongest economies. Singapore's burgeoning biomedical science sector has played a central role: output in 2004 was US $9.7 billion, a 33.2 per cent increase on the previous year.[26] This is not limited to investment on the part of established western pharmaceutical companies, as a host of younger indigenous R&D companies are also scaling up their operations.[27] Singapore's emergence as a significant location for value-added R&D has also contributed to the search for new medicines for diseases endemic to poor countries. A high profile investment in Singapore is the Novartis Institute for Tropical Diseases, which opened in July 2004. It will focus initially on researching treatments for dengue fever and drug resistant tuberculosis.

Hypothetical: Creating a market for malaria treatment

To evaluate the impact of improved IP protection on incentives to develop and market a new drug for one of the diseases of poverty, consider the potential market for a new malaria treatment.

While the costs of researching and developing a new drug in the US and other wealthy countries are estimated to be US $800 million, the costs of developing a drug in a less developed country would be far lower. Because of comparative advantages of producing in those countries, we assume that the cost would be around US $100 million (taking into account failure rates, etc.).

Currently, approximately 300 million people suffer from malaria each year. If 10 per cent of those pay for a new treatment, that amounts to 30 million treatments per year. Although patents are valid for 20 years after filing, the effective life of a patent for a new drug is on average cut to about 10 years because of the time it takes to develop, test and comply with regulatory requirements (IFPMA, 2004). That means a total of 300 million courses of treatment while the drug is under patent.

Assuming a discount rate of 15 per cent, each course of therapy needs to yield a margin of only 62 cents in order for the developer to break even on sales. The average cost of production for a course of Artemisinin Combination Therapy treatment is currently estimated at US $2.40.[28] Assuming that a new drug would cost a similar amount, the total cost of one course of treatment need be only around US $3.50 for the developer of the drug to cover the cost of development, production and marketing – and even make a profit (albeit a relatively small amount). At such a price, a new, patented malaria therapy would be competitive in the market and might plausibly sell the necessary 30 million courses per year.

If it were possible effectively to patent a new malaria drug in relevant markets, it seems plausible that there would exist a private sector company which could produce a cost-effective and efficacious new malaria treatment.

Sadly, however, the barriers to innovation and access described in this chapter mean that the discovery and development of drugs for the diseases of poverty is currently not financially viable for private sector firms, except as part of their philanthropic efforts.

Inappropriate levels of intellectual property protection in developed countries

From the above, it is clear that intellectual property protection in most lower-income countries is almost certainly too weak, with the result that the level of for-profit development of medicines for the diseases endemic to those countries is too low.

However, concerns have been raised that in certain respects, intellectual property protection in some wealthier countries may be too strong. In particular, we are concerned that in some cases patents are granted for what appear to be mere discoveries rather than genuine innovations. For example, in some cases a genetic sequence has been patented even though the use of that sequence has not been identified. This might have the perverse effect of creating too broad a patent, blocking downstream innovations. On the other hand, it is possible that without such patents, investments in biotech research would be far lower, and the discoveries that form the basis of downstream pharmaceutical products would never come into being.

Likewise, there has been much criticism of patents granted for research tools. These, it is argued, raise the cost of research without providing any substantive benefits. On the other hand, it is again possible that without the possibility of patents, there would be insufficient incentives to invest in the development of the research tool in the first place.

After the fact, it is often easy to argue that an invention was 'obvious.' To engineers who develop laser-guidance systems, the light bulb no doubt seems 'obvious.' To the developers of modern hybrid cars, perhaps the internal combustion engine seems 'obvious'. But the reason the innovations seem obvious after the fact is that they are already there and in some sense have been factored into all downstream innovations. What is not clear is whether they – and the downstream innovations upon which they depend – would in fact have been developed had there been no means by which the inventors could have captured the rewards of their investments.

Nevertheless, the question remains as to how best to ensure that patents that are granted are not too broad. This may be addressed in various ways. Some, for example, argue that greater pre-grant scrutiny of patents would reduce the number of egregious patents that are granted. In our opinion this is not a good solution. In a TRIPS-compliant system where patents are granted for 20 years after filing, it would likely further delay the granting of patents. This would both delay investments in R&D related to the patented innovation and reduce the effective life of the patent once granted. In the context of medicines, this would mean fewer new drugs and longer delays in their appearance on the market.

Others argue that the rules applied by patent examiners should be changed. For example, it has been suggested that patent applications should be evaluated not only on the basis of the three standard criteria (novelty, non-obviousness, and utility)[29] but also on the basis of their effectiveness. This, however, presupposes that effectiveness can be measured prior to the development and testing of a product, which usually it cannot – especially in the case of new molecular entities. In such circumstances, the requirement of 'effectiveness' will lead to arbitrary decisions by patent examiners and judges, and patents will not be granted to many potentially effective products.

We believe that there are better solutions, including:

◆ **Simplified procedures for granting patents.** At present, many countries have highly bureaucratised patent agencies, which are extremely slow in making decisions on the granting of patents; streamlining procedures along the lines of international best-practice could improve the situation.
◆ **The introduction of regional patent granting agencies.** Where resource constraints are a problem for patent offices, such agencies could reduce costs and increase throughput, thereby increasing the competitiveness of the whole region.
◆ **Improved incentives for patent agents to make decisions.** For example, introducing a performance related pay system (appropriately constrained by quality requirements) might increase throughput of patent applications; contracting out the service to the private sector could have a similar effect.
◆ **Simplified procedures for challenging patents in courts.** This would enable more rapid and less costly resolution of disputes.
◆ **The introduction of petty patents or 'utility models.'** This would be useful for certain classes of product where a full

patent might not be justified – these might apply, for example, to research tools and certain genetic sequences.

♦ **Competition between patenting authorities.** While it may be desirable to have common minimum standards for patents, such as those to which members of the WTO have agreed under TRIPS, it is important also to retain a degree of competition between authorities in order to ensure that the appropriate breadth of patents may be discovered.[30]

Pre-market regulations

Companies are required to comply with an increasing number of regulations before they can launch a pharmaceutical product onto the market. This drives up the costs of supply, making the end product more expensive and thus less affordable for customers in lower-income countries. According to a survey of 20 leading pharmaceutical companies conducted by the CMR Institute for *Regulatory Science* in 2003, 65 per cent of companies felt that the change in the regulatory environment over the preceding three years had increased the cost and time of bringing new medicines to market. Furthermore, 23 per cent of those surveyed felt that the increasing regulatory burden was directly responsible for the decline in NME submissions (CMR, 2004). In South Africa, the situation is exacerbated by the Department of Health's stipulation that it approve all new drugs, even if they have been approved already in the EU, US or Japan. This can add delays of two or more years before new medicines are available in South Africa.

Because regulatory bodies are beholden to national governments, their tendency is to ensure that the potential side effects of new drugs are minimised as far as possible. This is because the publicity surrounding the discovery of an unsafe drug in the market leads to a public outcry, resulting in high political costs for national regulatory authorities. The missed gains from new medicines that are delayed or refused approval are less obvious (or even intangible) to the general public, so regulators have an incentive to err on the side of caution. However, if the regulator only considers potentially harmful side effects, this will have the unintended consequence of raising the cost, and delaying or preventing the approval of new drugs.

One consequence of an excessively precautionary approach is that regulatory authorities allow new medicines or vaccines to be sold to the public only after extensive pre-clinical and clinical trials have been performed. These trials examine the safety, quality and efficacy of the new drug in treating or curing diseases. Estimates of the average time it takes to for a new drug to go through these trials range from 8.5 to 13.5 years, a process which adds considerable costs to the drug development process (DiMasi, 1995; Adams & Brantner, 2003; Dranover & Meltzer, 1994).

Estimates of the cost of bringing a new drug to market vary; some researchers suggest that the total cost is over US $800 million (DiMasi et al., 2003). As such, manufacturers have strong incentives to concentrate their resources on developing 'blockbuster' drugs that will provide a return on that significant investment. Meanwhile, there is less incentive to invest in drugs for rarer conditions in the richer world (such as psychiatric disorders) and even for relatively common diseases in lower-income countries.

Professor Sir Michael Rawlins, Chairman of the UK's National Institute for Health and Clinical Excellence, has argued that many of the preclinical and clinical studies required by various regulatory agencies add little to the safety of the final product, but instead contribute unnecessarily to the estimated US $300–450 million cost of clinical development (Rawlins, 2004). Clearly removing excessively precautionary regulatory barriers would speed up drug development and reduce costs, creating stronger incentives to invest in the development of new drugs for diseases that may otherwise be relatively unprofitable.

To some extent, the length of time it takes for new drugs to enter the market, and the consequent cost to society of delays, is an issue recognised by regulatory agencies. The FDA has adopted 'fast-track approval' and 'accelerated approval' for certain classes of drugs, while the European Medicines Agency has instituted stiff targets for the marketing approval of orphan drugs. These represent a step in the right direction, but governments are often tempted to impose further regulations on drugs manufacturers when they come under political pressure. A recent example comes from the United Kingdom, where the health minister Lord Warner revealed that he is considering a fourth stage of clinical trials to alleviate safety fears surrounding new drugs. Legislators should resist the temptation to assuage public fears through such excessive regulation, because it would increase the time and expense of getting a drug to market. This would be most harmful for the development of drugs for regions or diseases where returns are the lowest – most typically, diseases endemic to lower-income countries.

One solution that would ensure new drugs reach markets as quickly as possible – in part by reducing the ability of local drug regulatory agencies to impose arbitrary and overly stringent requirements on new registrations – would be to enable competition between existing national drug regulators, as well as between private certification boards (Sauer, 2005).

Such accountable, competitive regulators would set the standards of regulation at levels demanded by those making choices about drug regimens. For many drugs, this would mean swifter approvals and a reduction in development costs, leading to an increase in the number of drugs developed for most diseases – especially those which affect the poorest and those which affect relatively smaller populations – while also reducing the price of medicines to all.

Public health would be safeguarded by the desire of these agencies to defend their own reputations. The importance of reputation in maintaining clients and attracting new ones, the existence of a free press engaging in investigative journalism, and expected penalties through the legal system for corrupt and dangerous decisions by these regulators, should lead to a well-functioning market in drug approval. A drug approval agency that bends to pressure from pharmaceutical companies, for example, would be quickly exposed, and the marketability of their future products would suffer.

Data exclusivity

Another aspect of pre-market regulation is the treatment of the data submitted to regulatory authorities. These data are submitted on the basis of 'data exclusivity,' an agreement that the authorities will not release them for a specified period and that during this period other firms may not rely upon the data as the basis for their applications for licenses.

This period of data exclusivity varies from 5 to 11 years.[31] Once it expires, competing companies are free to access and rely upon the data and thereby avoid having to conduct duplicative research (and associated costs).[32]

It has been alleged that these periods of data exclusivity hinder generic competition, thereby keeping the price of medicines unnecessarily high. But while the introduction of competition typically leads to price reductions on medicines, the net effect will depend on the impact it has on the incentives to invest in research and development. Companies invest heavily in the development of the data they supply to regulators during the approval process. If these data are then shared with other companies, the value to the originator is reduced. This erosion of value has negative consequences for the ability to raise the funds required to conduct future tests, and is likely to act as a disincentive to companies which might otherwise bring new, therapeutically beneficial medicines to the marketplace.[33]

Unclear rules governing the submission of data to regulatory authorities will only increase legal disputes between research-based companies and their generic counterparts. These disputes are already common and their frivolous costs must now be factored into the rapidly rising total cost of delivering a drug to the marketplace. While great effort is being expended towards containing these costs, the failure properly to address data exclusivity arrangements threatens not only to increase costs, but also to reduce the incentives to innovate as well.

Price differentiation

The ability to sell a product at different prices to different consumers enables companies with a degree of market exclusivity to ensure that their products reach as many consumers as possible while still maximising revenue. If a company is able to segment markets precisely according to each individual's willingness to pay, then every consumer willing to pay at least the marginal cost of production for the product should be able to purchase that product. This would both maximise the number of people who benefit from the product and would also maximise revenue to the company, which in principle would enable more to be spent on R&D.

Perfect market segmentation means that the number of consumers served and the price paid by the poorest consumer are the same as that which would exist in a perfectly competitive market (Appendix Figure 5).

In practice, market segmentation is costly to enact – primarily because of the need to prevent low-price purchasers reselling to higher-price purchasers – and the larger the number of market segments, the greater the cost. So, firms weigh up the benefits of adding a segment with the cost of enforcing the additional segmentation. Typically, firms segment markets first by overall market (which is usually a country or trading bloc) and then by sub-categories, such as: individuals (which may be further segmented by age and income), businesses, charities, and governmental bodies. So, for example, drug prices in South Africa are far lower than in Europe and the US (Reekie, 1997). This means that market segmentation can be particularly beneficial for patients in poorer countries.

Where the overall market for a product is very large and where that market is readily segmented (i.e. the cost of enforcing the segmentation is low compared to the benefits), companies may set the lowest price close to the marginal cost of production. In the context of a disease such as HIV/AIDS, where the total market for medicines is massive and the humanitarian case for widespread distribution is great, companies may even choose to sell below marginal costs in some markets, provided that sufficient profit is recuperated in others (Danzon & Furukawa, 2003).

Market segmentation is underpinned by intellectual property – especially patents and trademarks – and contracts. If the intellectual property rights and contracts are respected,[34] firms can operate freely within the marketplace without running the risk of having separate national or international markets compromised by the resale of the lowest priced medicines into markets where prices are relatively higher.[35] However, infringements upon intellectual property rights mean that firms cannot control their own pricing schemes, with serious consequences. Not only does this act as a disincentive for firms to sell their products in poor countries, it may also inhibit future innovation.

In short, price differentiation allows companies to cater for people who otherwise could not afford to purchase their products. It allows countries that are not able to shoulder the costs of R&D themselves to afford expensive medicines. It also means output is higher than the level that would occur if no differentiation were possible. Moreover, the innovator is able to generate more revenue, providing a greater pool of resources for investing in new drug development.

Price controls

Unfortunately, governments often restrict the ability of companies to implement differential pricing strategies. For example, they frequently impose price controls on drugs, capping the price of drugs and making any other sales price illegal. Nearly all economically advanced countries – with the notable exception of the United States – impose price controls on medicines in one form or another (Danzon & Furukawa, 2003). Because the controlled price is effectively the *only* price, this prevents competition that would drive the price lower; in other words, the price 'ceiling' becoming a price floor (U.S. Dept of Commerce, 2004).

Drug price controls discourage companies from registering products in certain markets, leading to shortages in supplies and illegal trade in medicines. This in turn provides a route for counterfeit medicines to enter the market. A 2003 study illustrated that one of the risks of parallel importation from countries which have regulations that ensure low drug prices is that medicine manufacturers prefer to delay or cancel the launch of a particular product in the price-controlling countries (Danzon et al., 2003). The study showed that between 1994 and 1998, there were 85 New Chemical Entities launched in the US and UK. However, out of a maximum possible 2,125 registrations of these NCEs in 25 countries, only 55 per cent (1,167) were actually registered. The research also showed that those countries with lower expected prices or a smaller expected market size – most typically lower-income countries – experience longer delays in drug registration.

Delays in registration of new medicines are particularly harmful to sufferers of HIV/AIDS. Research shows that one new anti-retroviral (ARV) HIV/AIDS drug prevents around 6,000 deaths in the US the following year and ultimately prevents around 34,000 deaths (Lichtenberg, 2003). Although new ARVs cost more than older, off-patent ones, they can substantially reduce the number of lost productive work days, so in many cases pay for themselves in a purely financial sense (one study estimated that 21.3 per cent fewer days were lost with the introduction of each new ARV) (Lichtenberg, 2003). Newer drugs also reduce the amount of time patients spend in hospital, negating any financial benefit from using older, off-patent drugs.

Price controls also have a number of other adverse impacts:

Reduced supply

Regulations on drug prices drive pharmacies into bankruptcy as their margins are squeezed, and make the distribution of drugs to remote and rural regions financially unviable. For example, the price caps forced on certain drugs in South Africa have been implicated in the closure of 103 pharmacies.[36] Price controls will likely reduce profit margins on controlled-price pharmaceuticals. As a result, wholesalers and pharmacies are likely to carry a smaller range of drugs. If the price controls are widespread or targeted at the most popular drugs, they may have such a negative impact on profits that it is not worth a wholesaler distributing them to far-flung pharmacies – and so pharmacies in rural areas will be more likely to close. The lack of profitability in the sale and distribution of medicines will also reduce the incentives for pharmacists to invest in training, which will make them less effective purveyors of healthcare advice. This would be particularly damaging to the rural poor, whose contact with professional healthcare is very often limited to local pharmacists.

Reduced innovation

In many countries (especially Canada, and countries in Europe and Australasia), government control over healthcare systems has led directly to price controls of one kind or another. Ageing populations, combined with more effective but more costly treatments for many diseases puts upwards pressure on healthcare costs. Politicians may be wary to increase spending on health, especially where the spending affects the incomes of taxpayers and can be seen as the result of their actions – because of the potential it could have on their chances to be re-elected.

The relatively short electoral cycle creates incentives on the part of politicians to achieve short-term savings, even when these will lead to longer-term costs or longer-term harm to health. The result has been strong pressures to restrict access to more costly new pharmaceuticals which are relatively more expensive, even though in many cases these new drugs would reduce the subsequent need for more expensive procedures and hospital treatment.

A striking example comes from Canada, whose Patented Medicines Review Board sets strict guidelines on the price of medicines. This board also has the power to compel a supplier to reduce prices if they exceed pre-determined levels (Menon, 2001). Likewise, Germany's government sets levels at which it will reimburse purchases of specific classes of drugs, with consumers paying any difference. This has the result that the consumer's perception of the cost of buying newer drugs is much greater than the real price differential. As a result, consumers have an incentive to buy older drugs that are less effective.

Price controls reduce the ability of producers to implement effective price differentiation strategies. In essence, fewer drugs are supplied at a price higher than would be paid by the poorest consumer but lower than would be paid by the wealthiest consumer. As a result, wholesalers and retailers are likely to carry a smaller range of drugs. If the price controls are widespread and targeted at the most profitable drugs, they are likely to have a substantial impact on profits throughout the value chain. That means not only fewer wholesalers and pharmacies, but also less investment in new drugs by pharmaceutical companies. (The economic consequences can be seen in Appendix Figure 6.)

Economic theory is backed up by increasing amounts of empirical evidence. Price controls have had a direct negative impact on the numbers of new drugs that are submitted for regulatory approval. A recent US Department of Commerce study found that the price controls used by a range of OECD countries have resulted in a significant decrease in spending on both old and new drugs (U.S. Department of Commerce, 2004). It found that these controls have decreased the price, pushing it closer to marginal production costs, which in turn leaves less revenue for future investment in R&D. The study estimated that, after extrapolating to a broader set of OECD countries, the diminished returns as a result of price controls are in the range of US $18 billion to $27 billion annually. If this lost revenue could be recouped through deregulated pricing strategies, the study calculates that an additional three or four new molecular entities (NMEs) could be developed every year. To put this into context, only 30 NMEs were approved by the FDA between 2000 and 2003.

Price controls in some European countries have also hindered

Europe's ability to develop new medicines. In 1992, six out of ten best selling medicines were developed in Europe; by 2002 only 2 out of 10 were of European origin. If the US were to introduce price controls, it is estimated that this would result in a reduction pharmaceutical R&D by some 30 per cent. This would translate into 330 to 365 fewer new drugs within a twenty-year period (Giacotto, 2004).

Compulsory licenses

Compulsory licenses – or the threat of issuing a compulsory license – can have a similar effect on innovation as price controls. In the interest of improving public health, compulsory licenses can be a way for extremely poor countries to procure relatively inexpensive medicines (when all attempts to secure such products voluntarily have been exhausted). The issuance of such licenses in a medical state of emergency has always been permitted under the original TRIPs Agreement for countries with manufacturing capacity. The 2001 WTO Doha TRIPS agreement extends this safeguard to countries without manufacturing capacity – enabling them to procure from companies with manufacturing capacity but where otherwise production would be restricted to patent holders – thereby protecting the interests of the poorest nations.

In practise, however, middle-income countries such as Brazil have often used the threat of compulsory licensing as a negotiating tool to secure lower prices. [37] While this can prove to be a politically popular move in the short term, it undermines the ability of innovator companies effectively to price differentiate. It also places increased strain on pricing strategies aimed at offering the cheapest medicines to patients in extremely poor countries, and acts as a further disincentive for firms to develop new and improved medicines for the diseases of poverty (Kremer et al., 2004). (Appendix Figure 4 shows what would happen if both demand and supply-side constraints were lifted.)

Discussion

Clearly, many urgent health concerns in the poorest parts of the world could be addressed if existing drugs and interventions were to be distributed properly. However, a variety of factors conspire to prevent people from receiving the medicines they need. As we have seen, poor road and electricity networks hinder the distribution of drugs, as does the shortage of medical facilities such as clinics, hospitals and pharmacies. Health insurance systems, which would enhance access to medical care, are currently inadequate because the governments of lower-income countries frequently fail to foster the kind of institutional environments in which they can thrive.

But people are also denied medicines in more insidious ways. Governments in lower-income countries impose burdensome taxes and tariffs on imported medicines, pricing many people out of treatment. Governments also impose often unjustifiable non-tariff barriers, such as arbitrary licensing restrictions. At the same time, governments nominally offer healthcare services to everyone, but in practice they do so in ways that primarily benefit a small number of citizens (mostly the elite) at a very high cost. As a result, government-financed healthcare systems in such countries are often poorly resourced and poorly managed. Meanwhile, the private sector often is over-regulated. These glaring failures of governance help to ensure that universal access to essential medicines remains a long way off for many regions of the world.

The manifold failures in drug distribution also have ramifications that reach beyond the immediate health needs. Because these failures diminish demand for medicines, they make it less likely that new medicines will be created. In richer countries this is less of a problem because effective demand is higher.

Producers respond to the perceived demands of consumers, whether those consumers are individuals, health agencies, insurance companies or governments. (This is illustrated in Appendix Figure 1.) This has led to the creation of a wide variety of drugs to combat the range of disorders suffered by consumers in rich country markets. However, in lower income countries the absolute size of the market is constrained by the weakness of distribution mechanisms, leading to a concomitant decrease in supply. If a medicine stands little chance of actually reaching its intended consumer, there is little point in risking large amounts of capital in developing a drug specifically designed for a poorer market. As a result, certain diseases endemic to these regions, such as the cluster of so-called 'neglected diseases,'[38] have failed to attract sufficient research from commercial drugs companies. More problematic is the fact that these same constraints also limit the distribution of all kinds of pre-existing medicines. Access to these medicines would improve if the many barriers to access identified in this chapter were addressed as a matter of priority.

Appendix

Figure 1 **Market equilibrium**

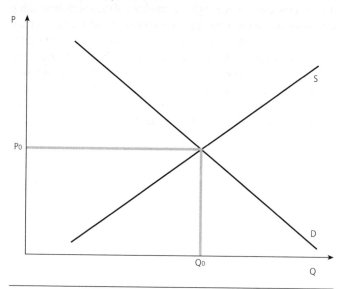

Figure 1 shows consumer willingness to pay, represented by the 'demand' curve, D, and industry willingness to supply, represented by the 'supply' curve, S. The intersection of these two curves shows the total quantity that will be supplied, Q_0 and the minimum price charged, P_0.

Figure 2 **Effect of taxes and tariffs on demand for medicines**

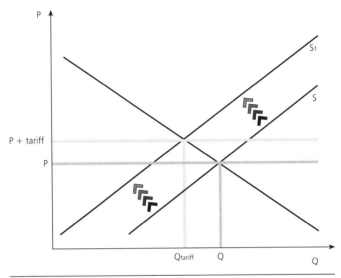

If a government imposes a tax on a medicine, this raises the minimum price artificially. Figure 2 shows the effect of adding such a tax; the supply curve is effectively shifted inwards because suppliers must now add the tax to the amount that they charge. As a result, the amount supplied falls from Q_0 to Q_{tariff}.

Figure 3 The impact of a rightward shift in the demand curve

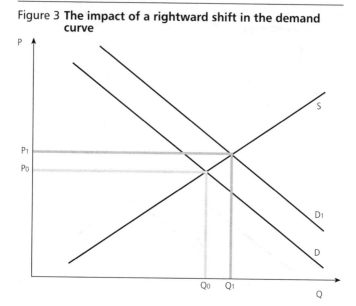

Figure 3 shows that when consumer willingness to pay increases (for example as a result of a rise in income), the demand curve shifts to the right. This leads to an increase in the amount supplied (from Q_0 to Q_1) and also to an increase in the minimum price (from P_0 to P_1). This is because the supply has been met by moving along the original supply curve, for which the cost of producing an incremental unit is assumed to rise as output rises — because more expensive production methods have to be brought on-stream.

Figure 4 **The impact of a rightward shift in the supply curve**

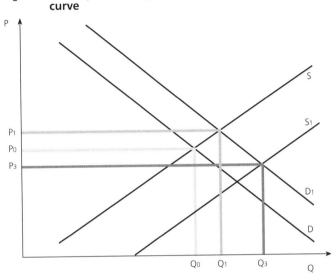

However, the rise in price (as a result of the expansion in the demand curve in Figure 3) is likely to be seen by entrepreneurs as an opportunity to make money by supplying the market using new technologies (these might be, for example, new production technologies, or they might be new drugs in the same class). As those entrepreneurs enter the market, supply increases to Q_3, and the price falls to P_3. This can be represented as a rightward shift in the supply curve (Figure 4).

Figure 5 **Perfect market segmentation**

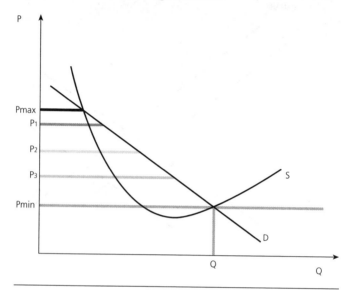

If a supplier has an element of market power (for example as a result of the temporary market exclusivity conferred by a patent), then in principle he is able to set prices and will do so in such a way as to maximise profits. The textbook economics analysis of such situations assumes that the supplier will choose only one price, which will be higher than the marginal cost of production. However, if the supplier is able to segment the market perfectly, then he will sell at a wide range of different prices to different consumers and will maximise profits by setting the minimum price (Pmin) at which he sells just above the marginal cost of production and the maximum price at Pmax. He will then sell total quantity Q, which is the same as the perfectly competitive quantity. This is shown in Figure 5.

Figure 6 **Regulated market**

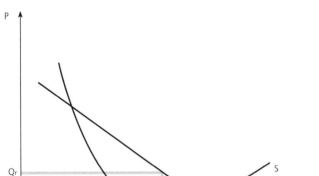

The quantity sold under a regulated market, Q_r, is lower than the quantity sold under a segmented market, Q_0, where the firm is able to price its product based on the willingness to pay of different groups of consumers. The price paid by the poorest consumer in the regulated market, P_r, is higher than the lowest price charged in a segmented market, P_0.

6 **Cost effective means of fighting the diseases of poverty**

Khalil Ahmed,[1] Franklin Cudjoe,[2] Eustace Davie,[3] John Kilama,[4] Martín Krause,[5] Andrés Mejia,[6] Barun Mitra,[7] Nonoy Oplas,[8] Martín Simonetta,[9] Philip Stevens,[10] Jose Luis Tapa,[11] Margaret Tse,[12] Jasson Urbach[13]

This chapter considers the cost-effectiveness of existing strategies for addressing the diseases of poverty promoted by the WHO and other intergovenmental organisations and compares these to other possible strategies. The first half examines the UN's response to HIV/AIDS and malaria. The second half looks at what might be done to tackle those diseases of poverty which have a lower political profile but nonetheless constitute a significant proportion of the disease burden of less developed countries – diarrhoeal diseases, acute lower respiratory infections and diseases associated with malnutrition.

HIV/AIDS: The WHO's '3 by 5' treatment plan

In September 2003, the World Health Organisation announced that it would ensure that by the end of 2005, 3 million HIV-infected people would be on anti-retroviral treatment. Since then, many billions of dollars have been spent attempting to achieve that goal. However, by December 2005, only 1.3 million people

Table 1 Doctors and nurses available and people living with HIV/AIDS for selected sub-Saharan countries

	Medical doctors per 100,000 pop	Nurses per 100,000 pop	PLWHAs (thousands)	Total population (thousands)	PLWHAs per 100,000 population	PLWHAs per medical doctor	PLWHAs per nurse
Malawi	1	26	900	12,105	7,435	7,435	286
Mozambique	2	21	1,300	18,863	6,892	3,446	328
Zimbabwe	6	54	1,800	12,835	14,024	2,337	260
Tanzania	2	37	1,600	36,977	4,327	2,164	117
Rwanda	2	21	250	8,387	2,981	1,490	142
Zambia	7	113	920	10,812	8,509	1,216	75
Swaziland	18	320	220	1,077	20,427	1,135	64
Botswana	29	241	350	1,785	19,608	676	81
Uganda	5	54	530	26,699	1,985	397	37
South Africa	69	388	5,300	45,026	11,771	171	30

Source: adapted from http://www.who.int/globalatlas/default.asp & http://www.who.int/hiv/universalaccess2010/en/

had access to these drugs – representing only 43 per cent of the WHO target of 3 million people by the end of 2005 (UNAIDS, 2006). In sub-Saharan Africa, only 11 per cent of those who needed treatment were receiving it in June 2005 (UNAIDS/WHO, 2005a).

Depressingly, the failure of the initiative was entirely predictable. The necessity of reaching its ambitious target led the WHO to scale up treatment despite the manifest absence of workable health infrastructure in the worst afflicted countries. The overwhelming majority of people living with HIV/AIDS (PLWHA) are in sub-Saharan Africa, where public health systems are fragmented, dilapidated or nearly non-existent. Most countries in the region lack sufficient qualified health workers and doctors, not to mention pharmacies, clinics and doctors. Figure 1 shows that some of the worst afflicted countries also have the fewest medical professionals.

Antiretroviral drugs are complex to administer, requiring specified regimens and oversight by knowledgeable professionals and testing equipment, both of which are in short supply in most of Sub-Saharan Africa. Seen in this light, the WHO's decision to push its mass treatment initiative as the key to solving the AIDS crisis was a gross strategic error. Without sufficient staff and facilities, there is a substantial risk that inappropriate doses will be handed out to patients, and patients will not adhere to regimens. This raises the spectre of resistance, which has the potential to render many of the currently available treatments ineffective (Blower et al., 2003). Samples taken before 1996 showed about 5 per cent drug resistance to existing HIV strains, rising to at least 15 per cent between 1999 and 2003. This all implies significant extra costs as drug-resistant patients have to be moved onto expensive second-line and third-line therapies (REF).

It is unlikely that the governments of these most afflicted countries, with a good knowledge of their infrastructural and human resource constraints, would have imposed such ambitious ARV treatment targets on themselves – indeed, the WHO never consulted or asked for approval from member states when it launched "3 by 5" in December 2003. Many extremely poor countries have enormous difficulty delivering simple vaccines and essential medicines to their populations, let alone delivering and monitoring complex ARV regimes.

Meanwhile a variety of factors – including the mismanagement of funds, inefficiency, waste, expensive technical assistance and corruption within recipient governments – has meant the cost of treating a developing-country patient for two years ballooned to $12,538 by the end of 2005 – nearly 10 times the $1,633 initially estimated by UNAIDS. Such inflated costs will be unsustainable if the UN is to meet its current target of placing 10 million PLWHA on ARV treatment by 2010.

It is not even clear that the WHO's efforts directly led to the achievement of 1.3 million on ARV treatment by the end of 2005, not least because many of the countries that have been most successful in scaling up treatment – such as Thailand and Brazil – were already running successful treatment programmes independent of WHO advice. Furthermore, it is recognised that by the end of 2005, some 716,000 people were receiving ARV treatment independently of "3 by 5" through the Accelerating Access Initiative, a partnership between the UN and several pharmaceutical companies.[14]

Prevention

Leading public health experts are virtually unanimous in concluding that prevention is of paramount importance in the fight against AIDS (Salomon et al., 2005). However, by making itself publicly accountable to meeting such ambitious treatment targets, the WHO has been forced to devote far more resources to treatment at the expense of prevention.

The overriding focus on treatment was one result of the 2000 international AIDS conference in Durban, South Africa. At about this time, advances in medical science were making AIDS in the west a manageable (but not curable) condition, as opposed to the automatic death sentence it was a few years previously. Health activists thought – not unreasonably – that if American AIDS patients could get the miracle drugs, why shouldn't people in poor countries? Previously, international agencies had focused on prevention out of a desire to contain the pandemic, but also because ARV therapies were too expensive. However, after voluble and emotive campaigns from AIDS activists following the Durban AIDS conference, governments and global agencies reoriented their strategies towards favouring treatment.

One outcome of this lobbying by pressure groups was the creation of the WHO's flagship "3 by 5" programme. But the presumption towards treatment has been further institutionalised by the creation of the President's Emergency Plan for AIDS Relief (PEPFAR) in 2003, which has been required by the US Congress to dedicate 55 per cent of the US $15 billion five year budget for HIV to treatment of individuals with HIV/AIDS. In financial years 2006 through to 2008, 75 per cent of those funds are to be spent on the purchase and distribution of antiretroviral drugs, with only 20 per cent of all funding to be spent on prevention.[15]

The prioritisation of treatment over prevention has had significant opportunity costs, by not curtailing new infections and increasing the pool of people with the potential to transmit the virus. The UN's own statistics indicate that more people became infected with HIV in 2005 than ever before, with an estimated additional five million new infections worldwide. The number of people living with HIV globally has also reached its highest level ever. By the end of 2005, global HIV prevalence had risen to an estimated 40.3 million people (UNAIDS, 2006), from a figure of 34.9 million in 2001 (UNAIDS, 2004). 4.1 million people were infected in 2005 alone, an increase from 3.9 million in 2003. According to UNAIDS, HIV prevalence is increasing in South Africa, China, Indonesia, Papua New Guinea, Vietnam, Bangladesh and Pakistan. While prevalence rates in many sub-Saharan African countries seem to be stabilising, very few countries are experiencing significant declines in prevalence (UNAIDS, 2006). Figure 2 illustrates the increasing numbers of infections globally.

Table 2 **Regional HIV and AIDS prevalence and infection rates, 2003 & 2005**

Region	Adults and children newly infected with HIV	Adult (15–49) prevalence (%)
Sub-Saharan Africa		
2005	2,700,000	6.1
2003	2,600,000	6.2
North Africa and Middle East		
2005	64,000	0.2
2003	54,000	0.2
Asia		
2005	930,000	0.4
2003	860,000	0.4
Oceania		
2005	7,200	0.3
2003	9,000	0.3
Latin America		
2005	140,000	0.5
2003	130,000	0.5
Caribbean		
2005	37,000	1.6
2003	34,000	1.5
Eastern Europe and Central Asia		
2005	220,000	0.8
2003	160,000	0.6
North America, Western and Central Europe		
2005	65,000	0.5
2003	65,000	0.5
TOTAL		
2005	4,100,000	1
2003	3,900,000	1

Source: UNAIDS, 2006.

This failure has been underplayed and deflected by WHO, which has justified the failure of its "3 by 5" programme on the grounds that it has galvanised further efforts towards achieving universal access to treatment, and has demonstrated the feasibility of providing HIV treatment even in the poorest parts of the world (UNAIDS, 2006).

However, the shortcomings of this strategy have been highlighted by a little-publicised external evaluation document commissioned by WHO following the end of the "3 by 5" programme. As the document states, "HIV prevention efforts are not containing the pandemic, since some 4.9 million more people became infected with HIV during 2005." The document continues:

> *HIV prevention has been a technical area within the "3 by 5" initiative that has received relatively little investment and effective prevention interventions, such as the prevention of mother–to–child transmission of HIV, were not properly prioritised"* (WHO, 2006b).

The WHO's focus on treatment has therefore allowed the pandemic to become even more out of control. In countries that have pursued active and sustained HIV prevention strategies, the numbers of infected people has generally decreased, thereby reducing both the economic burden of caring for PWLHA, as well as reducing the potential human tragedy of a worsening AIDS pandemic. In Uganda, one of the few countries in sub-Saharan Africa where HIV prevalence has fallen in the last decade, education played the key role. The country's ABC programme ('Abstain, Be faithful, or Condomize') emphasised the risks of casual, unprotected sex, and has had a dramatic effect on patterns of sexual activity, contributing to an 80 per cent reduction in HIV prevalence (Singh et al., 2003). Brazil and Thailand have also managed to reverse the spread of HIV through early prevention efforts. More recently, there is some evidence the decline of HIV prevalence in Cambodia, Zimbabwe, and in areas of Tanzania, Haiti, Kenya and Burkina Faso are partly due to HIV prevention efforts (UNAIDS, 2005b).

An increasing body of evidence shows how the expansion of prevention programs could save millions of lives. One study calculates that if prevention programmes are scaled up sufficiently, 28 million new HIV infections could be averted between 2005–2015. As well as preventing an impending human tragedy, this would also generate significant cost savings. Although the authors estimate that it would cost $3,900 to avert each infection, this would save $4,700 in treatment and care costs for each individual, resulting in savings of $780 per infection averted (Stover *et al.*, 2006). Furthermore, this paper also demonstrates that the data reveals that a lack of attention to prevention between 2001 and 2005 has resulted in a huge missed opportunity to save lives; indeed, as of 2003 prevention services were only partially available globally.

Even if HIV prevalence is brought under control, we are still left with the issue of how best to distribute antiretroviral drugs to infected patients. A remarkably successful public private partnership in Botswana between the Gates Foundation, several western drug companies and the government offers some lessons. This initiative involved the construction of clinics to distribute high-quality antiretrovirals, while schools and colleges have undertaken public education programmes (Ramiah & Reich, 2005). Botswana now has more people on ARV treatment than any other country in sub-Saharan Africa and is the only such country to provide free treatment for all.

Private philanthropy can be an effective stop-gap measure. In the medium to long term, however, Africa needs self-sustaining, efficient health-care systems that allow effective distribution of life saving medicines, as well as the propagation of vital health education.

Malaria

In order to combat the global malaria problem, the WHO and associated agencies kicked off an ambitious plan to 'Roll Back Malaria' (RBM) in 1998, with the goal of halving malaria incidence by 2010.

It proposed to achieve this by a combination of judicious use of medicines and the distribution of insecticide-treated bed nets.

Seven years in, there are some indications that the global malaria problem is not improving and may be getting worse. Although problems associated with collecting accurate data make it difficult to determine precisely how many people suffer from malaria, in 2002 an external evaluation of RBM set up by the WHO said:

Anecdotal evidence and the strong consensus among experts suggests that, at the very least, the malaria burden has not decreased. What is more likely, and believed to be the case by most of those involved, is that malaria has got somewhat worse during this period. (Malaria Consortium, 2002)

More recently, scientists from the University of Oxford suggested, on the basis of improved measurements, that more than half a billion people – nearly double previous estimates – were infected by the deadliest form of malaria in 2002 (Snow et al., 2005). Clearly, the Roll Back Malaria campaign is failing to achieve its stated goal.

But the real tragedy is that malaria might be far less of a problem today if the WHO had adopted a different strategy from the beginning. An important part of such a strategy would have included spraying the inside walls of residential buildings with insecticides such as DDT. Remarkable control was achieved in the 1950s and 60s, even in regions where transmission rates were unusually high. But since the cessation of such activities the disease has returned to many such areas, often with devastating impact on human mortality. Residual treatments are far more effective than using bednets, but have been rejected because of environmental concerns. Such indoor residual spraying (IRS) helps prevent mosquitoes from entering dwellings and it repels or kills those insects that do manage to enter. Because it minimises the chances of humans being bitten, IRS effectively prevents the transmission of the malarial parasite, which makes it an excellent tool for preventing the spread of the disease. In the years following World War II, the WHO put DDT at the centre of its malaria eradication plan, saving an estimated 50 to 100 million lives through prevention alone (Roberts et al., 1997).

Many countries have tamed malaria through IRS with DDT (Roberts et al., 2000). India, for example, started a nationwide programme of IRS with DDT in the 1960s. In that decade, India deployed around 18,000 tonnes of DDT and reduced malaria cases from 75 million per year to less than 100,000. Unfortunately, the caseload increased significantly when the use of DDT was reduced in subsequent decades (Sharma, 1987).

More recently, Namibia, Botswana, Mozambique and South Africa have been somewhat successful in reducing the incidence of malaria through IRS programmes utilising DDT and alternating with other pesticides (Baird, 2000). Uganda is determined to utilize this powerful tool, despite potentially being threatened with trade sanctions by the EU.[6]

Over the last few decades, however, the WHO has discouraged the use of DDT in member states – encouraged by environmentalists, who have often massively overstated the negative effects of DDT on human and animal health (Roberts et al., 2000). Until recently, most Western aid agencies discouraged the use of DDT and indoor residual spraying generally, and the WHO has provided little financial assistance to those governments that wish to go down this route.

Recently, however, USAID has re-evaluated its support of IRS, deciding to allocate more funding to such projects. The WHO also undertook something of a *volte face* in November 2005, when it announced that IRS with DDT would form a key plank of its Roll Back Malaria programme. In September 2006, the WHO announced that it would henceforth strongly recommend to member states the use of DDT for IRS.

In terms of prevention, the WHO's Roll Back Malaria strategy has largely focused on the distribution of insecticide treated bednets, claiming that they provide the most effective means of vector control. It has historically funded bednets almost to the exclusion of other preventative measures.

While bednets may have a role in preventing transmission of malaria (Premji et al., 1995; Philips-Howard et al., 2003), they are far from perfect, particularly in the poorest areas where they are most needed but can only be obtained at considerable expense. Mosquitoes tend to be most active in the hottest parts of the year, and few people relish the thought of covering themselves in a net during these hot nights. In certain parts of Africa, people are reluctant to sleep in nets because they resemble a shroud. People also often misuse bednets, with enterprising individuals using them as fishing nets. Even when bednets are used properly they are a far from perfect barrier, not least because mosquitoes, being opportunistic, will take advantage of any occasion when a person happens to get out of bed during the night (Bean, 2001; Choi, 1995).

Bednets also face the hurdle of effective distribution. While public health authorities in many parts of Africa find it difficult to distribute routine and simple vaccines and treatments, so too are they failing to get the nets out to all people who need them. These problems are compounded by the fact that the nets need to be retreated with insecticide every three months, or else they lose much of their utility.[17] According to one study, fewer than five per cent of children in malarial areas currently sleep under a bednet (Hamel et al., 2001).

Indoor residual spraying alone is not enough. The most successful malaria control strategies have been those which have combined indoor spraying with education campaigns to encourage people to eliminate breeding sites, such as used tires which can collect stagnant water, and changes in the management of animals in order to reduce the proximity of these malaria parasite reservoirs to people.[18]

In combination with these strategies, prophylactic drugs can play an important role in reducing the pool of malaria parasites in the human population and thereby reduce transmission rates. This is especially important for the most deadly species of human malaria parasite, *Plasmodium falciparum*. In addition, effective drug treatment can help to reduce the number of deaths.

However, the WHO has also mishandled treatment recommenda-tions. Until as recently as 2004, it advocated the use of chloroquine in Africa, even in the face of increasing resistance to that drug by the *P. falciparum*. This was despite the existence of a far more effective – albeit more expensive – alternative, Artemisinin Combination Therapy (ACT). In fact, the WHO recognised the benefits of ACT and named it a central plank of its RBM strategy, only then to approve the use of the nearly useless chloroquine in many African countries because it is cheaper (Attaran et al., 2004). The WHO only recently started heeding its own advice and properly approving ACT after it came under pressure from malaria experts and the international press. But in part because of the abruptness of WHO's belated change in strategy, artemisinin supply is now unable to keep up with increased demand.

Clearly, the availability of appropriate and effective medicines is of great importance to helping those already infected with the malarial parasite. However, sensible and wide-scale prevention techniques could remove much of the need for medication, largely because there would be far fewer infections in the first place. Reducing the prevalence of malaria would then free up considerable resources for the purchase of the most effective, modern medicines and avoid debacles such as occurred with RBM and chloroquine.

Diarrhoeal diseases

Diarrhoeal diseases are one of the major causes of premature childhood deaths in lower-income countries. According to the World Bank, three million children die every year from cholera and other water-borne diarrhoeal disorders (World Bank, 2002). Much suffering could be averted with effective use of treatments such Oral Rehydration Therapy (ORT). In addition, antibiotics could be used to eliminate more serious bacterial infections. Finally, vaccines have been and are being developed against viral causes of diarrhoea, such as rotavirus; if these vaccines were deployed widely, the incidence of such diseases could be reduced dramatically. In the case of rotavirus, a vaccine could prevent some 500,000 childhood deaths annually.[19] Unfortunately, at present even inexpensive treatments such as ORT do not reach those most in need (Rao et al., 1998).

Another, more fundamental approach to controlling these diseases focuses on improving the quality of drinking water. Currently, water resources in most countries are owned and controlled by the state (typically municipal governments). Yet in poor countries, the state has shown itself to be a very poor provider of water, with some respite from dry or non-existent taps being provided by informal private suppliers (Okonski, 2006). Where ownership and/or management have been transferred to the private sector, access has typically improved considerably, as has been shown for Chile (Rosegrant & Gazmuri, 1994), Argentina (Galiani et al., 2003) and Guinea (Menard and Clarke, 2000; Noll et al., 2000; Brook Cowen, 1999). In Argentina, in particular, there is strong evidence that privatisation of supply has led not only to improved access but also to reduced incidence of water-borne disease, especially in the poorest districts (Galiani et al., 2003).

Finally, much could be done to improve sanitation in poorer countries, including improvements in sewerage. In addition, this means educating people to use soap and other cleansing agents. Such education could in principle be provided by the private sector – for example, by companies who have a material interest in selling soap – but this is often inhibited by a political environment hostile to commercial enterprise.

Acute lower respiratory infections

Another major contributor to premature deaths in lower-income countries is acute lower respiratory infections (ALRI). One of the leading causes of such infections is inhalation of smoke from dirty energy sources such as wood, dung and crop residues burnt in poorly ventilated dwellings. Exposure to such smoke increases the risk of ALRI (such as pneumonia), especially in children and women.

This problem afflicts up to half of the world's population, almost entirely in the poorest countries. Globally, ALRI represent the single most important cause of death in children under five years of age, and contributes to approximately two million deaths annually in this age group (Bruce et al., 2002).

Thus, if the poor were able to use more efficient, cleaner forms of energy, the positive impact (in terms of reducing the global disease burden) would be immense. Unfortunately, governments tend to restrict the ability of people to use cleaner fuels and technologies such as electricity, liquefied petroleum gas (LPG) or even kerosene. The impact of these restrictions falls primarily affects poorer households, who must then resort to burning wood, low-grade coal, crop residues and animal dung, which in turn exacerbates both indoor and local air pollution.

In India, for instance, the country's 2001 census revealed that less than 44 per cent of households have an electricity connection (Goswami, 2004). Because the national and state governments have intervened extensively in the supply of electricity, the country has an artificial shortage – so merely possessing an electricity connection does not mean that a household actually receives electricity.

Policies of the Indian government have also contributed heavily to a shortage of petroleum-based fuels in the country, which particularly affects the rural poor. Kerosene is subject to government rationing. Only two government-run companies in India supply LPG – thus, these companies are not competing in a dynamic, competitive market. Although LPG production is in principle subsidised by the state, it is unclear whether these subsidies are passed on to consumers (in the form of lower costs) or whether the companies inflate their production costs (thus absorbing the subsidy). Moreover, there is little if any distribution network for LPG – so private suppliers are unlikely to enter the market. This explains why rural access to LPG is extremely low; India's 2001 census revealed that fewer than 10 per cent of rural households utilize LPG (Goswami, 2004).

These examples show why government policies towards can

have harmful side effects for health – contributing directly or indirectly to the prevalence of ALRI in poor countries such as India.

While prevention is almost certainly preferable to cure, there are also many inexpensive medicines that can be used to treat pneumonia and other ALRI. However, these often are not available.

Diseases associated with malnutrition

Poor nutrition contributes to 53 per cent of deaths associated with infectious diseases among children under five years of age in lower-income countries (Black et al., 2003). Many cases of malnutrition could be prevented if people were able to produce and distribute food more efficiently, yet in Africa especially this has been difficult because of weak property rights.

In agrarian communities, strong property rights enable more efficient farming practices. First, the ability freely to buy and sell land means farmers are better able to achieve economies of scale. Second, clearly defined property rights enable land owners to access low-cost capital, in the form of mortgages, that otherwise would not be available. Such loans enable people to invest in more capital-intensive forms of production, both on farm and off. The result is higher yields, greater investment – and profit from – non-farm forms of economic activity, and generally an increase in wealth.

In addition to improving the efficiency of agricultural production, many technologies exist that could help improve this situation. One such technology – biofortification – entails breeding specific traits into a plant such that it produces and contains essential micronutrients that can be utilized by the human body.

One example of biofortification is Golden Rice, which was developed as a humanitarian project to address Vitamin A deficiency. This deficiency kills at least 6,000 children every day and leads to irreversible blindness in 500,000 children each year (WHO, 1995). Traditional interventions such as the distribution of vitamin A capsules by the WHO are helpful but have not substantially reduced these figures.

In 1999, a 15-year project culminated when two teams of

European scientists successfully modified the starchy tissue of rice (the part consumed by humans) to produce pro-Vitamin A (the chemical that is converted into Vitamin A in the body).

However, activists who are opposed to GM foods more generally objected that the fortified rice, when eaten in normal quantities, would not provide a poor person with the necessary levels of dietary Vitamin A. However, a new strain of the rice (Golden Rice II) has been developed that would provide 23 times more pro-Vitamin A compared to Golden Rice I, effectively solving this problem (Paine et al., 2005).

Since 1999, the inventors of Golden Rice have sought to transfer the benefits from this technology to the poor in lower-income countries – e.g. the people for whom it was intended. Governments and charities were able to finance the entire project research, but not the subsequent development and regulatory stages. Attempts to take Golden Rice to its next phase, with field trials and tests for nutritional compatibility in individual countries, have been thwarted by an overly precautionary approach by regulators, fuelled by the sentiments and actions of activists. The same fate befalls many other genetically modified crops (Paarlberg, 2006).

The field trials have been delayed because opponents of Golden Rice insist that the plants must pose no risk to the environment. For humanitarian projects, such barriers create unnecessary expense and delay. This is not to suggest that Golden Rice should be exempted from normal regulatory procedures. The problem is that regulators have focussed on hypothetical and mostly non-existent risks rather than reasonably assessing the actual risks alongside the real benefits, in particular, the potential to immediately reduce Vitamin A deficiency and thereby save human lives. As a result, researchers will be less inclined to use biofortification to solve other micronutrient problems – such as iron, protein and zinc deficiency.

Conclusion

In tackling diseases of poverty such as malaria and HIV/AIDS, global public authorities such as the WHO have a track record of prioritising grandiose but unachievable schemes over more practical approaches. Billions of dollars have been spent in recent decades, with little discernible impact on mortality rates.

In the context of HIV/AIDS, intervention by the WHO seems to have exacerbated the problem by neglecting prevention in its aspiration to achieve 'treatment for all,' with the result that new infections are soaring.

In the context of malaria, public health experts have long advocated indoor residual spraying with insecticides such as DDT, yet the WHO and aid agencies have until recently provided little practical support for those nations wishing to adopt this practice. The failure to date of the WHO's Roll Back Malaria programme also reveals the limitations of the argument that intellectual property rights are standing in the way of improving human health. The price of patented drugs has little (if anything) to do with the failure of public health agencies to reduce the impact of the disease. RBM failed because WHO was responsive to special interest groups whose concerns seemingly had no relationship to actions which would actually improve the lives of the poor.

The burden of both HIV/AIDS and malaria could be significantly reduced with sensible prevention strategies and careful treatment programmes. While new medicines for these diseases would obviously be beneficial, in order to address the inevitable development of resistance to available treatments, we must recognise that effective distribution of those treatments will be practically impossible until the physical and human aspects of health infrastructures are improved.

The cases of ALRI and diarrhoea reinforce the fact that there is a need for greater focus and more appropriate strategies in tackling all the diseases of poverty. Policies pursued by intergovernmental agencies, national governments, and humanitarian charities would benefit from an improved understanding of the root causes of extreme poverty and ill health. In this regard, a growing body of literature implicates corruption, weak or non-existent rule of law and limits on economic freedom (see e.g. Greenspan, 2003; Gwartney & Lawson, 2004; Kasper, 2006). The reform of governance structures must therefore be a priority; that means strengthening property rights, liberating markets and entrenching the rule of law.

Admittedly, the reform of governance in sovereign states is outside the bounds of WHO policy. But the fact that so many African governments are corrupt and ineffective does not excuse the WHO from promulgating the disastrous strategies it has followed. Indeed, the very fact that health infrastructure is so weak in the world's poorest countries makes many of these strategies all the more absurd.

7 Counterfeit medicines in LDCs: problems and solutions

Julian Morris and Philip Stevens

Much of the debate surrounding counterfeit medicines to date has focused on how to prevent them seeping into the supply chains of developed-country markets. The majority of counterfeit medicines originate in Less Developed Countries (LDCs), including most of those that end up in the US and EU. Steps should be taken to change the incentives faced by counterfeiters in LDCs participating in the production and trade of counterfeit pharmaceuticals.

The scale of the problem

While counterfeit medicines in wealthy markets are a growing concern for physicians and law-enforcement agencies, their prevalence pales in comparison to their penetration of less developed markets. According to the World Health Organisation (WHO), 25 per cent of all medicines in LDCs are counterfeit.[1] In some countries, the prevalence is far higher:

- Counterfeit medicines constitute between 40 and 50 per cent of total supply in Nigeria and Pakistan.[2]
- In China, authorities have found that some products have a counterfeit prevalence ranging between 50 and 85 per cent.[3]
- 36.5 per cent of antibiotics and anti-malarials on WHO essential drugs list in Thailand and Nigeria are substandard (Shakoor *et al.*, 1997).

♦ A recent survey by the WHO of seven African countries found that between 20 and 90 per cent of all anti-malarials failed quality testing. These included chloroquine-based syrup and tablets, whose failure rate range from 23 to 38 per cent; and sulphadoxine / pyrimethamine tablets, up to 90 per cent of which were found to be below standard (WHO, 2003).

In spite of a lack of hard data (Cockburn *et al.*, 2005), it is clear that counterfeit medicines are not confined to a handful of therapeutic classes. This is especially true in LDCs, where the range of fakes on the markets encompasses treatments for a diverse range of conditions and ailments. The top five counterfeited medicines in the Philippines provide some illustration of this point:

1. Antihypertensive drugs (Adalat Gits 30mg Tablet).
2. Anti-asthma drugs (Ventolin Expectorant syrup).
3. Analgesic medicines (Ponstan 500).
4. Anti-diarrhoea (Diatabs Reformulated).
5. Vitamins (Propan with Iron Capsule, Ceelin 100 mg/5 ml Syrup, Enervon C and Iberet 500).[4]

This list is certainly not exhaustive. Other favourites for counterfeiting include drugs for treating anaemia, HIV, schizophrenia, as well as growth promotion hormone (used in the treatment of HIV). The problem also extends beyond fake pharmaceuticals to medical consumables such as non-sterile syringes and gauze and even substandard electronic medical equipment.

Where are counterfeit medicines being produced?

A large proportion of the world's counterfeit medicines originate in Asia. China in particular is a production centre, although precise data about the scale and scope of the problem within this country is neither widely available nor reliable. In 2001 it was reported that China had 500 illegal medicines factories[5] and while no newer data is available, it is safe to assume that number has since increased. Also in 2001, it was reported that Chinese authorities "closed 1,300 factories while investigating 480,000 cases of counterfeit drugs worth $57 million."[6] Most Chinese counterfeit medicines that find their way into foreign supply chains first pass through the ports of Hong Kong and Shenzhen.

South East Asia more generally is a major source of counterfeit medicines. According to the WHO, Cambodia had 2,800 illegal medicine sellers and 1000 unregistered drugs on the market in 2003. The same report showed that Laos had about 2,100 illegal medicines sellers, while in Thailand, substandard medicines account for approximately 8.5 per cent of the total market.[7]

One 2002 study by government officials showed that 9 per cent of all drugs tested in **India** were substandard.[8] Some 15,000 generics manufacturers operate in India.[9] Although the majority are legitimate, a small minority are likely to be 'fly by night' operations that do not comply with proper standards. Most of the counterfeit medicines in **Nigeria** originate in India, a fact that lead the Nigerian authorities to threaten to ban the import of all drugs from India in 2003 (Raufu, A., 2003). However, it should be noted that 70 per cent of the Indian domestic market is supplied by around 20 companies that regularly pass inspections from visiting officials from Western countries.[10]

Counterfeit medicines also abound in **Latin America**, with instances reported in Argentina, Brazil, Colombia, Venezuela, Mexico, Peru and Guatemala: **Mexico** is a major global source of counterfeit medicines, with the trade standing at an estimated value of US$650mn per year – equal to around 10 per cent of total drug sales in the country.[11]

In **Russia**, it is estimated that counterfeits constitute between five and ten per cent of the total market.[12] In 1999 alone, 1,500 lots of Russian-made drugs failed to pass quality tests.[13]

The impact of counterfeit medicines

Counterfeit medicines can cause harms in various ways: the presence of toxic chemicals frequently causes injury or death; inappropriate delivery systems and/or inadequate amounts of active ingredient prevents the drugs from working effectively and, again, can lead to injury or death; more broadly under-dosing fosters resistance to the active chemical. In the cases of HIV/AIDS and malaria, this latter aspect is particularly worrying.

Harmful

Counterfeit medicines often contain agents that are injurious to health, as for example when 89 people in Haiti died after ingesting cough syrup manufactured with diethylene glycol (a chemical commonly used as anti-freeze). This particular product was made in China, transported through a Dutch company to Germany, before winding up on the Haitian market. A similar case occurred in Nigeria in 1995, resulting in the death of 109 children and again in Bangladesh (Hanif et al., 1995).

The dangers of widespread counterfeiting were illustrated in 1996 during a meningitis epidemic in Nigeria. Some 60,000 people were inoculated with counterfeit vaccines, resulting in the deaths of 2,500 people (Pecoul *et al.*, 1999).

More importantly, counterfeits medicines typically provide inadequate doses of drugs, either because too little active ingredient is included in pills or because the delivery vehicle (including otherwise 'inactive' ingredients) are inappropriate (for example, chemicals that are not water-soluble). As a result, patients receive too little medicine and die or are far sicker would have been the case if they had received an adequate dose.

It is estimated that in China between 200,000 to 300,000 people die each year due to counterfeit or substandard medicine. However, this "official" statistic may over- or under-state the true number of cases.[14]

Drug resistance

Perhaps one of the most worrying implications of the global boom in counterfeit medicines is the acceleration of new, drug resistant strains of viruses, parasites and bacteria. If drugs contain too little of the active ingredient, not all the disease agents are killed and resistant strains are able to multiply and spread.

Malaria

This is already being observed in the treatment of malaria. Counterfeiters around the world have cashed in on the massive demand for the latest and most effective antimalarial drug, artemisinin. A field survey conducted in 2004 showed that 53 per cent of artemisinin-based antimalarials in a range of South East Asian countries contained incorrect levels of active ingredient (Dondorp et al., 2004), which implies that swathes of patients are receiving the incorrect dose. The direct consequences are death and serious injury resulting from improper treatment.

In addition, malaria parasites exposed to inadequate (subtherapeutic) concentrations of artesunate may result in the multiplication of parasites resistant to the drug (White, 1999). Even though Artemisinin has only been widely available since the late 1990s, scientists are already reporting cases of resistance. According to Dr Dora Akunyili, the head of Nigeria's national drug regulator, the racket in fake medicine is directly responsible for this resistance, and is a contributing factor to the doubling of malaria deaths over the last 20 years.[15]

HIV AIDS

HIV/AIDS treatment is also under threat from counterfeit medicines. The recent discovery of counterfeit antiretrovirals (stavudine-lamivudine-nevirapine and lamivudine-zidovudine) in the Congo (Ahmad, 2004) raises the prospect that the first line therapies for treatment of HIV/AIDS could soon be rendered useless. With few new research leads in the pipeline, this could have grave implications for the people of sub-Saharan Africa.

Bird flu

Finally, counterfeit medicines could be undermining our ability to contain and treat a potential avian flu pandemic. As demand has grown for the anti-viral drug Tamiflu, one of the best current treatments for the disease, counterfeiters have ramped up production of illegitimate versions. Already, the Internet is awash with spurious Tamiflu, while consignments have been discovered as far apart as New York and Beijing. The risk is that copies containing sub-therapeutic levels of active ingredient could facilitate the development of drug resistant forms of the avian flu virus, leaving very few tools to contain a potential pandemic.

Undermining R&D

Counterfeiting can also undermine the incentives of R&D based companies to invest in future innovation. Even near-perfect copies of on-patent medicines cause harm by competing with legitimate supplies of medicines from originating companies, which reduces revenues and undermines incentives to invest in future R&D.

Underlying causes of LDC counterfeiting

♦ *Absent or defective IP protection.* One way to prevent the sale of unauthorised copies of medicines is to enable companies to register and enforce trademarks. These enable vendors to signal the quality of their product to potential purchasers. Trademark owners have strong incentives to ensure that the quality of their product is maintained because their reputation and hence future profitability depend upon it.In many LDCs, it is difficult to enforce trademarks – even for local companies. Where trademarks cannot be enforced, cheaply produced poor quality copies will typically crowd out good quality drugs.

♦ *Lack of adequate civil liability.* Civil law protects the consumer against mis-sold or defective goods. By enabling consumers (or their relatives) to obtain redress from the manufacturer or supplier of a harmful product, such liability both compensates those who are harmed and discourages manufacturers and suppliers from selling counterfeits. In many LDCs, however, civil law is either poorly defined or difficult to enforce.

♦ *Inability to resolve disputes over property rights and contracts in independent courts.* Underlying the lack of civil liability and weak IP protection are costly and inefficient legal systems As a result, it can often take years for cases to be heard. Many courts in LDCs are hampered by a lack of basic things such as reliable electricity and inefficient processes, causing delays.

In many LDCs, law enforcement is also corrupt. In such places, criminal counterfeiting gangs may be able to pay corrupt law enforcement agents to turn a blind eye to their activities. If a case does make it to court, the gangs may be able to pay off the judge and thereby induce a favourable judgement.

♦ *Weak or absent rule of law:* In LDCs with a weak rule of law, political and legal decisions tend to be arbitrary and designed to benefit the elite. As a result, regulation designed to combat counterfeiting is often ineffective. Corruption within regulatory agencies and police forces exacerbates this problem, so that the enforcement of regulations is seen as an opportunity to collect bribes.

♦ *Price controls.* The imposition of price controls by governments prevents companies from selling goods at different prices to different consumers. Also, where prices are controlled at different levels in different markets, traders exploit these price differentials through arbitrage. Such trade (called parallel trade) may create gaps in the supply chain which can be exploited by counterfeiters. For example, it is often necessary to repackage drugs in order to sell them in a different market, which requires that the packages will require relabelling in the correct language. This creates opportunities for unscrupulous intermediaries to infiltrate the supply chain with fakes. Price controls in wealthy country markets therefore increases the

Duties and taxes on retail medicines

Country	Combined total duties and taxes
India	55%
Sierra Leone	40%
Nigeria	34%
Pakistan	33%
Bolivia	32%
Bangladesh	29%
China	28%
Jamaica	27%
Morocco	25%
Georgia	25%
Mexico	24%

Table adapted from European Commission, 2003

chance that copies of patented medicines produced in LDCs will leak back into wealthy country markets.

In addition, companies have less incentive to register products in markets where their drugs are subject to price controls, leading to shortages in supplies. They also reduce the margins made by pharmacies, making the distribution of drugs to remote and rural regions financially unviable. For example, the price caps forced on certain drugs in South Africa have been implicated in the closure of 103 pharmacies.[16] If markets are left unsupplied in this way, it presents a clear incentive for counterfeiters to fill in the unmet demand.

♦ *Taxes and tariffs.* LDC governments also stimulate demand for cheaper fakes by artificially driving up the price of legitimate drugs through taxes and tariffs, which can inflate the retail price of drugs by up to 50 per cent (see table below). Many of the high tariff countries also have a significant indigenous counterfeit medicine industry and / or problem. It is unlikely that this is entirely coincidental.

What can be done in Less Developed Countries?

In order to contain the global counterfeiting scourge, it is necessary to address those dynamics which encourage the manufacture and supply of counterfeit medicines. Since the majority of these drugs originate in LDCs, it should be a matter of priority to address those lacunae of governance which allow LDC counterfeiters to ply their trade with relative impunity.

Most importantly, it is essential that contracts, property rights and the rule of law be upheld in the countries in which the majority of these drugs are produced. When properly upheld, these formal market institutions enable entrepreneurs to participate freely in the market, leading to economic growth and technological development. When these institutions are not upheld, as is the case in most lower-income countries, people are forced into the informal economy as a way of side-stepping the cost and difficulty of conducting business formally. And when the majority of the population subsist within the informal economy, they are unable to avail themselves of the protection that would otherwise exist from contracts or the implied reputation of trademark-protected products.

Some concrete steps to overcome these problems in LDCs include the following:

- Adjudication of disputes over contracts should be simpler and cheaper, so that contracts may be more readily enforced.
- Bureaucratic restrictions on doing business should be removed.
- The manufacturers of brand goods should be able more effectively to protect their trademarks.
- Most fundamentally, courts of law should be granted greater independence, so that their rulings are more impartial and less influenced by powerful vested interests.
- The legislature should not have the power to interfere with judicial decisions.
- The power of law enforcement agents should be curtailed and their actions subject to judicial review.

- The actions of other government agents (e.g. regulators) should
  be subject to judicial review.
- Regulation restricting the supply of medicines should be
  improved or scrapped. [17]
- Governments should reduce taxes and tariffs on all
  medicines.[18]

What can be done? Internationally

TRIPs

At the international level, the agreement on trade related aspects of
intellectual property rights (TRIPs), which is part of the WTO Agreements of 1994 and is mandatory for all World Trade Organisation
members, requires that the trademark laws of member jurisdictions
are compatible with each other, a quality which is known as 'harmonisation.' LDCs that are members of the WTO should therefore
have TRIPs-compliant trademark recognition.

However, the only way for aggrieved countries to enforce
breaches of the TRIPs agreement is through trade sanctions. This is
often not a particularly desirable option, for several reasons. First,
trade sanctions hurt both parties – people in the offending country
will lose much-needed export revenue and associated employment
opportunities, while people the aggrieved country will lose the
economic benefits of importing goods from a country that has a
comparative advantage in production. To the extent that employment falls in the offending country, more people may end up with a
smaller disposable income and thereby more likely to purchase
cheaper counterfeit medicines.

Secondly, the enforcement of TRIPs can, in certain cases, undermine popular support for intellectual property protection, making
future enforcement more difficult politically. For example, in 2001
the research-based pharmaceutical companies sought to challenge
in the courts a South African law that seemingly contravened TRIPS.
In response to a very vocal campaign by AIDS activists, the pharmaceutical companies withdrew their case. While the dispute was

not brought in the WTO, the negative PR given to it created a persistent fear of the possible fall-out from bringing such a WTO dispute.

Bilateral trade agreements

An alternative way of persuading LDCs to institute intellectual property regimes is through tempting them with bilateral and regional free trade agreements (FTAs). Most FTAs involving the United States contain provisions that require signatory countries to bolster their intellectual property regimes. By promising access to large and lucrative markets, these agreements can be a way of persuading LDCs to respect the fundamentals of intellectual property protection, which is a vital step for curtailing counterfeiting.

Although these agreements are not as beneficial as unconditional free trade, they are a step in the right direction, freeing up trade and thereby improving economic well-being. However, they do raise complications in the form of 'rules of origin' issues, which are costly to monitor and administer. Furthermore, an overly-complex 'rules of origin' system may lead to the development of illicit trade routes which could be exploited by traders in illegitimate goods such as counterfeit medicines.

Conclusion

The counterfeiting of drugs is a global problem which will not be eliminated until the supply-side issues are addressed. The majority of counterfeit drugs are manufactured in LDCs, so reform in these countries is absolutely vital if progress is to be made. The most pressing area for reform in the majority of LDCs is the application of the rule of law, the definition and enforceability of property rights and the enforceability of contracts. Without such reforms, counterfeiters will continue to kill hundreds of thousands of people every year.

8 **The value of vaccination**

David E. Bloom, David Canning, and Mark Weston[1]

Introduction

> *You let a doctor take a dainty, helpless baby, and put that stuff*
> *from a cow, which has been scratched and had dirt rubbed into*
> *her wound, into that child. Even, the Jennerians now admit that*
> *infant vaccination spreads disease among children. More mites*
> *die from vaccination than from the disease they are supposed to*
> *be inoculated against.* (George Bernard Shaw, 1929)

The world has come a long way since George Bernard Shaw fulmi-
nated against vaccination in the 1920s. Vaccines are now widely
regarded as an effective and cheap tool for improving health.
Children in all countries are routinely immunized against major
diseases, and the practice has become a central plank of global
public health efforts.

Despite these advances, however, immunization coverage
remains far from universal, and the developing world in particular
remains vulnerable to vaccine-preventable illnesses. For example,
global coverage for DTP – the vaccine for diphtheria, tetanus, and
pertussis (whooping cough) – had reached 70 per cent in the 1990s,
but in Sub-Saharan Africa it stood at just 53 per cent. In Somalia,
Nigeria, and Congo, moreover, coverage halved between 1990 and
2000 (WHO, 2002). Vaccination against measles also falls short; the
disease caused 660,000 deaths in 2002 (WHO, 2004) In all, 3 million
people die each year from vaccine-preventable diseases (Centre for
Global Development, 2005).

In the developed world, too, vaccination efforts face obstacles. The rise of a well-organized anti-vaccine movement has persuaded some parents not to immunize their children. Vaccines, the campaigners claim, cause more harm than good: in societies where vaccine-preventable disease prevalence is minimal (ironically as a result of past immunization efforts, although this is rarely acknowledged by campaigners), the side effects of vaccines pose a greater health threat than the diseases themselves. Why, they ask, should everyone be vaccinated in order to protect the relatively small number of people that might contract the disease in the absence of mass immunization?

It is not just populist activists who overlook the positive effects of vaccination. More scientific estimates of the effects of vaccines also tend to underplay the benefits, disregarding the broad economic impacts of immunization in favor of a predominant and narrow focus on the averted costs of medical treatment and health care. With other human capital investments, such as education, economic analysis of the impacts focuses on the effect on earnings. This has not occurred, however, with vaccination, and until recently it did not occur for health in general. Public health specialists generally perceive vaccination as a hugely beneficial investment as it is both cheap and very effective at a population level (the influential 1993 World Development Report, 'Investing in Health', listed the World Health Organization's Expanded Program on Immunization as the first component of "the essential public health package"(World Bank, 1993)). Because of the narrow view of its impacts taken by the rest of the policy-making community, however, policy emphasis on vaccination is weaker than it might be if the full range of benefits were taken into account.

Health economists have long used two well-established tools to evaluate health interventions in economic terms. Both types of analysis are widely used and appropriately respected. Cost-effectiveness analysis (CEA) seeks to determine the cost of an intervention (e.g., vaccination) in relationship to a particular outcome. How much does it cost to save a certain number of lives, or to avert a certain number of illnesses, for example? Averted medical costs (at least those that would be incurred in the short run in the absence of vaccination) are also typically taken into account. Cost-benefit analysis (CBA), by contrast, makes a direct comparison between costs and benefits by monetizing the value of the latter. This technique facilitates comparison of two or more interventions, particularly when there is a range of discrete outcomes.

There are several problems with both types of analysis, as they have been used to date. First, neither type typically takes account of the cost of averted infections that may occur years later. This is understandable, since such infections are hard to predict, but that does not make future cost savings any less important.

Second, both types of analysis take a narrow view of the benefits of vaccination that fails to take account of recent academic work on the effects of health on incomes. The experience of development over the past half-century shows that good health fuels economic growth, just as bad health strangles it. Healthy children perform better at school, and healthy adults are both more productive at work and better able to tend to the health and education of their children. Healthy families are also more likely to save for the future; since they tend to have fewer children, resources spent on them go further, thereby improving their life prospects. Finally, healthier societies may be a stronger magnet for foreign direct investment and tourism than those where disease poses a constant threat.

Third, neither type of analysis factors in the effects that improved health has on triggering lower fertility rates. The combination of lowered mortality rates followed by lowered fertility rates leads to a baby boom generation that, when it reaches working age, can help bring about a significant economic boom (as happened in East Asia). In the case of vaccination, the consequent boost to health can catalyze a change in the age structure of the population (via the lowered fertility rates) that can lead to significant economic benefits.

Our research looks at all CEA and CBA studies listed in Pub. Med. for 2004 and 2005. The wide range of published results emphasizes the difficulties inherent in such work. However, since all of these studies fail to address the broader considerations described in the preceding two paragraphs, they all either overstate the cost of achieving a given beneficial outcome or underestimate the net benefits. It is this insight that spurs the current work.

With the spread of immunization having stalled in many parts of the world, a wider look at its benefits is timely. In this paper, we discuss the value of vaccination from a broad perspective. As well as the health benefits, we examine the cost of vaccine programs and their economic impacts. Vaccination has proved a cost-effective and remarkably efficient way of improving health, and has saved millions of lives. It has the potential, however, to be more effective still, and renewed efforts are needed if the momentum is to be regained.

Part 1 of the paper provides a brief summary of the history of vaccination and its impacts on human health. Part 2 looks at the state of play today and at the reasons why progress on vaccine delivery and development has slowed, and part 3 outlines why rate of return analysis and calculations of economic impacts suggest policy makers should direct more resources toward vaccination. Part 4, which reviews both cost-effectiveness analysis and cost-benefit analysis, indicates that a broader view of the long-term benefits of vaccination makes immunization programs much more worthwhile, in terms of their economic consequences, than has been thought in the past. Part 5 details our study on immunization and cognitive development, which has, in turn, been linked to higher earnings. Part 6 estimates the rate of return to one of GAVI's prospective investments, showing that this return is quite high.

A glorious past

The theory behind vaccination was brought to the West from Asia. The Chinese had observed that certain illnesses could only be contracted once, so they experimented with giving healthy individuals doses of diseases such as smallpox that would be too small to make them ill but large enough to stimulate immunity. The process was known as variolation and, in the case of smallpox, usually involved injecting powder from smallpox scabs into the vein. Although some individuals fell ill or died during the process, smallpox rates among communities that had been variolated were significantly lower than elsewhere.

Variolation was introduced to Britain by Lady Mary Wortley Montagu, who had observed the process in Turkey, where her husband was British ambassador, in the early 18th century. Several decades later, Edward Jenner, who had undergone variolation as a child, noticed that people who contracted cowpox after working with cows became immune to smallpox. To test this observation, he injected a small child with cowpox. The child fell ill with cowpox but, when later injected with smallpox, did not contract the latter disease. Jenner published his findings in 1798, and named the process 'vaccination', from the Latin word for cowpox (The Hutchinson Encyclopaedia, 1999).

In 1890, Emil von Behring and Shibasaburo Kitasato gave substance to Jenner's observation when they discovered antibodies. Injecting a small amount of a disease organism into an uninfected individual, they found, stimulated the production of antibodies, which fought off the initial attack and thereby prepared the body to fend off infection later in life. At around this time, vaccines for rabies, cholera, typhoid, and the plague were developed, although it was not until after the World War II that vaccines became a widespread tool for improving health. Today, 26 diseases are vaccine-preventable.

Since World War II, vaccination has had a major impact on global health, as the following list of successes shows:

* Smallpox, which had killed two million people per year until the late 1960s, was wiped out by 1979 after a massive worldwide immunization campaign.
* The number of polio cases fell from over 300,000 per year in the 1980s to just 2,000 in 2002 (Global Alliance for Vaccines and Immunization website, 2002).

- Two-thirds of developing countries have eradicated neonatal tetanus (WHO, 2002)
- Since the launch of the World Health Organization's Expanded Program on Immunization (EPI) in 1974, the number of reported measles deaths has dropped from 6 million to less than 1 million per year.
- Whooping cough cases have fallen from 3 million per year to less than a quarter of a million.
- Diphtheria cases have declined from 80,000 in 1975 to less than 10,000 today (Birmingham & Stein, 2003).
- The haemophilus influenzae B (Hib) vaccine has reduced the incidence of Hib meningitis in Europe by 90 per cent in ten years (Ehreth, 2003).

The EPI includes six vaccines, covering diphtheria, tetanus, whooping cough, measles, polio, and tuberculosis. Before 1974, only 5 per cent of children were vaccinated against these diseases. Today over 70 per cent are vaccinated (WHO, 2002). The program has reduced the share of the six diseases it tackles in the total burden of disease in young children from 23 per cent to less than 10 per cent since the mid-1970s (WHO, 2001). It has been estimated that declines in diphtheria, measles, and whooping cough have averted well over a million deaths in developing countries (Birmingham & Stein, 2003).

In 2000, in an effort to maintain the EPI momentum, the Global Alliance for Vaccines and Immunization was launched. GAVI comprises United Nations agencies, governments, donors, foundations, private companies, and academic institutions. It has six core strategic objectives: GAVI

- Improve access to sustainable immunization services
- Expand the use of all existing safe and cost-effective vaccines, and promote delivery of other appropriate interventions at immunization contacts
- support the national and international accelerated disease control targets for vaccine-preventable diseases

- Accelerate the development and introduction of new vaccines and technologies
- Accelerate research and development efforts for vaccines needed primarily in developing countries
- Make immunization coverage a centerpiece in international development efforts

As we will see part 2 of the paper, such an initiative is urgently needed.

A difficult present

Lost momentum

The rapid progress towards universal vaccination coverage in the 1970s and 1980s has slowed in recent years.

Declining funding for immunization has been mirrored in stagnating or falling coverage. UNICEF funding for vaccination fell from $182 million to $51.4 million between 1990 and 1998 (Gauri, 2002). Global coverage of the diphtheria, tetanus, and pertussis (DTP3) vaccine has stalled at around 74 per cent since 1990 (GAVI, 2003). Fifty-seven developing countries have yet to eliminate neonatal tetanus, and 200,000 babies died of the disease in 2000 (WHO, 2002). Yellow fever has made a comeback, despite the availability of an effective vaccine; the number of outbreaks increased sharply after governments curtailed programs in the belief they had vanquished the disease (GAVI, 2001).

Developing countries lag behind the West in terms of vaccination coverage. Measles immunization rates are over 90 per cent in Europe but below 70 per cent in South Asia and below 60 per cent in Sub-Saharan Africa (see figure 1) (World Bank, 2004). Ten developing countries reported cases of polio in June 2005, despite the massive (and largely successful) global effort to eradicate the virus (WHO, 2005). Sixty-two per cent of countries, meanwhile, had still not achieved full routine immunization coverage in 2003, with GAVI estimating that at least 9.2 million additional infants need to be reached to achieve full coverage (GAVI, 2003).

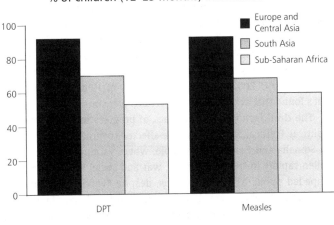

Figure 1 **Disparities in immunization rates**
% of children (12–23 months) immunized

Source: World Bank, 2004

There are several factors behind this loss of momentum. First, although dramatic progress has been made in increasing worldwide vaccination coverage from below 5 per cent to above 70 per cent, the task has inevitably become harder now that the easiest-to-reach populations have been vaccinated. Many of those whom campaigns have not yet reached are either living in inaccessible areas, out of range of clinics and health services, or reluctant to be vaccinated or to vaccinate their children. Because these communities are more elusive, the average cost per vaccination has increased, and it may be that other apparently cheaper health interventions have become more attractive.

Second, there are many practical problems impeding vaccine delivery. Delivering vaccines to patients requires functioning freezers and refrigerators (which in turn require a constant supply of energy); good roads and reliable transport to move the vaccines from port to clinic; clinics with access to people who need to be immunized; parents who know the value of vaccination; trained medical staff to deliver the dose; and sterile syringes.

Many of the poor countries where vaccine coverage has stalled lack all or part of this infrastructure. In Burkina Faso and Niger for example, 23 per cent of refrigerators used for storing vaccines were found to be non-functioning (GAVI, 2003). Only 16 per cent of vaccine-importing countries could guarantee vaccine safety and quality, (WHO, 2002) while a further study of 19 developing countries found that at least half of injections were unsafe (WHO, 2002).

The third factor behind the lack of progress in recent years is political. Political disruptions have affected coverage in some areas. In Somalia and Congo, for example, where vaccination rates have fallen rapidly in the past decade, war and social breakdown have impeded public health campaigns, despite "vaccination days" in Congo that temporarily halted fighting. Gauri et al. have found that the quality of institutions and governance are positively correlated with vaccination coverage (Guari, et al. 2002). Immunization campaigns do not operate in isolation – they are dependent on the prevailing political and social environment. As that environment is altered, immunization may be interrupted.

Politics in the developed world have also played a part. According to a report by the US Institute of Medicine, in 1982 the US vaccine industry was forced to stop offering low-price vaccines to developing countries following congressional hearings that "savaged" the industry for "allegedly subsidizing vaccines for the poor children of the world by charging high costs to US families and taxpayers" (Institute of Medicine, 1997). As the Institute of Medicine points out, this move was based on a flawed premise, as the US vaccines would have been developed anyway to protect American children and travelers.

The fourth reason for the lost momentum relates to public perceptions of vaccination. As coverage spreads through a community, it reaches a point at which those who are unvaccinated are highly unlikely to catch a disease because herd immunity has set in. At this juncture, it may be more rational for an individual to refuse vaccination in order to avoid any risk of side effects. With oral polio vaccine, for example, there is a 1 in 1 million chance of paralysis, and in societies where mass vaccination has eliminated the disease, the risk of paralysis is greater than that of catching polio itself. What had once been a public and private good is now a public good but a private risk. As more and more people choose to avoid this risk, of course, overall coverage rates decline, and the community is once again exposed to the threat of the disease.

Public perceptions have been influenced by vaccine scares. Controversy and the attendant bad publicity about the safety of vaccines has been abetted by incidents such as the withdrawal of half the US supply of flu vaccines in 2004 due to contamination at the manufacturer, Chiron's UK plant (Los Angeles Times, 2005) and by the swine flu vaccine, which led to deaths of some of those immunized (while the flu itself did not arrive).

In addition, alarms over the safety of vaccines such as that for measles, mumps and rubella (MMR), which some believe to cause autism, have further fanned the anti-vaccine movement's flames. In the United States, disputes continue to rage about the scientific basis of such claims, but the preponderance of the evidence, according to the US Centers for Disease Control, says that the MMR vaccine is safe (Kennedy, 2005). In the UK, physician Andrew Wakefield caused alarm over the MMR vaccine for the same reason. Rates of MMR coverage dropped in Britain and elsewhere in the wake of this scare, before Wakefield's case was to a large extent discredited and the journal that had published his research, *The Lancet*, partially retracted the study.

A survey of public reactions to Wakefield's findings showed that 53 per cent of people believed that, because media coverage gave roughly equal space to support and rejection of the autism theory, the scientific evidence base must be similarly balanced (Hargreaves et al., 2003). Only 25 per cent, moreover, were aware that no link between MMR and autism had been found in the overwhelming majority of studies (Lewis & Speers 2003). A similar scare occurred over the hepatitis B vaccine, which in the mid-1990s was briefly believed to cause multiple sclerosis in some who received it. Subsequent cohort and case-control studies found no link between the two (Halsey 2003).

Vaccine scares do not always lack foundation. The Rotashield vaccine for rotavirus, which was approved in the US in 1998, was withdrawn a year later after reports were received of acute intussusception (a potentially serious bowel condition) occurring shortly after delivery of the vaccine. A study later confirmed this relationship – between 1 in 5,000 and 1 in 10,000 infants developed intussusception within two weeks of vaccination (Mulholland & Bjorvatn, 2003). Such events, as well as causing enormous financial losses to the company that developed the vaccine, can have negative effects on public trust in immunization. They also increase pressure on governments to tighten regulation of vaccines, thereby making their production even more costly.[2]

In response to these types of controversies in the United States, the Institute of Medicine has called for independent oversight of vaccine safety studies to ensure the fairness and openness of the Vaccine Safety Datalink program, which is overseen by the CDC.[3]

Imperiled innovation

As well as vaccine coverage, development of new vaccines has also stalled in recent years. The number of major western pharmaceutical companies making vaccines fell from 26 in 1967 to five today, although some of the slack has been taken up by developing-country manufacturers (Washington Times, 2005). As profit margins for rich-world vaccines have outpaced those for vaccines needed by poor countries, drug developers have concentrated ever more on diseases of the developed world.

The profitability deficit for developing-world vaccines is huge. The developing-world vaccine market is estimated at just 10–15 per cent of the world total and less than 0.2 per cent of the entire global pharmaceutical market (Siwolop, 2001). The total volume of all vaccine doses acquired by UNICEF and the Pan American Health Organization (PAHO) for distribution in the developing world, moreover, is 100 times greater than the number of doses of Prevnar (a vaccine for diseases caused by streptococcus pneumoniae) delivered in the US, but brings in less than half the revenue.

Rich and poor countries have different immunization needs. Parents in rich and poor countries alike are concerned with the safety of vaccine delivery; but governments in poor countries are concerned with its cost, too. Products have therefore begun to diverge, even when they tackle the same illness, and the new vaccines that respond to developed-world demands are often too expensive for poor countries. In the 1990s, for example, developed countries began to use the DTaP instead of DTwP vaccine. DTaP (which incorporates an acellular pertussis vaccine) is more expensive and no more effective than DTwP (which contains a whole-cell pertussis vaccine), but it has fewer side effects and has therefore proved more popular with developed-world consumers. Similarly, the oral polio vaccine has been replaced in countries such as the US by inactivated polio vaccine (IPV), which is delivered by injection. Unlike OPV, the IPV vaccine cannot cause paralysis (Batson et al., 2003).

Pharmaceutical companies have found it difficult to persuade shareholders of the value of continuing to develop vaccines for poor countries. The pharmaceutical giant Glaxo SmithKline, for example, reported in 2001 that it was planning to allocate its freeze-drying capacity to haemophilus influenzae B (Hib) vaccine rather than the less profitable meningitis A/C vaccine. Doses of the DTwP vaccine offered to UNICEF, moreover, declined from 600 million in 1998 to 150 million two years later (GAVI, 2001).

Intellectual property rights present a further challenge to vaccine development. Unlike many other drugs, people generally need only one dose of a vaccine or vaccine booster. Manufacturers therefore need to gain a return on their investment from a single use, rather than over a full course of treatment as in the case of antibiotics or over a patient's entire lifetime as in the case of antiretroviral drugs for AIDS. Companies are thus particularly zealous about protecting vaccine patents – monopoly over production of a vaccine is, they believe, the best way to profit from it. Generic drug producers in poor countries, however, threaten these patents and increase the risk that vaccine developers will not gain a satisfactory return on their investment. Compulsory drug licensing, moreover, which some countries have introduced for antiretroviral treatment for AIDS, may deter future investment in drugs for the developing world. If pharmaceutical companies cannot guarantee a return on their research and development costs through the end of the patent period, the attraction of vaccines for developing countries may weaken further.

There is a lively and important debate regarding the costs of drug development and how they should be assessed. The pharmaceutical industry has long claimed that the enormous costs of development are only sustainable by the prices charged for the subset of drugs that are finally approved. Critics have argued that the development costs are overstated, with Relman and Angell (Relman & Angell, 2002) pointedly stating that "… research and development (R&D) constitutes a relatively small part of the budgets of the large drug companies. Their marketing and advertising expenditures are much greater than their investment in R&D." In addition, they argue that the pharmaceutical companies are not as innovative as generally assumed – and that much of the spending on truly new drugs is taxpayer-supported. DiMasi et al. respond to some of the drug industry's critics, (DiMasi et al., 2004) carefully critiquing their methodology, and offer new estimates of drug development costs (Di Masi et al., 2003). (Relman and Angell also critique DiMasi et al.)

As Relman and Angel note, not all investment in vaccines comes from the private sector. Government research agencies and academic institutions are responsible for much investment in basic scientific research. A widely promoted means of filling the gap between the needs of developing countries and the demands of pharmaceutical firms' shareholders is for public organizations to step in and guarantee a market for vaccines once private companies have developed them. GAVI is currently coordinating this effort internationally but, as the downfall of an earlier initiative shows, encouraging diverse organizations to work together to achieve a common goal is a task riven with complexities.

William Muraskin has detailed the demise of the Children's Vaccine Initiative (CVI), which was launched by the World Health Organization in 1990 in response to the slowdown in development of new vaccines and poor distribution of existing ones (Muraskin, 1998). The CVI's efforts to bring together public and private sector scientists and organizations to work towards solutions were unsuccessful. As Muraskin explains, there was a "great gulf of distrust, often bordering on contempt," between public and private sectors. Public sector scientists saw their private sector counterparts as being purely driven by profit, while the latter saw the public sector as a wasteful and untrustworthy partner. The WHO closed the CVI down in 1999. Such experience reinvigorates the question of government's responsibility for ensuring the timely development and production of vaccines – both for old diseases and new. One alternative is that governments themselves could create greater vaccine development and production capacities. Another option is for governments to offer major financial incentives to pharmaceutical corporations in exchange for guaranteed increases in development efforts and actual construction of vaccine production facilities. Under this latter scenario, a government could promote competition among companies for contracts of this type. The case of avian flu, which could soon burst onto the world scene on a terrifying scale, brings this discussion into sharp focus: governments must assess whether they can rely on the private sector to take the initiative in guaranteeing public health when the steps needed to make such guarantees currently look unprofitable.

Developing and delivering vaccines, then, are by no means straightforward tasks. The progress in eliminating smallpox and drastically reducing cases of polio shows that with will and effort immunization campaigns can be successful, but the momentum for mass immunization has stalled in recent years. In the next section we examine the case for a renewed global effort to extend vaccination coverage, focusing on the economic impacts of vaccine programs.

An uncertain future

The narrow perspective

Assessment of the benefits of vaccines has traditionally focused on a specific range of health-related impacts. Cost-effectiveness and cost-benefit analyses of the numbers of averted illnesses, hospitalizations and deaths; disability-adjusted life years (DALYs) gained; and medical costs avoided are the most common assessment methods. Cost-effectiveness analysis looks at the cost of a health intervention per life saved (or per DALY gained, etc.); cost-benefit analysis takes into account the value of each life saved or the extra years of healthy life gained, and compares the total value of those benefits to the cost of the intervention.

The World Health Organization, for example, has estimated that polio eradication will save governments $1.5 billion per year in vaccine, treatment, and rehabilitation costs. The elimination of smallpox is thought to have saved $275 million per year in direct health care costs (GAVI, 2003); Barrett estimates that the $100 million invested in eradicating the disease in the ten years after 1967 "saved the world about $1.35 billion a year" (Barrett, 2004). And the US Institute of Medicine reports that for every dollar spent on the MMR vaccine, $21 is saved (Institute of Medicine, 1997).

Other cost-effectiveness studies have also found that vaccination campaigns lead to substantial savings in medical costs,[4] but a recent review of 60 studies on the effectiveness, cost, and cost-effectiveness of immunization programs in developing countries concluded that the literature base on cost-effectiveness was flimsy. Only three of the studies addressed cost-effectiveness, and most studies were riddled with weaknesses. Few provided confidence intervals for their findings, follow-up was limited, data sources were not clearly defined, and there was little discussion of confounding variables. Studies on costs, moreover, found wide variations depending on the setting in which a vaccine was being delivered, making estimates of cost-effectiveness difficult to generalize (Pegurri et al., 2005).

The available literature on DALYs suggests immunization is a highly cost-effective intervention. The total cost of the EPI vaccine package is less than $1 (Gauri et al., 2002). According to GAVI, most vaccination campaigns cost less than $50 per year of healthy life gained. By contrast, treatment for diseases such as hypertension in the US costs between $4,340 and $87,940 for each DALY gained (GAVI, 2003). Jamison et al. estimated that the EPI vaccine program costs $14–20 per year of healthy life gained in low-income countries (Jamison et al., 1993). Miller and McCann show a similar cost for the Hib vaccine in Africa, and that Hepatitis B immunization in low-income, high-prevalence countries costs just $8–11 per DALY gained (Miller & McCann, 2000).

Although cost-effectiveness provides a robust demonstration of the extent to which vaccines reduce medical costs, it does not take account of the wider range of benefits that are covered by cost-benefit analysis. The latter also has the advantage of being comparable with investments that take place outside the health sector.

Many cost-benefit analyses of vaccination have shown positive effects. In South Africa, a study of the mass measles immunization campaign of 1996 and 1997 found a benefit-cost ratio of 2.27 in the province of Mpumalanga (Uzicanin et al., 2004). In Japan, the benefit-cost ratio of subsidized influenza vaccinations for the elderly was estimated at 22.9 (Ohkusa, 2005). Purdy et al. found that most of the costs related to pertussis are due to lost productivity at work and that the benefit-cost ratio of the immunization of 10 to 19 year olds is strongly positive (Purdy et al., 2004).

Some studies, on the other hand, have shown higher costs than benefits. In the study of measles immunization in South Africa, the benefit-cost ratio in the Western Cape province was 0.89 (Uzicanin, 2004). And a study to assess the incorporation of the pneumoccocal 7-valent conjugated vaccine into the routine immunization program in Spain found a benefit-cost ratio of only 0.59 (Navas et al., 2005).

A wider view
Neither cost-effectiveness nor cost-benefit analysis has so far taken full account of the broader economic impacts of immunization. These impacts stem from the fact that immunization

protects individuals not only against getting an illness per se, but also against the long-term effects of that illness on their physical, emotional, and cognitive development. For example, by stunting physical growth, childhood diseases can curtail opportunities for carrying out manual labor during adulthood. In developing countries, where manual work is frequently the only option, physical handicaps are particularly damaging. Cognitive development may also be affected by vaccine-preventable disease. Measles, for example, can cause brain damage or impair learning abilities, with severe impacts on a child's life prospects.

The importance of these effects is borne out by recent work demonstrating the link from improved health to economic growth. This research has made clear the importance of health interventions for achieving growth and suggests that cost-effectiveness analyses, as currently conducted, are likely to underestimate the benefits of vaccination.

There are several channels through which health improves wealth. The first is through its impact on education. Healthy children are better able to attend school and to learn effectively while in class. Studies have found that health interventions such as de-worming programs and iron supplementation reduce absenteeism from school (Miguel et al., 2004). Curing whipworm infection, meanwhile, has been found to lead to improved test scores (Nokes et al., 1992).

The second channel is through health's impact on productivity. Like schoolchildren, healthier workers have better attendance rates and are more energetic and mentally robust. Workers in healthy communities, moreover, need to take less time off to care for sick relatives. Body size, which is greatly influenced by one's health during childhood, has been found to have large impacts on long-term productivity (Fogel, 1991). Bloom et al. have calculated that a one-year increase in life expectancy improves labor productivity by 4 per cent (Bloom et al., 1998).

The third means by which health improves wealth is through its effect on savings and investment. Healthier people expect to live longer, so they have a greater incentive to save for retirement. They are also able to work productively for longer, giving them more time to save. Workers and entrepreneurs therefore have a larger capital base to draw on for investment, leading to greater job creation and higher incomes. The savings booms in the East Asian "tiger" economies in the last quarter of the 20th century were largely driven by rising life expectancy and greater savings for retirement.

Finally, health can boost economies via a demographic dividend. The transition from high to low rates of mortality in many developing countries has been rapid. Largely brought about by medical and dietary improvements, the transition has contributed to falls in fertility as parents realize they need fewer children to attain their ideal family size. The boom in young dependents that occurs when mortality falls is therefore followed by a decline in fertility. At this stage, parents can concentrate their resources in nurturing fewer children, thus increasing the latter's prospects of receiving a good education and effective health care. As the boom generation reaches working age, and provided it encounters a policy environment that is favorable to job creation, it can give a large boost to an economy by swelling the ratio of workers to dependents. It has been estimated that the demographic dividend accounted for as much as one third of East Asia's "economic miracle" (Bloom et al., 1998).

A more thorough investigation of the impacts of vaccination, then, should look not just at direct medical cost savings and averted illness, but also at the effects on cognitive development, educational attainment, labor productivity, income, savings, investment, and fertility.

The benefits of vaccination – new evidence
The effect of GAVI
We have carried out calculations for two vaccination campaigns, taking into account the broader economic impacts of immunization. The first study assesses GAVI's program to extend the use of the traditional basic childhood vaccination package; increase coverage of the underused Hib, hepatitis B, and yellow fever vaccines; and help

finance the introduction of anticipated vaccines covering pneumo-coccal disease, rotavirus, and meningococcal A/C conjugate. This program will operate in 75 low-income countries with a combined population of 3.8 billion from 2005–2020, and will cost $13 billion. We examine the likely effect of the program on worker productivity at the individual level. The second study covers efforts in the Philippines to immunize children with DTP, TB, polio, and measles vaccines. It measures vaccines' effects on children's cognitive development, an important determinant of adult earnings.

The countries involved in the GAVI immunization program suffer from high rates of child mortality. In countries that are not covered by the program, there are fewer than 10 child deaths per thousand live births. In the GAVI countries, there are over 65 deaths per thousand. GAVI estimates that its program will reduce child mortality by 4 deaths per thousand live births in 2005, rising to 12 per thousand by 2020 as the campaign expands.

We used a life table to translate averted deaths into increased probability of adult survival (the proportion of 15 year olds who reach age 60), and found that the GAVI program will increase the adult survival rate by 5 per 1,000 initially and by 16 per 1,000 by 2020 (life expectancy will increase by half a year initially and by one and a half years by the end of the program).

To translate the latter into growth of wages and income per capita, we used estimates in the economics literature from Shastry and Weil (2003) and Weil (2005) (Shastry & Weil 2002) that show the link between health and wages in individuals.[5] This analysis shows that for a group of 1000 adults, for each additional person surviving from age 15 to 60, average wages rise by 0.179 per cent. Based on the assumption that labor productivity and wages account for two-thirds of national income (Hall & Jones, 1999), we calculate that each extra surviving adult in a group of 1000 boosts income per capita by 0.119 per cent.

From this figure, we calculate that the average percentage increase in income for the children whose immunization coverage increases through the GAVI program will rise from 0.78 per cent in

2005 to 2.39 per cent by 2020. This equates to an increase in annual earnings per child of $14 by 2020 (see table 1). The total increase in income per year once the vaccinated cohort of children start earning will rise from $410 million in 2005 to $1.34 billion by 2020 (at a cost of $638 million in 2005 and $748 million in 2020).

We estimate the internal rate of return to the program by calculating the interest rate that would make the net present value of the flow of future benefits equal the initial costs. The rate of return amounts to 12.4 per cent in 2005, rising to 18 per cent in 2020 as vaccine costs decline. These are conservative estimates, since they do not take account of averted medical costs, the value of reduced pain and suffering among survivors, welfare benefits associated with averted deaths, or demographic dividend effects.

If these additional benefits of vaccination had been included, it is likely that the rate of return would be higher still, and possibly much higher, but even these conservative estimates compare favorably with the average rates of return to schooling. A review of 98 country studies from 1960 to 1997 showed that the average returns for primary, secondary and higher education were 19 per cent, 13 per cent and 11 per cent respectively (Psacharopoulos & Patrinos, 2002). This finding suggests that the benefits of vaccination have been greatly underestimated and amounts to a strong argument for increased immunization in developing countries.

Immunization and cognitive development – evidence from the Philippines
In the Philippines study, we examined the effect of immunization on productivity by looking at its impact on test scores that measure the cognitive ability of ten year olds. There is robust evidence that childhood illness can impair cognitive development, and that the latter affects adult productivity and earnings. Since our data cover children born in 1983–1984 and thus do not offer information on wages, we take scores in cognitive tests at the age of ten as an indicator of likely productivity in adulthood.

Our study involves a sample of 1975 children from the Cebu

Longitudinal Health and Nutrition Survey (CLHNS). CLHNS is part of a longitudinal survey of Filipino women and their children born in the year following 1 May 1983. The women lived in 33 districts of the metropolitan Cebu area. Bi-monthly interviews carried out over two years allow us to track immunization activities in the first two years of a child's life, while a follow-up study conducted between October 1994 and October 1995 provides us with scores on language, mathematics, and IQ tests.

We compared the test score results of children who had received the basic six vaccines (DTP, polio, measles, and TB) in the first two years of life with those who had had no vaccinations. It is important to recognize, of course, that children who are immunized have other advantages that make them more likely to succeed in cognitive tests. For example, they may receive a better education or hail from families that place a great emphasis on health in general, meaning they would score well whether or not they were immunized. In order to eliminate these effects, we used a propensity score matching method that matches each child in the treatment group with a similar control group. We matched children on the probability that they would be vaccinated given their characteristics – that is, their "propensity scores". Groups of children with a certain propensity score were matched with control groups whose propensity scores are close to their own, with the closest-matched groups given more weight (Canning & Seiguer, 2005).

After controlling for these observed characteristics we found that immunization was associated with significantly improved scores in IQ, language, and mathematics tests. The effect was stronger (significant at the 5 per cent confidence level) for IQ and language scores than for mathematics (where the effect was significant at the 10 per cent level). Childhood vaccination appears to have positive and long-term health impacts that translate into increased cognitive ability in ten year olds, which in turn is associated with higher earnings in adulthood.

In both our studies, then, we found significant positive impacts of vaccination programs. As well as improving health, vaccines have long-term effects on the development of an individual. These individual effects, which are produced at a remarkably low cost, are likely to translate into lasting impacts on economies.

Summary

Clearly there is scope for more research to be conducted on the diverse benefits of vaccination. The Miller and McCann study cited above shows that rates of return differ by country and by income group. It is likely they also differ by the type of vaccine delivered. Further research is needed to calculate the value of vaccination for different countries and at different stages of development. However, immunization does appear to be an important tool for improving survival and strengthening economies. By boosting cognitive abilities, it improves children's prospects of success when reaching working age. And it does so in an extremely cost-beneficial way. Immunization provides a large return on a small investment – higher than most other health interventions, and at least as high as non-health development interventions such as education.

There is a strong case, therefore, for a renewed international commitment to vaccination. The impressive progress towards universal basic vaccine coverage in the 1970s and 1980s has stalled in the past decade, and several damaging childhood illnesses have begun to return as a result. A revived commitment to vaccination requires action on several fronts. First, the public health establishment must communicate clearer and more compelling messages about the value of vaccination. The targets of such communication should include governments in developed and developing countries, as well as donors that fund vaccination in the latter. Second, these messages should move beyond explanation of the effect of immunization on health and on medical costs to address the broader impacts on economies. Vaccination is not purely a health sector issue – it has resonance for wider economic planning and for long-term economic progress. Apprising finance ministries of its importance is vital for cementing its position in development policy.

The third area where renewed action is needed relates to leadership. At an international level, GAVI has begun to increase awareness of the value of vaccination and to push multiple partners toward expanding its breadth and scope. At the national level, politicians' commitment is important in driving immunization campaigns forward. Traditionally, individuals have submitted to state encouragement to vaccinate because they have trusted government to act in their best interests. Recent problems with vaccines, along with efforts (valid or not) of those who continue to argue that vaccines are unsafe, are weakening this trust. Politicians are not elected on vaccination platforms, so there is no pressure on them to champion vaccines once in power. However, the confusion caused by British Prime Minister Tony Blair's refusal to reveal whether his own son had received the MMR vaccine at the height of the MMR scare highlights the dangers of equivocal leadership on such sensitive issues. Blair's lack of clarity, which was the subject of extensive media coverage, may have increased uncertainty over the vaccine (Lewis & Speers 2003) Public complacency, as measles outbreaks that have followed declines in vaccination coverage in the developed world show, can quickly imperil health, and governments and donors that recognize the benefits of immunization must continually hammer the point home.

Traditionally, governments and donors have only considered the health impacts of vaccine-preventable illnesses, and their effect on overall welfare has been underestimated. However, new evidence on the importance of health as a driver of economic development and poverty reduction suggests the need for a re-think. Vaccines in particular, as the evidence presented in this paper shows, are an inexpensive and extremely effective means of improving health and overall welfare. Their impacts, moreover, are much greater than previously thought.

Making the push to complete worldwide vaccination coverage will be a difficult task, and finding ways of ensuring the continued development of effective vaccines in the future potentially more complex still. Vaccines should be seen not as a cost that swells

Table 1 Projected costs and economic benefits of the expanded GAVI immunization program

	2005	2006	2007	2008	2009	2010	2011	2012	2013	2014	2015	2016	2017	2018	2019	2020
Total cost ($million)	638	652	583	659	790	862	761	762	1,023	1,051	1,059	994	896	769	727	748
Deaths averted	732,673	855,998	923,529	993,247	1,052,696	1,125,275	1,229,883	1,349,584	1,608,999	1,741,284	1,913,958	1,955,902	1,973,229	1,990,757	2,002,458	2,014,390
$ cost per death averted	871	761	632	663	750	766	619	565	636	604	553	508	454	386	363	371
Reduction in under 5 mortality rate (per 1000)	4.10	4.89	5.43	6.00	6.45	7.11	7.82	8.60	10.20	11.08	12.24	12.43	12.49	12.54	12.56	12.57
Total increase in adult survival rate (per 1000)	6.61	7.87	8.74	9.64	10.37	11.43	12.56	13.81	16.38	17.80	19.65	19.97	20.06	20.14	20.17	20.19
Increase in life expectancy (years)	0.58	0.69	0.77	0.85	0.91	1.00	1.10	1.21	1.44	1.56	1.73	1.76	1.76	1.77	1.77	1.78
Average percentage increase in income for all children in that cohort	0.78	0.93	1.03	1.14	1.23	1.35	1.48	1.63	1.93	2.10	2.32	2.36	2.37	2.38	2.38	2.39
Increased annual earnings per child in the cohort	4.61	5.49	6.10	6.73	7.24	7.98	8.77	9.64	11.43	12.43	13.72	13.94	14.00	14.06	14.08	14.10
Increase in total cohort income per year, once earning starts ($millions)	410	492	550	610	661	732	809	895	1068	1168	1297	1326	1340	1355	1365	1376
Internal rate of return	12.4%	13.2%	14.4%	14.3%	13.8%	13.8%	15.0%	15.5%	14.9%	15.2%	15.8%	16.2%	16.9%	17.8%	18.2%	18.0%

public health budget requirements, but as an investment with enduring and large-scale impacts. The benefits of a push for increased immunization are likely to heavily outweigh the costs, and policy makers who neglect immunization will be missing a great opportunity for promoting development.

9 The World Health Organisation: a time for reconstitution

Richard E. Wagner

The World Health Organisation (WHO) was established in 1948 as one of several global organisations that were created in the aftermath of World War II. Among those other organisations were the International Monetary Fund, the International Bank for Reconstruction and Development (which became the World Bank), and the General Agreement on Tariffs and Trade (which became the World Trade Organisation). While this essay is concerned with the WHO and its activities as these are revealed in an examination of its budget for 2006–07, much of the underlying argument that informs this examination applies to international organisations generally.

This chapter unfolds in five stages. The first stage asks what would constitute reasonable performance for the WHO, and does so by postulating two concepts of performance that would surely command wide assent: smallpox and Mother Teresa.

The second stage examines the WHO's budget for 2006–07, exploring the extent to which those concepts can be identified within the WHO's line items. While this exploration does not show that the WHO has been an abject failure, it nonetheless gives the agency a low grade. To some, this might constitute a minimal pass while to others it would mean that the agency has failed.

The third stage examines the collectivist presuppositions on which the WHO was founded, and which to this day shape its performance.

According to those presuppositions, free markets are weak arrange-ments for societal organisation, and require domineering government intervention to secure tolerable performance. These collectivist pre-suppositions are now generally recognised to have been false, yet they still inform the WHO's conduct.

The fourth stage examines the WHO's guiding political and bureaucratic incentives, which lead it to support the intervention-ist agenda that prevails in the environmental and public health bureaucracies of the Western social democracies.

The fifth stage explains that since the WHO was initially consti-tuted upon false presuppositions, securing improved performance requires a re-constitution of the agency. Fundamentally, this means that government ought to provide a supporting, and not a leading, role in social and economic activities which generate health of a people as one of their many outcomes.

Images of the WHO: smallpox and Mother Teresa

How are we to appraise the activities of the WHO? The WHO is a large organisation with a presence throughout the world. Its head-quarters are in Geneva, and it also has six regional headquarters: Brazzaville for Africa, New Delhi for Southeast Asia, Manila for the Western Pacific, Cairo for the Eastern Mediterranean, Washington for the Americas, and Copenhagen for Europe.

Its budget for 2006–07 calls for an expenditure of $3.185 billion, distributed across 37 distinct line-items of activity, as shown in Table 1. Judging by its budget, about 31 per cent of the WHO's activities take place at its Geneva headquarters, another 28 per cent are dis-tributed among its six regional headquarters, and the remaining 41 per cent take place within individual countries throughout the world.

Specific observations about some of these budgetary line items will be offered later, but any effort to examine those line items in great detail would quickly become mired in numerous complex issues that could obscure an overall vision of the organisation.

A coherent evaluation of the WHO's activities must start with some overarching vision of the organisation. This vision can be conveyed reasonably well by two simple concepts: smallpox and Mother Teresa (Wagner, 1997). Smallpox, a disease that was eradicated with the WHO's participation, represents communicable diseases which do not respect national boundaries and thus present potential issues of global concern. Mother Teresa represents charity towards impoverished people by those who are relatively well off. These two concepts represent valuable points of reference against which the WHO's activities can be appraised.

Before evaluating WHO's activities, however, it is worth putting into perspective more generally the role of the private sector, government and inter-governmental bodies in addressing health issues.

The first thing to be said about a market-based economy is that it will generate a wide variety of health-related products and services. The situation in this respect is no different for health than it is for food, shelter, amusement, or anything else. There is an underlying logic of economic relationships that governs such things as relative amounts of human activity directed at such services. That logic also informs the relative emphases which people give to inventing and developing new technologies in those varied areas of market activity. Entrepreneurs seek to develop, in a cost-effective manner, services that consumers will want to buy. Some entrepreneurs will develop exercise equipment; others will develop medications to combat diseases; and yet others will publish books about diet, exercise and other health-related matters.

To be sure, a governmental presence operates in the background of all market-generated activity. One of government's prime responsibilities is to maintain the framework of property rights and contracts that is essential for a well-functioning market economy. For instance, as a matter of formal principle, people will invest in medical research so long as they believe the return they anticipate receiving will make the investment worthwhile. The extent of this anticipated return, however, will depend on factors such as the terms on which patents can be secured and the extent to which they are subsequently enforced. Hence, the pace of health-related research within a market economy depends on how successfully government discharges its background presence.

The difference between government in the background and in the foreground is extremely important. The world may be a stage, as Jacques asserts in *As You Like It*, but market participants populate the foreground while political officials remain in the background. That background entails essential work, for the play cannot go forward without the work of the stagehands. But it is background work nonetheless, out of the public's sight.

The foreground is occupied by those market participants (firms, entrepreneurs, customers, consumers) who establish hospitals and pharmaceutical companies, as well as the myriad other enterprises and transactions, which contribute to the generation of health-related enterprises and outcomes within a market economy. In the background, government facilitates commerce between these participants by protecting relationships established through the principles of property and contract.

Two categories of activity, conveyed by smallpox (to represent communicable diseases) and Mother Teresa (to represent charity towards the poor), might provide a justification for government agencies to move out of the background and into the foreground.

In dealing with communicable diseases, the presumption of market efficiency that generally obtains for non-communicable diseases becomes questionable. It is a truism to say that people will buy protection against diseases to the extent that they perceive such protection to be worthwhile. For non-communicable diseases, this creates a situation where people will rely on market-generated options to secure protection, so long as the cost of securing additional protection is less than the benefit they believe that additional protection will provide. In this benefit-cost sense, market-based outcomes with respect to health generate efficient levels of protection against non-communicable diseases.

However, the situation does not necessarily apply to communicable diseases. Someone who acquires a communicable disease imposes a prospective cost on those with whom he comes into contact. Similarly, someone who reduces their own likelihood of acquiring a communicable disease thus also confers benefits on other people. Economists describe this phenomenon as an "externality," and it provides a plausible (though not conclusive) argument in support of some role for government in the foreground of health-related activity. Allthough individuals will purchase protection to the extent that they judge such protection to be worthwhile, their calculation of benefits does not account for the benefits or costs that their own choices confer on other people.

Influenza provides a good illustration of this point. There are several things people can do to protect themselves against influenza, none of which is perfectly effective but each of which offers some measure of protection. People can increase the frequency with which they wash their hands. They can reduce the amount of time they spend in crowded places. They can wear respirators in public. Most visible among these protective measures is inoculation. While inoculation is available for influenza, it may work well against some strains of the disease but not against others.

Each of these measures involves costs and entails some perception about the degree of protection secured. In a market economy, inoculation must be paid for, and thus carries a price. In some instances, inoculation will also involve negative side effects, and may not provide total immunity. When people take these various considerations and perceptions into account, they will purchase some volume of inoculation, which in turn will generate some level of protection against influenza within the society.

This account of individual choice and market outcomes does not account for the effect of one person's choice on other people. A person who increases his level of protection, whether through inoculation or changes in conduct, reduces the chance that he will contract the disease and subsequently transmit it to others. Formally speaking, that person would seek protection against communicable disease to the point where the cost of that added protection is equal to the perceived benefit from that protection. Ideally, however, that

Table 1 WHO's budget by line item, 2006–2007, $000s

Area of Work	Total
Communicable disease prevention & control	152,983
Communicable disease research	108,457
Epidemic alert and response	131,119
Malaria	137,509
Tuberculosis	134,526
HIV/AIDS	260,650
Immunization and vaccine development	381,211
Noncommunicable disease surveillance	56,103
Health promotion	48,146
Mental health & substance abuse	29,764
Tobacco	29,193
Nutrition	24,098
Environment & health	90,412
Food safety	23,717
Violence, injuries, and disabilities	17,505
Reproductive health	65,867
Making pregnancy safer	64,017
Gender, women, and health	17,703
Child and adolescent health	100,500
Essential medicines	61,968
Essential health technologies	31,182
Policy-making for health in development	39,533
Health systems policies & service delivery	116,349
Human resources for health	77,631
Health financing & social protection	42,975
Health information & research policy	57,586
Emergency preparedness & response	105,400
WHO's core presence in countries	197,776
Knowledge management & information technology	138,180
Planning, resource coordination, & oversight	27,590
Human resources management	51,873
Budget and financial management	46,155
Infrastructure and logistics	133,682
Governing bodies	37,388
External relations	35,126
Direction	39,433
Miscellaneous	71,797
Total	**3,185,104**

Country	Regional	Headquarters
63,481	50,976	38,526
3,275	6,397	98,785
52,121	44,423	34,575
55,767	47,167	34,575
68,147	38,719	27,660
163,010	68,004	29,636
193,318	123,682	64,211
25,019	14,982	16,102
17,731	9,670	20,745
13,696	8,659	7,409
12,778	9,204	7,211
8,990	8,193	6,915
38,287	25,947	26,178
8,652	8,348	6,717
6,672	4,610	6,223
12,599	7,036	46,232
33,982	19,169	10,866
5,656	4,144	7,903
42,769	34,022	23,709
25,236	11,048	25,684
11,312	8,016	11,854
19,300	10,552	9,681
58,813	33,432	24,104
42,701	22,384	12,546
19,864	12,245	10,866
27,021	17,723	12,842
77,634	19,863	7,903
176,145	16,692	4,939
21,140	47,890	69,150
4,961	9,787	12,842
479	16,819	34,575
330	23,598	22,227
2,193	55,424	76,065
58	11,646	25,684
2,183	13,383	19,560
488	11,945	27,000
1,178	12,119	58,500
1,316,986	**887,918**	**980,200**

protection should be extended to the point where the cost is equal to the combined benefit to the person choosing the protection *and* to all the others who in turn receive some enhanced protection.

While there is plenty of controversy over the extent to which government should be involved in the provision of health-related services, there is widespread agreement that communicable diseases provide a justification for some form of government participation in preventative measures.

Communicable diseases that originate in poorer regions of the world present more severe problems of global coordination than those that might originate in wealthier regions. Within a wealthier society, people are likely to achieve a level of care against communicable disease that exceeds what people in poorer societies would be able to attain.

In a setting of global mobility, this means that an externality exists. People in poorer societies will tend to take fewer precautions against contracting communicable diseases than people in wealthier areas might desire them to take. If residents of wealthier societies feel that they are threatened by contagious diseases when not enough precautions are taken by poorer societies, a case can be made for richer societies to support control of communicable diseases in the poorer societies.[1]

This justification based on contagion across national boundaries is independent of and distinct from any justification that might arise from poverty. It is clear that the most severe health problems in any society are found among its poorest members. This negative relationship between health and poverty holds throughout the world just as it holds within any single nation.

A society's wealthier members generally possess and display some charitable attitude towards fellow people who experience significant deprivation. Charity is a natural human sentiment, and it is plausible that charitable sentiments would find some expression on a global level.

To be sure, however, it does not follow that charitable sentiments should necessarily entail governmental participation. There is plenty of charitable activity organised through voluntary arrangements of all kinds. Furthermore, it is doubtful to what extent charitable sentiments are truly expressed when the contributions are extracted from taxpayers by force, rather than by voluntary donation.

In general, the collectivist spirit that dominated much of the 20th Century has been replaced by recognition that free and liberal arrangements and institutions are the best way to enable human flourishing. Nevertheless, an organisation like the WHO might still play a role in the foreground of health-related activity, due to the existence of communicable diseases which ignore national boundaries, and possibly to carry out charitable sentiments directed towards the poor.

Communicable disease and charity, smallpox and Mother Teresa, moreover, are not independent of each another with respect to health. The places where communicable diseases are most prevalent are also the poorer places in the world. In any case, smallpox and Mother Teresa provide clear conceptual images to examine the WHO's budgetary activities.

The WHO's budget for 2006–07

Table 1 portrays the WHO's budget for 2006–07 in terms of 37 line items, along with the location of the expenditure as between Geneva, one of the six regional headquarters, or within individual countries. It would be a reasonable experiment to give the WHO's budget, along with the descriptive detail that accompanies the budget to a disinterested observer. The observer would be asked to reach a judgment about the extent to which the concepts represented by smallpox and Mother Teresa are reflected in the agency's budget.

Two conclusions would surely emerge out of such an examination. One is that the WHO's budget does contain some activities that reflect those concepts of combating communicable diseases and offering health assistance to impoverished people. The second, obverse, conclusion is that many of the WHO's activities have nothing at all to do with those activities, and reflect instead an image of an interfering, self-absorbed bureaucracy that is involved in promoting anti-market ideologies and activities.

An initial analysis of the 37 lines of the WHO's budget could lead an impartial observer to distinguish between the first seven items, and the remaining 30. Judging by their titles, the first seven line-items convey clear images of smallpox and Mother Teresa. To be sure, those are not the only concepts that are conveyed; a bureaucratic image is also present in those seven items. For one thing, there is very little work to be done in Geneva that would reflect the images of either smallpox or Mother Teresa.

Comparatively speaking, however, the extent of bureaucracy is less for those first seven items than for the remaining 30. For instance, 25 per cent of the WHO's spending on these seven items is designated for the WHO's headquarters in Geneva. By contrast, 35 per cent of the spending takes place in Geneva for the other 30 items. On a comparative basis, the first seven items reflect a stronger orientation towards controlling communicable disease and providing assistance for the impoverished than do the remaining budget items. At the same time, those first seven activities constitute but 41 per cent of the WHO's budget. The remaining items occupy 59 per cent of the WHO's budget, and these more fully reflect an anti-market health bureaucracy at work. This is elaborated in subsequent sections.

The devolution of expenditure away from Geneva to the country level does not necessarily imply that the WHO's activities more fully reflect the concepts represented by smallpox and Mother Teresa. For instance, the third-largest item in the WHO's budget is "WHO's core presence in countries." This item is exceeded only by budget entries for "HIV/AIDS" and "immunisation and vaccine development." True to its name, moreover, 89 per cent of WHO's spending for its "core presence in countries" occurs at the country level.

At first glance, there might seem to be little bureaucracy evident here. The WHO's account of what this activity actually entails, however, suggests the image of a lobbyist. Its purpose is to cultivate support for the WHO and its agenda of comprehensive health planning. For instance, one of the listed objectives for this line-item is to triple the number of countries "that have an updated WHO Country Cooperation Strategy." The other listed objectives within this line-item are likewise aimed at polishing the WHO's image in individual countries. The image reflected in this activity is one of bureaucratic self-promotion.

Some criticisms can be made about the budget entry for "policy-making for health in development," where three-quarters of expenditure occurs outside of Geneva. For that item, the WHO announces that it "seeks to influence a wide range of national and international policies, laws, agreements, and practices." In seeking to accomplish this, the WHO asserts that it not only pushes the Millennium Development Goals (a UN-sponsored adventure in development planning), but it also occupies the policy foreground with respect to "such issues as the relationship between health and human rights, poverty, aid instruments, macroeconomics, equity, ethics, globalization, trade and law."

If this is not sufficient testimony about bureaucratic self-promotion, the WHO's budget reveals objectives such as achieving a five-fold increase in the "proportion of low-income countries in which WHO has played an acknowledged role in enabling national authorities to develop Poverty Reduction Strategy Papers [and] national poverty reduction plans." Even its line-item for "essential medicines" seeks to promote medical nationalisation, and adopts as one if its objectives an increase in the "number of countries with public-sector procurement based on a national list of essential medicines."

The same bureaucratic imperative is present in the line-item called "health promotion." This item is dominated by the WHO's assertion that "governments must play a stronger role in developing health public policies; health ministries need to take the lead by advocating for the development and adoption of these [WHO-advocated] policies." Those policies have numerous objectives. At various places in the WHO's budget, we see that the WHO is concerned with high blood pressure, cholesterol, weight, diabetes, heart disease, cancer, and smoking. While this may seem extensive, it is not the limit of the WHO's activities: it is also involved with depression, drug abuse, neurological disorders, violence, and traffic safety and numerous other issues.

Another line of inquiry would be to probe the effectiveness of the WHO's activities, by analysing the overall structure or pattern of its budgeted activities to examine the details of its operation. At a structural level, it could be concluded that approximately 40 per cent of the WHO's activities are described reasonably well by the concepts of smallpox and Mother Teresa. The details of how that 40 per cent is allocated and spent, however, might well reveal that those funds are being used relatively ineffectively. If so, a transfer of those funds to organisations that perform those activities more effectively would accomplish both more comprehensive control of communicable disease, and would provide a greater measure of health assistance for impoverished people.

Consider the line-item for "communicable disease research." By definition, this spending fits the concept of smallpox and to some extent the image of Mother Teresa, since problems of communicable disease are most severe in impoverished parts of the world. Yet a close examination might conclude that the $108.5 million spent in this category – 90 per cent of which is spent in Geneva – could do more good if it were redirected to other activities.

The WHO's spending on communicable disease research is a tiny portion of such spending worldwide. The issue here is the marginal contribution of the WHO's effort, especially when compared to other efforts the WHO might have undertaken with the same resources. It is likely that more would be accomplished if the WHO reduced its emphasis on research and redirected those funds to dealing with malaria, tuberculosis or HIV/AIDS.

It is even conceivable that the WHO's marginal contribution to the advancement of knowledge about communicable disease is negative. The agency's own description of this line-item suggests that it prefers a hierarchical approach to scientific inquiry. Its vision of research on communicable disease is that the agency leads the way in articulating what research should be pursued, and individual researchers then follow the WHO's lead.

Yet scientific inquiry follows the same organisational principles as ordinary economic activity, which means that progress occurs more rapidly through open competition than through central direction or regulation. By attempting to centrally direct research, the WHO narrows the lines of inquiry that are pursued. In most cases, this retards progress (Kealey, 1997; Tullock, 1967).

Suppose the WHO were to shift resources away from research on communicable diseases into activities represented by its line-items for malaria, tuberculosis, or HIV/AIDS. There is no guarantee that extra money devoted to those specific diseases will accomplish much. The WHO's activities regarding malaria, for instance, are of dubious value. Since the WHO started its 'Roll Back Malaria' program in 1995, the global toll from malaria has actually increased. To be sure, this post hoc statement does not constitute proof of the WHO's ineffectiveness – but the agency has been reluctant to clearly support the use of DDT as a form of vector control, despite its clear success in controlling malaria in India, South Africa and many other countries (Roberts et al., 2000). Instead, it has almost exclusively promoted alternative measures such as insecticide-treated bed nets. These are several times more costly, as well as generally less effective than DDT. With such an implicit rejection of other methods to prevent malaria, the WHO has followed the expressed desires of environmental and health activists in the first world. Deaths from malaria now exceed one million annually, and some estimates are far higher (Snow et al., 2005).

Similarly, the WHO's attempts to scale up antiretroviral treatment for HIV/AIDS sufferers have been far from successful. Its '3 by 5' initiative – a plan to put three million people on life-extending antiretroviral (ARV) treatment by the end of 2005 – is arguably the single largest effort that any multilateral body has yet undertaken to tackle the disease.

However, by February 2005 only 700,000 people were receiving ARV treatment, well short of the 3 million proposed when the initiative was started in 2003, and a drop in the ocean compared with the minimum of six million people in Africa, Asia and Latin America who need the treatment.[2] Bowing to pressure from Western health activists, the WHO relied heavily on untested triple drug fixed-dose combinations in order to meet its self-imposed targets. In late 2004, it was forced to de-list these drugs, produced mainly by otherwise-reputable Indian drug companies, because of safety concerns.

There is no doubt that the concepts of smallpox and Mother Teresa can be observed in some of the WHO's work – but those images constitute a minority of the full range of its activities. Judging from its budget, the control of communicable disease and the provision of health assistance to the impoverished are secondary activities of the agency.

The primary activities of the WHO would seem to be of two interdependent sorts. One sort is simply bureaucratic self-promotion. However, this requires allies within the environmental and public health bureaucracies of the first-world nations, which are the WHO's largest source of budgetary support.

The majority of activities of the WHO seem to be focused on bureaucratic self-promotion. This appeals to the environmental and health bureaucracies that guarantee much of the agency's funding, and it explains why some of the WHO's primary activities involve promoting and supporting the agendas of those interventionist bureaucracies.

The heritage of a collectivist half-century

With the collapse of communism now receding quickly into the background of our memories, it is becoming increasingly difficult to recall the collectivist nature of the climate of opinion that reigned throughout the West during much of the 20th century. Though Western societies were grounded in individual liberty, with private property and limited government providing the framework for a market economy, many intellectuals, including economists, were socialists even in the 19th century.

The Russian Revolution and formation of the Soviet regime early in the 20th century gave a huge boost to those socialist sympathies. While a few renegade economists like Ludwig von Mises and Friedrich Hayek argued that communist and collectivist planning systems could never generate the human flourishing that liberal, free-market capitalism had generated, the overwhelming climate of opinion sided with the socialists (Hayek, 1935; Roberts, 1971; Boettke, 1993).

To be sure, the Western-style socialist psyche recoiled at some of the regimentation that characterised Soviet-style socialism, and sought instead to establish a more humane form of market-friendly socialism. In this search, there was thought to be a grave trade-off: socialist planning might promote faster economic growth but would restrict liberty beyond what Western traditions would countenance. While traditions can always change, the Western concern was focused on expanding government's role in and control over economic and social life to boost economic progress, but stopped short of Soviet-style socialism.

Even as late as 1989 in the 13th edition of his renowned textbook *Economics*, Paul Samuelson described the splendid economic properties of a collectivist economic system which allowed the Soviet Union to grow at a significantly faster rate than the Western democracies, by asserting "the Soviet economy is proof that . . . a socialist command economy can function and even thrive." (Samuelson & Nordhaus, 1989). The challenge for those in the West who rejected Soviet-style collectivism was to find a middle way that would retain margins of modest liberty alongside a good deal of government participation in economic affairs.

Much of the Western concern about how much collectivism to embrace was based on predictions about the speed at which the Soviet Union's economy might surpass that of Western countries. Most intellectuals and economists were convinced that this would happen unless effective (but gentle) collectivist counter-measures were undertaken. Economist Warren Nutter was a rarity: he studied the Soviet Union carefully and concluded that the majority of Western economists were wrong (Nutter, 1961): the Soviet economy was not a looming powerhouse but was economically puny (although militarily dangerous). While Nutter was pilloried at the time by most other 'experts' (who sided with Paul Samuelson's appraisal of the situation), the evidence that surfaced since the disintegration of communism shows that even Nutter over-estimated the economic performance of the Soviet Union: it was even weaker than he had suggested.

The WHO and the other international organisations were founded at a time in history when belief in collectivism and the distrust of free markets were at their peak in the West. As the Iron Curtain came crashing down, it was recognised that Soviet-style collectivism should be opposed.

However, the presumed success of its economy was used as a justification for a Westernised version of collectivism; ostensibly, Western-style liberalism of the old order was out-dated in our modern age. The Western tradition of private property and individual liberty that underpinned free markets was widely thought to be a weak and fragile institutional arrangement. Unless they embraced some of the features of collectivist control that characterised the communist empire, Western societies would be plagued continually by instabilities, monopolies and externalities.

The WHO and its siblings were created among this widely prevailing climate of opinion: they were promoted as global instruments of collectivist intervention which, when combined with similar intervention in the individual national economies, would create a kinder and gentler alternative to Soviet-style collectivism. This is often characterised as a mixed economy, to indicate some mixture of liberalism and collectivism as the social equivalents of oil and water (Littlechild, 1978; Ikeda, 1997).

It is generally recognised that the ideas which governed Western societies in the post-war period were false. Free markets are not fragile and unstable institutional arrangements: they are robust arrangements that promote creativity and progress. Fragility and instability do appear in human societies, but when this happens the heavy hand of government is also close at hand.

This is true at a macro and micro level. On a large scale, the Great Depression is perhaps the prime instance of economic instability in the 20th century. For a long time this catastrophe was presumed to be the archetype of systemic market failure. Now, it is accepted that it was an outstanding and prolonged example of systemic government failure; the only remaining issues relate to the relative contributions of the various paths that government took in promoting depression.[3] Whatever the path, however, the Depression's origin lays with governments and not with free markets.

On a small scale, claims of market failure are voluminous. The argument is that externalities create market failures, which can only be corrected with some form of government regulation. Such claims often seem sensible on the surface, and equally often are shown to be wrong upon careful examination.

In a similar vein, it appeared reasonable for millennia to conclude that the sun rose in the west and set in the east. It wasn't until Copernicus examined the matter carefully that people came to realise that the surface impression was wrong. One of the archetypical claims of market failure – regarding bees and pollination (a situation that bears some resemblance to communicable disease) – was advanced by Nobel Laureate James Meade (Meade, 1952). Meade illustrated his argument with beekeepers and apple farmers, and claimed that markets would fail to secure efficient production. On the one hand, apple growers will plant too few trees because they do not account for the value that their trees provide to beekeepers. On the other hand, beekeepers will supply an insufficient number of hives because they do not consider the increased apple production that results from the pollination services the bees provide.

At first glance, this story seems sensible. Yet a closer examination of market relationships where honey and apples are produced shows this conclusion to be absolutely wrong: A wide variety of contractual agreements exist among beekeepers and apple growers (Cheung, 1973).

For instance, apple blossoms provide little honey but bees do offer valuable pollination services, so apple growers pay beekeepers to provide their bees for such services. On the other hand, clover does not require pollination but yields much honey, so beekeepers pay to bring their bees into fields of clover. In either case, there is no market failure that leaves us with too few apples and too little honey. This illustration, replicated numerous times in different settings, is testimony to the economically robust character of market-generated commercial arrangements.

With respect to the subject of this essay, it is often claimed the sparse supply of new drugs to treat diseases common to poorer parts of the world is an illustration of market failure. Governmental intervention, including intervention on an international level, is thus advanced as a remedy to redress the situation.

However, a closer analysis reveals myriad ways, through regulation and taxation, that government failure has weakened the commercial viability of efforts to develop such drugs (Morris et al., 2005). For instance, Third-world governments often imposes taxes and tariffs on imported drugs that can boost the price by as much as 50 per cent. When combined with price controls, the incentive for the market-based supply of drugs may range between weak and dead. Furthermore, those countries often have poorly developed institutional arrangements regarding the protection of property rights and the fulfillment of contractual obligations.

The WHO, along with the other international organisations, was founded at a time when the central analytical presupposition was that market failure was ubiquitous and that governments were guardians against such failure. Over the past 40 years, this standard presupposition has been reversed from two directions. One direction has been a growing appreciation of market-based arrangements. The other direction entails recognition that government agencies and bureaucracies often lack the knowledge or incentive to promote well-functioning markets, and tend instead to promote market failure. This suggests that government failure, not market failure, is often the source of observed societal problems and difficulties.

These considerations are relevant to a consideration of the WHO. The WHO was built upon a collectivist foundation which still guides the agency's work and activities. What it needs is not a renovation of its collectivist structure, but a new foundation that reflects the primacy of liberty and the supporting (rather than leading) role of government in the organisation of economic and social affairs.

A comparison of the experiences of South Korea and the Philippines over the past fifty years is a salient illustration of this point. Fifty years ago, each country had similar levels of per capita income, and each seemed to most analysts to face similar future prospects for economic growth and development. Today, per capita income in South Korea is around four times as large as that of the Philippines, due to a considerably faster rate of growth in the former. The Philippines' economy has been much more thoroughly plagued by interventionist government policies than that of South Korea.

Adam Smith claimed in the 18th century that "little else is requisite to carry a state to the highest degree of opulence from the lowest barbarism, but peace, easy taxes, and a tolerable administration of justice; all the rest being brought about by the natural course of things."[4] Smith's claim clashed severely with the collectivist orientation that was dominant throughout much of the 20th century, but in the post-socialist era, its wisdom has been reaffirmed as the most prosperous and robust economies are those where people have the greatest measure of liberty.[5]

A market economy grounded in private property and freedom of contract has two overwhelming advantages that are taken away increasingly as the blanket of collectivism spreads over an economy.[6] One advantage resides in the division and use of knowledge that characterises a market economy. In a famous essay entitled *I, Pencil*, economist Leonard Read noted that no single person could describe how to make a simple pencil, let alone actually make one. The task exceeds our mental capacities, for the ability to buy a pencil is the result of achieving a coordination among the actions of millions of people throughout the world, and extends across a period of many years. We take for granted our ability to buy pencils because no one dictates our ability to buy pencils.

It is no paradox to find that when we are unable to buy a product, we will also find that some person or office is using the power of government, purportedly to assure a steady supply of the product in question. For instance, in the United States in the mid-1970s, the federal government took on the task of assuring Americans that they could obtain petrol for their cars. Sure enough, it became difficult (and often impossible) to buy petrol.

During the same period, there was an even greater proportional reduction in production of coffee than there was of oil – yet everyone was able to buy coffee. The only difference was that there was no person or office in charge of assuring Americans that they could buy coffee. The amount of knowledge that must be brought to bear in organising the supply of petrol, coffee, or pencils is far too complex for any person or office to master. The effort at such mastery overloads the capacity of the mental and organisational circuitry, creating bottlenecks that result in government-generated market failure.

This brings us to the second advantage of market-generated arrangements: the fact that they offer superior incentives to producers and consumers. In a market economy, a producer might initially allocate too much petrol to one region rather than another, or might produce too much kerosene relative to petrol. The producer has a strong incentive to revise the initial decision, for otherwise sales and profits would be lost. A public official, however, has no such incentive, because he or she will not suffer any lost profit by failing to reconsider and revise an initial decision. That official, moreover, may well be insulated from personal inconvenience because governments typically have the first claim on petrol for their vehicles.

Adam Smith was right: there is nothing mysterious about the positive relationship between freedom and prosperity. The place of government in a flourishing society is mostly to occupy background positions. It is human nature, however, to seek the limelight of the foreground, and with this comes the age-old problem of the relationship between people and governments. Societies are more likely to flourish when governments and their officials occupy the background, but government offices are staffed by people who seek to occupy the foreground. Ideally, those governmental offices and officials work to maintain the framework of property and contract within which market participants interact to generate commodious living standards in free societies.

It is not their responsibility to ensure comfortable lifestyles for people in developed countries, for that comfortable living is generated through the creative, entrepreneurial efforts of all who engage in commercial activity. The contribution of government is important but modest, and it is clearly has a supporting but not a leading role in that process. Yet governmental officials are continually tempted to muscle their way into the foreground of economic and social activity. If they are too successful, taxes and regulation rise and prosperity is undermined.

What is true for wealth is also true for health: both are most effectively generated through free and open markets, with governments providing some important background services. But the WHO seeks to occupy the foreground of the stage of health-related human activity. While the WHO's Constitution lists 22 specific functions, the raison d'être of the agency is found in the agency's Preamble.

The Preamble asserts that "Health is a state of complete physical, mental, and social well-being and not merely the absence of disease or infirmity." Nothing, it would seem, is outside the purview of the WHO. This assertion of omnipresence is followed by the assertion that "the enjoyment of the highest attainable standard of health is one of the fundamental rights of every human being. . . ." After several more such assertions, the list ends with the assertion that "governments have a responsibility for the health of their peoples which can be fulfilled only by the provision of adequate health and social measures."

Such assertions could be regarded simply as wishful thinking, much like wishing for a peaceable kingdom where lions would lie down peacefully with lambs. Such a statement of wishes would never be confused with reality, and moreover, would hardly be suitable material for a Preamble to a constitution.

Yet these assertions must be taken as serious objectives and not just as fond wishes about some 'end of history.' The Preamble reveals that the WHO's self-identity is that of an entity which possesses primary responsibility for health conditions throughout the world. Within such an orientation, the WHO has primary responsibility for health, though as the first item in its Preamble states, health is not just as the absence of disease, but is everything that might be thought of as curtailing human happiness.

Consider the WHO's concluding assertion that "governments have a responsibility for the health of their peoples." If we generalise this statement about health to a statement about wealth, it would read that governments have a responsibility for the wealth of their inhabitants. These formulations suggest that people cannot secure wealth and health without government, for such things are beyond personal reach. Unfortunately, the WHO is mired in the same ideas that dominated in the West at the end of World War II, which (while fading) are still a threat to liberty and prosperity.

The bureaucratic gap between vision and reality

The WHO, like the other international organisations that were established after World War II, is a global bureaucracy. The gap between the vision characterised by the concepts of smallpox and Mother Teresa and the reality of the WHO's actual conduct is an understandable result of the institutional arrangements within which it was constituted. By now, a considerable literature has developed to explain the performance properties of public bureaucracies at the national level. A brief consideration of the central themes of that literature can provide a foundation on which to consider the WHO and other international bureaux.[7]

Public sector organisations do not have the same incentives as commercial firms for efficient supply of goods and services. This weaker incentive reveals itself in a variety of ways. It often results in a more costly service, because there is no owner who can capture the gain that greater efficiency will create. If a private enterprise becomes more efficient, its owners gain, but they lose if the firm becomes less efficient. If a public-sector organisation becomes more efficient, the gain accrues to taxpayers as a general class, but they also bear the loss as a class if it becomes less efficient. Numerous studies show that services provided by government bureaux are more costly than similar services provided by commercial enterprises.

There are also substantial differences along many dimensions in the qualitative characteristics of the services offered by government and commercial firms. Commercial firms are highly responsive to the desires of their customers, for it is the customers who supply revenue to the firms. In a government bureau, the people who receive its services do not supply revenue to the bureau, except to the generally small extent that user charges accrue to the bureau (and even here user charges never operate as effectively as market prices) (Wagner, 1991). Government organisations respond not to the individuals who receive the services the government supplies, but to the legislators who provide the organisation's budgetary support. Effectively, these legislators are the "customers" whom the organisation must please.

What this means is that a government bureau will focus on activities that its key legislative sponsors and overseers deem important. In some cases those activities might coincide with customer desires more generally, but this is by no means always the case. A national health bureau, for instance, will be especially responsive to desires expressed by the legislators which can most directly influence its fortunes.

On other matters, bureaux will have wide leeway to do as they choose. For instance, some cost-conscious legislators may believe that a publicly-funded hospital should not exceed private hospitals in the length of patient treatment. To pursue this thought, those legislators may examine average hospital stays for various categories of diagnosis. If this is the case, we may feel reasonably assured that the public hospital will generate the desired pattern of outcomes, or will have a good explanation for any discrepancy.

A closer examination might show that the public hospital achieved this outcome by selectively admitting patients, or perhaps by exercising discretion in its use of diagnostic codes, or perhaps by changing its standards for discharge. However, these kinds of issues are outside the range of oversight; what really influences the behaviour of a public-sector organisation is the interests of its political sponsors.

An international bureau is even less subject to oversight because it receives funding from a large number of donor nations. The WHO, for instance, receives funding from the largest and wealthiest first-world nations. Because the agency's budget is derived from many national governments (not just one), the WHO is less susceptible to political oversight than its national counterparts. Still, the agency must attract participation and contributions, and necessarily will be responsive to the strongly-held desires of its major donors and supporters. If those donors had a strong desire that the WHO acted according to the concepts of smallpox and Mother Teresa, its budget would look quite different.

The current budget reflects the variety of concerns and interests that inform the expansive health agendas of contemporary social democracies in the Western world. Part of that agenda includes an expansion of the meaning of "public health", away from communicable disease to practically anything that fits within the modern rubric of the therapeutic society. Thus, as communicable diseases have receded in significance, the WHO concentrates on activities relating to obesity, smoking, depression, and myriad other things in which now interest the public health bureaucracies of the rich world.

WHO transformed for a liberal world order

Our world has shrunk greatly over the past half-century, and will continue to do so through technological innovation. Electronic communication is instantaneous, and aeroplanes can now carry 800 people half-way around the world at several hundred miles per hour. This shrinkage presents both opportunities and threats.

The opportunity before us is to witness human flourishing on an unprecedented scale. To achieve this opportunity requires a functioning social order on a global scale. Such order must be generated largely in bottom-up fashion, through the promotion of human flourishing through market-generated economic relationships.

As Smith noted in the 18th Century, human flourishing is largely the product of the self-ordering activities of a free people. It requires that governments operate mostly in the background, facilitating people's ability to generate commercial enterprises and civic associations. The primary threat to human flourishing is the hubris of collectivist control, which results when politics escapes its proper location in the background and muscles its way onto centre stage.

The WHO was founded at the apogee of collectivist belief in the West, but the strength of that belief has been steadily weakening for a generation. Meanwhile commerce is continually expanding and borders are continually shrinking, and simultaneously the world order is moving in a liberal direction (even if in jerky fashion). Nevertheless, collectivism still informs the activities of many national governments and international agencies. The UN's Millennium Development Goals project is a dying effort to salvage a collectivist order with government dominating the foreground.

There will be a role for a WHO-type organisation within a liberal world order, as communicable diseases will probably always be present even if the intensely geographical pattern of poverty someday disappears. In the interim, though, the presently constituted WHO presents a danger to that liberal order insofar as it retards the pace of development with ideological efforts to promote development planning at the expense of free markets and entrepreneurship.

One option for the future is the outright abolition of the WHO. Abolition would not eliminate efforts to control communicable disease or to provide health assistance for the very poorest. The rich nations have the means to deal with communicable diseases, and do not need to funnel such efforts through the WHO. Many bodies exist that could co-ordinate actions at a supranational level, probably more effectively and in a less costly manner. A good number of privately organised charitable organisations already provide such services, and they would surely expand should the WHO shrink or die.

One example of how private organisations can successfully tackle global public health crises comes from Rotary International. The defeat of polio in the 20th century was largely the result of their funds and mass vaccination programmes. Twenty years ago, there were a thousand new cases of polio every day. Now polio strikes only about 1,000 children a year, and its complete eradication is imminent. By the time polio is entirely eradicated, Rotarians will have directly contributed at least $600 million – more than any other single organisation apart from the US government.

It is hard to see how the WHO could be reformed internally while maintaining the same character, at least as long as the agency is influenced by the interventionist policies advocated by the primary environmental and health bureaucracies of the Western world. One possibility along these lines would simply be to banish the WHO from the developed world. If the agency lost contact with those environmental and health bureaucracies, its attention would almost surely be devoted to matters of most immediate interest to those who inhabit poorer nations. This banishment would do no harm, even if there is no assurance about how much good it would do.

Whether the WHO is abolished or transformed, its focus should be on controlling the global transmission of communicable disease and not on promoting the expansive and interventionist agendas of the Western public health bureaucracies. As for whatever charitable activities the WHO might practice, other than what might emerge as a by-product of its work with communicable disease, such charity is far better for its intended recipients when it is conducted by private organisations. Mother Teresa, after all, was not an international bureaucrat.

Notes

Introduction

1 The UN Human Development Report of 2005 is one recent example.
2 http://www.who.int/hpr/NPH/docs/declaration_almaata.pdf.
3 This theory is set out more clearly by, for example Sachs *et al.*, 2004.

1 Wealth, health and the cycle of progress

1 In this paper, I will use GDP per capita, per capita income, income, wealth and affluence interchangeably. All data pertaining to GDP will be in terms of constant International (PPP-adjusted) dollars. International dollars are obtained using a special conversion methodology utilizing "purchasing power parity" which is designed to reflect more accurately the purchasing powers of different currencies. Conversion is based on the number of units of a country's currency required to buy the same amounts of goods and services in the domestic market as $1 would buy in the United States. In contrast, the market exchange rate (MXR) of a currency in U.S. dollars is the amount of the currency one can buy with one U.S. dollar on the open currency market.

2 The logarithm of per capita income is used to moderate the impact on the index from additional increases in income.

3 Data on per capita food supplies and GDP per capita are from World Resources Institute (2005) and the World Bank (2005b), respectively. Income is given in constant (2000) PPP-adjusted International dollars.

4 The smoothed curves in this figure were generated by regressing FS against the logarithm of income based on the following "log-linear" relationship: FS = A + B_D + C_log(income). D is a dummy variable to represent observations for different years (D = 0 for 1975, and 1 for 2002), and A, B and C are constant coefficients. A total of 263 observations were used for the two years (i.e., N = 263), the adjusted R^2 = 0.65, and the coefficients of the log(income) term and the dummy variable are significant at the 99.9 per cent level (i.e., $p < 0.001$). In other words, the dependence of FS on GDP per capita is significant, as is the upward shift in this indicator as we go from 1975 to 2002.

5 Technology is defined here broadly to include tangible tools and machines as well as intangibles such as skills and knowledge (see Goklany 1995). It includes hardware, software, as well as management practices, competence and know-how. Over time, all these aspects of technology can be, and generally are, improved, perfected and diffused, that is, time is a surrogate for technological change (so defined). Thus the entire upward displacement is attributable to the passage of time.

6 The smoothed curves for 1990 and 2002, based on data from World Bank (2005b), were generated using log-log regression analysis, that is, by regressing the logarithm of ASW against log(income) and a dummy variable to distinguish 1990 data from 2002 data. N = 241 for both years (combined). Because ASW cannot exceed 100 per cent, and some countries had reached that limit, a Tobit regression was used with truncation at this upper limit. The untruncated log-log regression had an adjusted R^2 = 0.52. The coefficients for the dummy variable and the log(income) terms, that is, the upward displacement of the ASW curve with time and the increase of ASW with income, are significant at the 95 per cent level for both the truncated and untruncated regressions.

7 See Table 1 and Figure 2.

8 See Table 3.

9 This figure, constructed using data from World Bank (2005b), uses the same methodology as is used for Figure 2 for food supplies per capita. See footnote 14. The smoothed curves in this figure are based on log-linear regression analysis. N = 268 for 1977 and 2003 cumulatively; adjusted R^2 = 0.56. The increase in life expectancy due to increase in income and the passage of time are both significant at the 99.9 per cent level.

10 And references therin. See Abstract and pp 13–15.

11 Health adjusted life expectancy is the life expectancy adjusted downward to account for the degradation in the quality of life due to ill health. It is calculated by subtracting a portion of years of ill-health (weighted according to severity) from the expected (unadjusted) life expectancy to give the equivalent years of healthy life.

12 Figure 5 uses data from WRI (2005) for 1950–55 and 1955–60 (plotted as 1952.5, and 1957.5, respectively). For Russia, it plotted the WRI data for 1960–65 and 1965–70 as 1962 and 1967 data. The multiple years reflect five-year averages. The rest of the data are from World Bank (2005b).

13 See, e.g., Pritchett and Summers (1996); World Bank (1993).

14 The curves in Figure 6 were fitted using a log-log relationship. N = 271 and adjusted R^2 = 0.77 with a dummy variable to distinguish data for the different years. The lowering of the curve over time is consistent with the creation and diffusion of new and existing-but-underused technologies. Both the lowering of the infant mortality with time and with the level of GDP per capita are significant at the 99.9 per cent level.

15 Figure 8 is based on data from 1990 and 2002 from World Bank (2005b) using log-log regression with a dummy variable to account for the data from the different years. The cumulative N = 180, and the adjusted R^2 = 0.58. The shift in the curve from 1990 to 2002 and the dependence of post-secondary enrolment on income levels are significant at the 99.9 per cent level and are probably owing to increasing knowledge about the benefits of education and the willingness and ability of families and societies to incur the costs of longer periods of education.

16 As noted previously, the index uses the logarithm of GDP per capita.

17 GDP per capita trends are based on constant, PPP-adjusted International dollars (World Bank 2005b).

18 The decline in their GDP per capita was largely due to a drop in the price of oil during this period.
19 The following data sources were used: for life expectancy, Haines (1994) for 1850–1900, Bureau of the Census (1975) for 1900–1970, Bureau of the Census (various years) for 1971–1979, CDC (2004) for 1980–2002; for literacy, Costa and Steckel (1997), and Bureau of the Census (1975) for 1900–1970; for GDP per capita (in constant 1990 International dollars), Maddison (2005a) for 1820 to 1990, and GGDC&CB (2005) for 1990–2002.
20 Figure 12, based on data from the World Bank (2005b), is constructed using linear regression for the smoothed curves, with a dummy variable to distinguish 1975 data from 2003 data. Cumulative N = 258, and adjusted R^2 = 0.47. The coefficients, which indicate that cereal yield increases with both time and economic development, are both significant at the 99.9 per cent level.
21 This is over and above their level of production and stocks at hand.
22 Bairoch defines manufacturing industry as industry in general except mining, construction, electricity, gas, and water.
23 This is calculated from GDPs provided by Maddison (2005a) for 1700 and 2001, and assumes a uniform (exponential) annual growth rate from 1700–1820 to calculate the GDP per capita for 1800.

2 South Africa's healthcare under threat

1 Republic of South Africa, South African Statistics 2004/05 (Pretoria: Statistics South Africa, 2005), p. 8.8, Table 8.3. Figures for private hospitals are dated June 2004 and those for semi-private and public hospitals August 2003. Mine hospitals are not included in the figures. According to Statistics South Africa there are 29 semi-private hospitals with 5 889 beds. For the purpose of this paper semi-private hospitals and beds have been included as public hospitals since they are "private" only in the sense that they are operated by private companies and charities under contract to government, with the bulk of funding from government. According to the Hospital Association of South Africa (HASA), which represents the majority of private hospitals in the country, there are 200 private hospitals with 26 000 private beds.
2 *Traditional medicine helps with Aids*, Mail and Guardian, 30 March 2004.
3 Deadly Denial, Time – Europe Edition: 19 April 2004, Volume 163, No 16. Also see: John Kane-Berman, *Beyond a Joke* (Johannesburg: South African Institute of Race Relations, Fast Facts No3 / March 2004.)
4 John Kane-Berman, *Beyond a Joke* (Johannesburg: South African Institute of Race Relations, Fast Facts No3/March 2004.)
5 Information on the contracts was posted on the company websites at the time of writing.
6 Anthony Browne, *NHS Cases pay for Quick Ops in South Africa* (London: The Observer, March 17, 2002.).
7 Thomas Sowell, *Tax cuts do what?* (New York: Opinion Journal – From the Wall Street Journal Editorial Page, 29 February 2004).

8 The author underwent MRI scans in 2000 and in 2005 and in both instances the procedures were done within hours after referral to the MRI facility by the doctor.

9 Waiting your turn: Hospital Waiting Lists in Canada (Vancouver, B.C: Fraser Institute: 2004), p.4.

10 James Bartholomew, *Six months wait for an MRI scan*. (April 19, 2005) Retrieved: August 22, 2005 from http://www.thewelfarestatewerein.com/archives/2005/04/six_months_wait.php. Also see: Nigel Hawkes, *Go private or wait 80 weeks, patient told* (London: The Times Online, 18 June 2005). Retrieved: August 22, 2005 from http://www.timesonline.co.uk/article/0,,2-1659149,00.html.

11 *Manto concerned about high cost of health care* (Johannesburg: Mail and Guardian, July 11, 2005.).

12 Treatment Action Campaign, *Minister Must Commit to Purchasing Interim Supply of Antiretroviral Medicines to Avoid Court Case*. Treatment Action Campaign Newsletter, 16 March 2004.

13 Republic of South Africa, *South African Yearbook 2003/04* (Pretoria: Government Communications: 2003), p. 374.

14 On the view that the introduction of new health-care technology is an obstacle to providing universal care and should be limited to make health care available to all see: National Department of Health, *Inquiry into the various Social Security Aspects of the South African Health System* (Pretoria: National Department of Health, May 2002.), p. 42.

3 Corruption in public health

1 When all three governance measures are jointly regressed on infant mortality and per cent measles immunization, only government commitment and is significant and consistently shows the expected sign.

2 Low demand for immunization occurs in developed countries as well, which accounts for the legal requirement in the US that children must be immunized before they enter day care or school. In the rest of the OECD governments take responsibility for ensuring immunization coverage.

3 It is counter-intuitive that only 15% of the Indian public and 9% of the Kazak public perceive corruption in the health sector when they ranked it so highly on perceptions of corruption in the sector. This bears further investigation.

4 They found that 26% of positions and 41% of physicians slots were vacant, suggesting that the total available stock was already below what was demographically required and budgeted.

5 The Bolivia survey collected data from 2888 women in 106 municipalities; the Moldova survey consisted of 390 interviews with physicians, nurses and patients in the capital, Chisinau, and two provinces; the Albanian household survey surveyed 3 provinces; the Poland survey was only of Gdansk and Wroclaw cities; and, the Kazakh hospital survey interviewed 1508 discharged patients from three Almaty City hospitals.

4 The diseases of poverty and the 10/90 gap

1 Available at http://www.who.int/intellectualproperty/documents/ thereport/en/index.html
2 Accessed at: http://www.aeras.org/
3 Accessed at: http://idri.org/page.php?pg_page_id=1
4 Drugs in development by the following PPPs: Bio Ventures for Global Health, Pharmaprojects, MMV, GATB, DNDi.
5 *Ibid.*
6 http://www.who.int/mediacentre/factsheets/fs117/en/
7 http://www.who.int/vaccines/en/pertussis.shtml
8 http://www.who.int/mediacentre/factsheets/fs101/en/
9 Victora CG., et al., *Applying an equity lens to child health and mortality: more of the same is not enough*, Lancet, 2003; 362: 233–41
10 The study assessed the size and impact of tariffs and taxes on drugs imported from the EU; taxes and tariffs on drugs imported from elsewhere may be subject to different rates of taxes and tariffs.
11 Poor countries are not members of the WTO Pharmaceutical Agreement, a 22 member agreement, concluded during the Uruguay Round, which has led to the reciprocal elimination of tariffs (dubbed 'zero-for-zero') on approximately 7,000 products (European Commission, 2003 and 2002).
12 The East African Community (EAC) is the regional intergovernmental organisation of the Republics of Kenya, Uganda and the United Republic of Tanzania with its headquarters in Arusha, Tanzania. The EAC website is: http://www.eac.int/
13 Information regarding the EAC Customs Union Tariffs scheme can be accessed at: http://www.eac.int/EAC_customs_U.htm
14 http://allafrica.com/stories/200502230903.html
15 European Commission, 2003. Applied customs rates were found for each of 27 HS numbers. To obtain and average customs rate per country, these numbers were arithmetically added without weighting them. The same process was used to calculate the average rates of VAT and other duties.

5 Increasing access to medicines

1 Alternate Solutions Institute, Pakistan.
2 Imani, Ghana.
3 Free Market Foundation, South Africa.
4 Global Biosciences Development Institute, USA.
5 ESEADE University, Argentina.
6 Instituto Libertad y Progreso, Colombia.
7 Liberty Institute, India.
8 Minimal Government, Manila, Philippines.
9 Fundación Atlas 1853, Argentina.
10 International Policy Network, UK.
11 Instituto Libre Empresa, Peru.
12 Instituto Liberdade, Brazil.

13 Africa Fighting Malaria, South Africa.

14 Jabu Mhlabane. Nearly 50 Mpumalanga doctors implicated in medicine theft (Middelburg, South Africa: *African Eye News Service, 13 February 2003). (Published on the website of LowveldInfo.com).*

15 The study assessed the size and impact of tariffs and taxes on drugs imported from the EU; taxes and tariffs on drugs imported from elsewhere may be subject to different rates of taxes and tariffs.

16 Poor countries are not members of the WTO Pharmaceutical Agreement, a 22 member agreement, concluded during the Uruguay Round, which has led to the reciprocal elimination of tariffs (dubbed 'zero-for-zero') on approximately 7,000 products (European Commission, 2003 and 2002).

17 The East African Community (EAC) is the regional intergovernmental organisation of the Republics of Kenya, Uganda and the United Republic of Tanzania with its headquarters in Arusha, Tanzania. The EAC website is: http://www.eac.int/

18 Information regarding the EAC Customs Union Tariffs scheme can be accessed at: http://www.eac.int/EAC_customs_U.htm

19 http://allafrica.com/stories/200502230903.html

20 European Commission, 2003. Applied customs rates were found for each of 27 HS numbers. To obtain and average customs rate per country, these numbers were arithmetically added without weighting them. The same process was used to calculate the average rates of VAT and other duties.

21 While there are some countries where the costs of introducing a patent system may temporarily outweigh the benefits, this applies only to those countries without a substantial knowledge-based industry. For those countries with incipient or extant knowledge-based industries, such as India, China, Brazil and South Africa, the benefits of introducing a patent system will quickly outweigh the costs.

22 McArthur (1999) shows that in industries with relatively stringent protection for intellectual property, capital spending is higher, the demand for high quality goods for export and the ratio of skilled to unskilled workers both increase over time.   Those same incentives that exist for investment in industries that do enjoy relatively high levels of intellectual property protection tend not to exist when that protection does not exist or is abandoned.   McArthur, W. M.D., *Intellectual Property Rights and the Pharmaceutical Industry*, The Fraser Institute, 1999, pp. 85–104.

23 SCRIP data.

24 http://www.businessweek.com/magazine/content/05_16/b3929068.htm

25 http://www.advocate.com/news_detail_ektid19293.asp

26 http://www.sedb.com/edbcorp/sg/en_uk/index/
    in_the_news/press_releases/2004/singapore_s_biomedical.html

27 http://drugresearcher.com/news/printNewsBis.asp?id=57722

28 http://www.rbm.who.int/cmc_upload/0/000/015/364/RBMInfosheet_9.htm

29 Or alternatively: novelty, inventive step and industrial application.

30 In the context of the debates over patents on genetic sequences and research tools, if some countries allow patents and others don't, then – other things being equal – over time it will become clear which countries are more conducive

to high-levels of research and development into down-stream innovations. Of course not all other things are equal, but to the extent that this competition is already taking place, the winner seems to be the country with the broader patent system: the United States. Time will tell.

31 Common practice for the Food and Drug Administration in the United States is 5 years, which is also the period agreed upon in many of the bilateral free trade agreements it has recently signed.

32 Potential cost savings for companies relying on data would be in the order of $450 million, the average costs associated with clinical trials for each approved drug. Some estimates show that these costs have more than tripled in the past fifteen years.

33 When data exclusivity is weak, it can also drive research-based pharmaceutical research industries out, as has happened in the past few years in Israel. A once thriving research destination, the lack of data exclusivity – the result of a powerful generics lobby – had driven research elsewhere. In September 2005, the legislation was changed to provide some data protection.

34 In legal terms, the specific element that is crucial to the firm's ability to price differentiate within a market is the international patent exhaustion principle. If patent rights are exhaustible the patentee must renounce the right to its product the moment it is first sold, giving the first purchaser the ability to potentially resell at a higher price. The TRIPS agreement does little to clear up this pressing issue. (http://www.wto.org/english/tratop_e/trips_e/factsheet_pharm02_e.htm)

35 A good example of successful price discrimination without re-exportation comes from the example of bronchodilators in South Africa. Here, Government purchases accounted for 66 per cent of sales volume, but only 33 per cent of revenues. In this case patents show that, if parallel importation is controlled for, good health can be promoted. Reekie, W.D., "South Africa's Battle with AIDS and Drug Prices", National Center for Policy Analysis, Dallas, TX, Brief 334, 2000.

36 http://www.freemarketfoundation.com/ShowArticle.asp?ArticleType=Publication&ArticleID=1093

37 The most recent example comes from Brazil, where the head of the country's AIDS program cited an increasingly high percentage of its AIDS budget, which is designed to offer Brazilians with the disease (some 600,000) free treatment, had to be devoted to pharmaceutical purchases. Because of this, Brazil threatened to issue compulsory licenses on the key drugs that combine to form anti-retro viral treatments. http://news.bbc.co.uk/1/hi/health/4059147.stm, accessed 06/01/2005

38 'Neglected diseases' are defined by the WHO as African Trypanosomiasis, leishmaniasis and Chagas disease.

6 Cost effective means of fighting the diseases of poverty

1 Alternate Solutions Institute, Pakistan.

2 Imani, Ghana.

3 Free Market Foundation, South Africa.

4 Global Biosciences Development Institute, USA.

5   ESEADE University, Argentina.
6   Instituto Libertad y Progreso, Colombia.
7   Liberty Institute, India.
8   Minimal Government, Manila, Philippines.
9   Fundación Atlas 1853, Argentina.
10 International Policy Network, UK.
11 Instituto Libre Empresa, Peru.
12 Instituto Liberdade, Brazil.
13 Africa Fighting Malaria, South Africa.
14 http://www.who.int/hiv/AAI_fs_4Q2005.pdf
15 United States Leadership Against HIV/AIDS, Tuberculosis, and Malaria Act of 2003.
16 http://online.wsj.com/article/0,,SB111644800426237250,00.html
17 WHO/CDS/WHOPES/GCDPP/2004.6, A generic risk assessment model for insecticide treatment and subsequent use of mosquito nets.
18 http://www.cdc.gov/malaria/control_prevention/vector_control.htm
19 http://www.rotavirusvaccine.org/vaccine-facts.htm

7 Counterfeit medicines in LDCs: problems and solutions

1   http://www.who.int/mediacentre/factsheets/fs275/en/
2   Liza Gibson, "Drug regulators study global treaty to tackle counterfeit drugs," British Medical Journal Volume 328, Number 486 February 28, 2004.
3   European Federation of Pharmaceutical Industries and Associations, "Counterfeit medicines", available at http://www.efpia.org/2_indust/counterfeitdrugs.pdf
4   http://www.manilatimes.net/national/2005/aug/16/yehey/life/20050816lif1.html
5   http://bmj.bmjjournals.com/cgi/content/full/327/7424/1126-a
6   Fackler M (2002 July 29) China's fake drugs kill thousands. San Francisco Examiner
7   http://www.who.int/entity/bulletin/volumes/81/12/WHONews.pdf
8   http://bmj.bmjjournals.com/cgi/content/full/327/7412/414-b
9   http://pharmalicensing.com/articles/disp/1120475327_42c918bf09048
10 Selling cheap generic drugs, India's copycats irk industry, available at http://chakra.org/articles/2000/12/03/indian/drugs
11 Latin America Battles Counterfeit Drug Threat, Daily International Pharmacy Alert: Washington Business Information, 2(292), 2006.
12 http://www.efpia.org/2_indust/counterfeitdrugs.pdf
13 Fake drugs worry authorities, firms, *The Russia Journal*, 2000, 3(4) 47
14 *South China Business Journal*, June/July/August, 2002.
15 http://www.prospect.org/web/page.ww?section=root&name=ViewWeb&articleId=10650
16 http://www.freemarketfoundation.com/ShowArticle.asp?ArticleType=Publication&ArticleID=1093
17 Very often, the supply of drugs is reduced by the Byzantine and tortuous regulations that emanate from local drug approval agencies. These regulations make it very difficult for manufacturers wishing to export to overseas markets

to register new products, thereby creating a gap in supply. This gap provides another opportunity for counterfeiters. One example is South Africa's Medical Control Council, which requires that all new medicines attain its own regulatory approval before they can be marketed in the country – even if they have already been approved by reputable foreign regulatory bodies such as the FDA. However, the extreme inefficiency of the FDA means that drugs that have already been registered for use in the US, EU and Japan wait an average of 39 months for approval in the South African system. If such delays occur on already existing medicines, it presents a clear incentive to counterfeiters to meet the artificially pent up demand in the market.

18 These artificial price inflators can price may patients out of treatment, and give them an incentive to look to cheaper counterfeit medicines to meet their needs. Abolishing these levies would return medicines to their natural prices, thereby undermining the potential profits – and incentives – of counterfeiters.

8 The value of vaccination

1 The authors thank Roger Glass, Tore Godal, Yuki Murakami, Sreekanth Ramachandra, Larry Rosenberg, and Josh Salomon for their assistance and comments. Financial assistance from the Global Alliance for Vaccination and Immunization is greatly appreciated. Earlier versions of this article were presented at the Sixth International Rotavirus Symposium in Mexico City (June 2004), a GAVI-funded seminar on "Development and Deployment of Vaccines Against Poverty-Related Diseases" in Bergen, Norway (September 2004), and the 23rd annual meeting of the European Society for Paediatric Infectious Diseases in Valencia, Spain (May 2005).

2 A notable sidelight to this story is that GlaxoSmithKline has now developed Rotarix, a new rotavirus vaccine (which does not appear to have intussusception as a side effect), which has already been introduced in Mexico and will soon be introduced in other developing countries. See *Technology Review*, June 2005, available at http://www.technologyreview.com/articles/05/06/tri/tri_vaccine.asp?p=1.

3 http://www4.nas.edu/news.nsf/6a3520dc2dbfc2ad85256ca8005c1381/e82b28891131e63e85256fab006fb1f3?OpenDocument

4 See, for example, Coudeville L (1999): The value of varicella vaccination in healthy children: cost-benefit analysis of the situation in France. *Vaccine* 1999 Jan 17:2 142–51; Ekwueme DU (2000) Economic evaluation of use of diphtheria, tetanus, and acellular pertussis vaccine or diphtheria, tetanus, and whole-cell pertussis vaccine in the United States, 1997. *Arch Pediatr Adolesc Med* 2000 Aug 154:8 797–803; Pelletier L (1998): A benefit-cost analysis of two-dose measles immunization in Canada. *Vaccine* 1998 May-Jun 16:9–10 989–96; Tormans HIV/AIDS (1998): Economic evaluation of pertussis prevention by whole-cell and acellular vaccine in Germany. *Eur J Pediatr* 1998 May 157:5 395–401; Hussain, I.HM.I , Syed Aljunid, Sofiah, A., Ong, L.C, Choo, K.E, Musa, M.N., Teh, K.H.& Ng, H.P. (1999): Cost-Benefit Analysis Of Haemophilus Influenzae Vaccination Programme In Malaysia. *Buletin Kesihatan Masyarakat Jilid 5, 1999*; Ulla K

Griffiths, Lara J Wolfson, Arshad Quddus, Mohammed Younus, Rehan A Hafiz (2004): Incremental cost-effectiveness of supplementary immunization activities to prevent neonatal tetanus in Pakistan. Bulletin of the World Health Organization, September 2004, 82 (9); Uyl-de Groot CA, Vermorken JB, Hanna MG Jr, Verboom P, Groot MT, Bonsel GJ, Meijer CJ, Pinedo HM. (2005). Immunotherapy with autologous tumor cell-BCG vaccine in patients with colon cancer: a prospective study of medical and economic benefits. Vaccine. Vol.23(17–18):2379–87; Navas E, Salleras L, Gisbert R, Dominguez A, Timoner E, Ibanez D, Prat A. (2005). Cost-benefit and cost-effectiveness of the incorporation of the pneumococcal 7-valent conjugated vaccine in the routine vaccination schedule of Catalonia (Spain). Vaccine. Vol. 23(17–18):2342–8; McIntosh ED, Conway P, Willingham J, Hollingsworth R, Lloyd A. (2005). Pneumococcal pneumonia in the UK – how herd immunity affects the cost-effectiveness of 7-valent pneumococcal conjugate vaccine (PCV). Vaccine. Vol. 23(14):1739–45; Jean-Jasmin LM, Lynette SP, Stefan M, Kai CS, Chew FT, Wah LB. (2004). Economic burden of varicella in Singapore – a cost benefit estimate of implementation of a routine varicella vaccination. Southeast Asian J Trop Med Public Health. Vol. 35(3):693–6; Uzicanin A, Zhou F, Eggers R, Webb E, Strebel P. (2004). Economic analysis of the 1996–1997 mass measles immunization campaigns in South Africa. Vaccine. Vol. 22(25–26):3419–26; Shepard DS, Suaya JA, Halstead SB, Nathan MB, Gubler DJ, Mahoney RT, Wang DN, Meltzer MI. (2004). Cost-effectiveness of a pediatric dengue vaccine. Vaccine. Vol. 22(9–10):1275–80. Two studies in developed countries, on the other hand, showed that programs were not cost-effective: Allsup S, Haycox A, Regan M, Gosney M. (2004). Is influenza vaccination cost effective for healthy people between ages 65 and 74 years? A randomised controlled trial. Vaccine. Vol. 23(5):639–45; Melegaro A, Edmunds WJ. (2004). The 23-valent pneumococcal polysaccharide vaccine. Part II. A cost-effectiveness analysis for invasive disease in the elderly in England and Wales. Eur J Epidemiol. Vol. 19(4):365–75.

5 This approach assumes that health is a uni-dimensional variable that is reflected in mortality and morbidity measures. Both microeconomic and macroeconomic studies of the effect of health on labor productivity use this approach, which enables a single measure to be used as an indicator of an individual's or a community's health. In our study, the health improvements generated by vaccination are therefore taken to have economic impacts similar to those of health improvements on average.

9 The World Health Organisation: a time for reconstitution

1 This statement reflects the practicalities of the situation. As a purely conceptual matter, the liability for that added protection could be placed on either the residents of the poorer lands or the residents of the wealthier lands. The reciprocal nature of externality relationships is developed in Ronald H. Coase, "The Problem of Social Cost," *Journal of Law and Economics* 3 (October 1960), 1–44.

2 Snow, B et al., "The global distribution of clinical episodes of Plasmodium falciparum malaria", *Nature* 434, 214–217 (10 March 2005)
3 For an emphasis on monetary contraction, see Milton Friedman and Anna J. Schwartz, *A Monetary History of the United States* (Princeton: Princeton University Press, 1963), esp. pp. 299–419. For an emphasis on credit expansion, see Murray Rothbard, *America's Great Depression* (Kansas City: Sheed Andrews, 1963). For an emphasis on regulation, see Robert J. Barro, "Second Thoughts on Keynesian Economics, " *American Economic Review*, Proceedings, 69 (May 1979): 54–59.
4 Lecture in 1755, quoted by Dugald Stewart
5 On the positive relationship between freedom and wealth worldwide, see James Gwartney and Robert Lawson, *Economic Freedom of the World* (Vancouver: Fraser Institute, 2004).
6 For a sample of valuable work on this matter, see William Easterly, *The Illusive Quest for Growth* (New York: St. Martin's Press, 2001); Peter Bauer, *From Subsistence to Exchange* (Princeton: Princeton University Press, 2000); Peter J. Boettke, ed., *The Collapse of Development Planning* (New York: New York University Press, 1994); Deepak Lal, *The Poverty of Development Economics* (Cambridge: Harvard University Press, 1983); and Peter T. Bauer and Basil S. Yamey, *The Economics of Underdeveloped Countries* (Cambridge: Cambridge University Press, 1957).
7 For exemplary treatises on bureaucracy, see Gordon Tullock, *The Politics of Bureaucracy* (Washington: Public Affairs Press, 1965); William A. Niskanen, Bureaucracy and Representative Government (Chicago: Aldine, 1971); Anthony Downs, *Inside Bureaucracy* (Boston: Little, Borwn, 1967); and Thomas E. Borcherding, ed. Budgets and Bureaucrats (Durham, NC: Duke University Press, 1977).

Sources

Introduction

Adelman, C., Norris, J., & Weicher, S., (2005), "The full cost of HIV/AIDS treatment", Hudson Institute White Paper, 2nd Edition, May 2005, Hudson Institute: Washington DC

Bloom, D., & Williamson, J., (1997), "Demographic change and human resource development", In Asian Development Bank, *Emerging Asia,* Manila

Bremen, J., (2001), "The ears of hippopotamus: manifestations, determinants, and estimates of the malaria burden," *American Journal of Tropical Hygiene,* 64 (1&2).

Center for Global Development (2005): "Making Markets for Vaccines: From Ideas to Action", CGD, Washington DC.

Dollar, D., (1995), "Outward-oriented developing countries really do grow more rapidly: evidence from 95 LDCs, 1976–85", *Economic Development and Cultural Change* 523–44.

Deaton, A., (2003), "Health, inequality and economic development", *Journal of Economic Literature,* 41: 113–58.

Dollar, D., & Kraay, A., (2001), *Trade, growth, and poverty,* Policy Research Working Paper No 2199, Washington DC: World Bank

Filmer, D., & Pritchett, L., (1999), "The impact of public spending on health: does money matter?" World Bank.

Frankel, J., & Romer, D., (1999), "Does trade cause growth?" *American Economic Review* June:379–99

Gramiccia, G., & Beales, P., (1988), "The recent history of malaria control and eradication," in Wersdorfer, W., & McGregor, I., eds. *Malaria: principles and practice of malariology.* New York: Churchill Livingstone

Gwatkin, F., (1980), "Indications of change in developing country mortality trends: the end of an era?" *Population and development review,* 6(4), 615–44

Kenny, C., (2005), "Why are we worried about income? Nearly everything that matters is converging", *World Development,* 33(1): 1–19.

Malaria Consortium, (2002), "Roll Back Malaria to Date," available at http://www.rbm.who.int/cmc_upload/0/000/015/905/ch2.pdf

Marmot, M., Shipley, M., & Rose, G., (1984), Inequalities in death – specific explanations of a general pattern? *Lancet;* i: 1003–6

Marmot M., Davey Smith, G., Stansfeld, S., Patel, C., North, F., Head, J., White. I., Brunner, E., Feeney, A., (1991), "Health inequalities among British civil servants; the Whitehall II study", *Lancet,* 337: 1387–1393.

Karoly, L., Greenwood, P., Everingham, S., Hoube, J., Kilburn, M., Rydell, C., Sanders, M., Chiesa, J., eds, (1998), *Investing in our children: what we know and don't know about the cost and benefits of early childhood interventions*, Santa Monica, California, RAND.

Noumba, I., (2004), "Are wealthier nations healthier nations? A panel data approach to the determination of human development in Africa", African Development & Poverty Reduction: The Macro-Micro linkage, Forum Paper, Cornell University

Pritchett, L., & Summer, L., (1996), "Wealthier is Healthier", *Journal of Human Resources*, 31(4): 841–868

Ridley, R., (2002), "Medical need, scientific opportunity and the drive for antimalarial drugs," *Nature*, 415(7).

Sachs, J. & Warner A., (1995), "Economic reform and the process of global integration", *Brookings Papers on Economic Activity* (1):1–118

Wagstaff, A., (2002), "Inequalities in health in developing countries: swimming against the tide?" World Bank Policy Research Working Paper 2795.

WHO, (2002), *World Health Report*, Geneva: WHO.

Wilkinson, R., (1999), "Putting the picture together: prosperity, redistribution, health and welfare", in *Social Determinants of Health*, eds Marmot, M., & Wilkinson, R., OUP, Oxford.

Williamson, J., (1990), *Coping with city growth during the industrial revolution*, Cambridge, UK: Cambridge University Press

World Bank, 2005. *World Development Indicator*s available at http://devdata.worldbank.org/dataonline/

Zumla, A. & Grange, M., (2001), "Multidrug resistant tuberculosis- can the tide be turned?" *Lancet Infectious Diseases*, vol. 1.

1 Wealth, health and the cycle of progress

Ausubel, J. H., and A. Grübler. 1995. Working Less and Living Longer. *Technological Forecasting and Social Change 50: 113–31.*

Barney, Gerald O., ed. 1980. Global 2000 Report to the President. New York: Pergamon Press.

Barro, R. J. 1997. *The Determinants of Economic Growth: A Cross-Country Empirical Stud*y. Cambridge, MA: MIT Press.

Bairoch, Paul. 1982. "International Industrialization Levels from 1750 to 1980." *Journal of European Economic History* 11: 269–333.

Barbour, I. G. 1980. *Technology, Environment, and Human Value*s. New York: Praeger.

Becker, Charles, and David Bloom. 1998. "The Demographic Crisis in the Former Soviet Union: Introduction." *World Development* 26: 1913–19.

Bhalla, S. 2002. *Imagine There Is No Country: Poverty, Inequality and Growth in the Era of Globalization*. Washibgton, DC: Institute for International Economics.

Bloom, Barry R. 1999. "The Future of Public Health." *Nature* 402 (supplement): C63–64.

Brown, Lester R. 1998. "The Future of Growth" in *The State of the World 1998*, ed. Lester R. Brown, Christopher Flavin, and Hilary F. French. New York: W. W. Norton, 3–20.

Bureau of the Census. 1975. *Historical Statistics of the United States, Colonial Times to 1970*. Washington, DC: Government Printing Office.

———. Various years. *Statistical Abstract of the United States*. Washington, DC: Government Printing Office.

———. 2004. *Statistical Abstract of the United States, 2004–2005*. Washington, DC: Government Printing Office.

Burnette, J., and J. Mokyr. 1995. "The Standard of Living through the Ages" in *The State of Humanity*, ed. Julian L. Simon. Cambridge, MA: Blackwell, 135–48.

Centers for Disease Control and Prevention (CDC) 2002. *HIV/AIDS Surveillance Report*, vol. 13 (no. 2), Table 31.

———. 2003. *HIV/AIDS Surveillance Report*, vol. 14 (no. 2), Table 7.

———. 2004. *Health, United States, 2004 With Chartbook on Trends in the Health of Americans with Special Feature on Drugs*. Table 27 (for life expectancy).

———. 2005. "Cases of HIV infection and AIDS in the United States, 2003." *HIV/AIDS Surveillance Report*, vol. 15, Table 7. Available at http://www.cdc.gov/hiv/stats/2003SurveillanceReport.htm.

Costa, Dora L., and Richard H. Steckel. 1997. "Long-Term Trends, Health, Welfare and Economic Growth in the United States" in *Health and Welfare during Industrialization*, ed. Richard H. Steckel and Roderick Floud. Chicago: University of Chicago Press, 47–89.

Daily Mail and Guardian. 1998. Zim Commander "Not Killed in DRC." December 15. Available http://www.mg.co.za/mg/za/archive/98dec/15decpmnews.html. Accessed July 26, 2000.

Dollar, David, and Aart Kraay. 2000. *Growth Is Good for the Poor*. Transition Newsletter. World Bank, Development Economics Research Group. Available http://www.worldbank.org/research/growth/absdollakray.htm Accessed September 3, 2000.

Easterlin, Richard A. 1996. *Growth Triumphant: The Twenty-First Century in Historical Perspective*. Ann Arbor: University of Michigan Press.

Easterly, William, and Sergio T. Rebelo. 1993. Fiscal Policy and Economic Growth: An Empirical Investigation. *Journal of Monetary Economics 32(3): 417–58.*

Economist. 2004. "More or Less Equal?" *The Economist*, March 11, 2004.

Ehrlich, Paul R. 1968. *The Population Bomb*. New York: BallantineBooks.

Floud, R., and B. Harris. 1997. "Health, Height, and Welfare: Britain, 1700–1980" in *Health and Welfare during Industrialization*, ed. Richard H. Steckel and Roderick Floud. Chicago: University of Chicago Press, 91–126.

Fogel, R. W. 1995. "The Contribution of Improved Nutrition to the Decline of Mortality Rates in Europe and America" in *The State of Humanity*, ed. Julian L. Simon. Cambridge, MA: Blackwell, 61–71.

———. 2000. *The Fourth Great Awakening and the Future of Egalitarianism*. Chicago: University of Chicago Press.

———. 2003. *Changes in the Process of Aging during the Twentieth Century: Findings and Procedures of the Early Indicators Project*. National Bureau of Economic Research Working Paper 9941, Cambridge, MA: NBER.

Food and Agricultural Organization (FAO). 1996. *Assessment of Feasible Progress in Food Security*. Technical Background Documents 12–15, vol. 3. Rome: Italy.

———. 2002. *The State of Food and Agriculture 2002*. Rome, Italy.

———. 2004. *The State of Food Insecurity in the World 2004*. December. Availablehttp://www.fao.org/documents/show_cdr.asp?url_file=/docrep/007/y56 50e/y5650e00.htm. Accessed July 12, 2005.

———. 2005. *FAOStat*. Available http://apps.fao.org. Accessed July 3, 2005.

Frankel, Jeffrey A., and David Romer. 1999. "Does Trade Cause Growth?" *American Economic Review* (June): 379–99.

Freedom House. 2002. *Democracy's Century*. New York: Freedom Hoise.

———. 2005. *Freedom in the World 2005*. New York: Freedom House.

Goklany, Indur M. 1995. "Strategies to Enhance Adaptability: Technological Change, Sustainable Growth and Free Trade." *Climatic Change 30: 427–49*.

———. 1998. "Saving Habitat and Conserving Biodiversity on a Crowded Planet." *BioScience* 48: 941–53.

———. 1999a. *Clearing the Air: The Real Story of the War on Air Pollution*. Washington, DC: Cato Institute.

———. 1999b. "The Future of Industrial Society." Paper presented at the International Conference on Industrial Ecology and Sustainability, University of Technology of Troyes, Troyes, France, September 22–25. Available from author, Office of Policy Analysis, Dept. of the Interior, 1849 C St. NW, Washington, DC 20240.

———. 1999c. "Meeting Global Food Needs: The Environmental Trade-Offs Between Increasing Land Conversion and Land Productivity." *Technology* 6: 107–30.

———. 2000. "Potential Consequences of Increasing Atmospheric CO2 Concentration Compared to Other Environmental Problems." *Technology* 7S: 189–213.

———. 2002. "The Globalization of Human Well-Being." *Policy Analysis* (no. 447), Washington, DC: Cato Institute.

Groningen Growth and Development Centre and The Conference Board (GGDC&CB). 2005. *Total Economy Database*. Available at <http://www.ggdc.net>.

Guardian. 2000. Malaria Impedes Development in Africa. May 12. Copy on file with the author.

Gwartney, James, Randall Holcombe, and Robert Lawson. 1998. "The Scope of Government and the Wealth of Nations." *Cato Journal 18: 163–90*.

Gwartney, James, and Robert Lawson. 2004. *Economic Freedom of the World 2004 Annual Report*. Vancouver, BC: Fraser Institute.

Haines, Michael R. 1994. *Estimated Life Tables for the United States, 1850–1900*. Historical Paper 59. Cambridge, MA: National Bureau of Economic Research.

Hill, K. 1995. "The Decline in Childhood Mortality" in *The State of Humanity*, ed. Julian L. Simon. Cambridge, MA: Blackwell, 37–50.

Lee, J., and W. Feng, W. 1999. Malthusian Models and Chinese Realities: The Chinese Demographic System, 1700–2000. *Population and Development Review 25: 33–65*.

Lerner, M., and O. W. Anderson. 1963. *Health Progress in the United States, 1900–1960*. Chicago: University of Chicago Press.

Maddison, A. 1995. *Monitoring the World Economy, 1820–1992*. Paris: OECD.

———. 1998. *Chinese Economic Performance in the Long Run*. Paris: OECD.

———. 1999a. "Poor Until 1820." *Wall Street Journal*, The Millennium, January 11, R54.

————— . 1999b. "Economic Progress: The Last Half Century in Historical Perspective." In Castles, Ian (ed), *Facts and Fancies of Human Development*, Occasional Paper Series 1/2000, Canberra: Academy of Social Sciences in Australia, pp. 1–22.

————— . 2005a. *The World Economy: Historical Statistics*. Available online at http://www.ggdc.net/~maddison/Historical_Statistics/horizontal-file.xls. Accessed July 1, 2005.

————— . 2005b. "Memorandum." In *The economics of climate change: 2nd report of session 2005–06: Vol. 2 Evidence*. House of Lords papers 2005–06 12-II. London: House of Lords Select Committee on Economic Affairs, pp. 249–256.

Malaria Foundation International. 2000. *Economic Analyses Indicate that the Burden of Malaria is Great*. Executive summary for Harvard University Center for International Development and the London School of Hygiene and Tropical Medicine. Available http://www.malaria.org/jdsachseconomic.html. Accessed October 2, 2000.

Marland, G., T.A. Boden, and R. J. Andres. 2005. Global, Regional, and National CO2 Emissions. In Trends: A Compendium of Data on Global Change. Carbon Dioxide Information Analysis Center, Oak Ridge National Laboratory, U.S. Department of Energy, Oak Ridge, Tenn., U.S.A.

Martin, Joyce A., Betty L. Smith, T. J. Mathews, and Stephanie J. Ventura. 1999. "Births and Deaths: Preliminary data for 1998." *National Vital Statistics 47(25)*.

McEvedy, C., and R. Jones. 1978. *Atlas of World Population History*. New York: Penguin.

Mitchell, B. R. 1992. *International Historical Statistics: Europe, 1750–1988*. New York: Stockton Press.

Mitchell, D. O., and M. D. Ingco. 1993. "The World Food Outlook." *Hunger Notes* 19(Winter 1993–1994): 20–25.

National Center for Health Statistics. 2005. National Vital Statistics Report: Births, Marriages, Divorces and Deaths: Provisional Data for 2004, vol. 53 (no. 21), June 28.

OECD. 1998. *Maintaining Prosperity in an Ageing Society*. Policy Brief 5-1998. Paris.

Paddock, W., and P. Paddock. 1967. *Famine 1975! America's Decision: Who Will Survive?* Boston, MA: Little, Brown.

Preston, S. H. 1995. "Human Mortality throughout History and Prehistory" in *The State of Humanity*, ed. Julian L. Simon. Cambridge, MA: Blackwell, 30–36.

Pritchett, Lant, and Lawrence H. Summers. 1996. "Wealthier is Healthier." *Journal of Human Resources* 31: 841–68.

Ravallion, Martin, and Shaohua Chen. 1997. "What Can New Survey Data Tell Us about Recent Changes in Distribution and Poverty?" *World Bank Economic Review* 11(2): 357–82.

Ravallion, Martin. 2004. "Pessimistic on poverty?" *The Economist*, April 7, 2004.

Sala-i-Martin, X. 2002. "The World Distribution of Income." National Bureau of Economic Research Working Paper 8933.

Seskin, E. P. 1978. "Automobile Air Pollution Policy" in *Current Issues in U.S. Environmental Policy*, ed. Paul Portney. Baltimore, MD: Johns Hopkins University Press.

Shalala, Donna E. 1998. "Eliminating Racial and Ethnic Health Disparities [sic]". Speech delivered at the Patricia Harris Public Affairs Program, Howard

University, March 13. Available http://www.hhs.gov/news/speeches/
HOWARDPH.html. Accessed February 3, 2001.

Simon, Julian L., ed. 1995. *The State of Humanity*. Cambridge, MA: Blackwell.

United Nations. 2000. "Security Council Extends Iraq 'Oil-for-Food' Program for
Further 186 Days." Press release SC/6872. June 8. Available
http://www.un.org/News/Press/docs/2000/20000608.sc6872.doc.html. Accessed
January 31, 2001.

United Nations Development Program. 1999. *Human Development Report 1999*. New
York: Oxford University Press.

———. 2000. *Human Development Report 2000*. New York: Oxford University Press.

———. 2004. *Human Development Report 2004*. New York: Oxford University Press.

United Nations High Commission on Refugees. 1998. *UNHCR Appeals for Funds for
Great Lakes Operations*. Press release. March 2. Available
http://www.unhcr.ch/news/pr/pr980302.htm. Accessed July 25, 2000.

———. 1999a. *1999 Global Appeal/Great Lakes*. Available
http://www.unhcr.ch/fdrs/ga99/overlake.htm. Accessed February 2, 2001.

———. 1999b. *1999 Global Appeal/Southern Africa*. Available
http://www.unhcr.ch/fdrs/ga99oversaf.htm. Accessed February 2, 2001.

United Nations Population Division (UNPD). 2004a. *World Population Prospects: The
2004 Revision*. United Nations Population Division. Available
http://esa.un.org/unpp/p2k0data.asp. Accessed July 2, 2005.

———. 2004b. World Population to 2300.

U.S. Department of Health and Human Services. 1997. *Active Aging: A Shift in the
Paradig*m. Office of Disability, Aging and Long Term Care. May 1997. Available
http://aspe.hhs.gov/ daltcp/reports/actaging.htm. Accessed August 7, 2000.

Watkins, Shirley R.1997. "Historical Perspective on the School Meals Programs: The
Case for Strong Federal Programs." Paper presented at Ceres Forum on School
Meals Policy, Georgetown University Center for Food and Nutrition Policy,
November 24, Washington, DC. Available
http://www.fns.usda.gov/fncs/shirley/speeches/
support/sw971124.htm. Accessed August 15, 2000.

World Bank. 1993. *World Development Report: Investing in Health*. New York: Oxford
University Press.

———. 1999. *World Development Indicators*. CD-ROM. Washington, DC: The World
Bank.

———. 2005a. Commodity Prices Pink Sheet, July 2005. Available at
http://siteresources.worldbank.org/INTPROSPECTS/Resources/Pnk_0705.pdf,
accessed July 12, 2005.

———. 2005b. *World Development Indicators* Online at
http://devdata.worldbank.org/dataonline/.

World Health Organization. 1999. *The World Health Report 1999*. Geneva.

———. 2000. *The World Health Report 2000*. Geneva, Available
http://www.who.int/aboutwho/en/promoting/nutrtion.htm. Accessed January 5,
2000.

World Resources Institute. 1998. *World Resources 1998–99 Database*. Washington, DC.

———. 2005. Earth Trends. Data online at www.wri.org. Accessed June & July,
2005.

2 South Africa's healthcare under threat

Cornell, J., Goudge, J., McIntyre, D., & Mbatsha, S., (2001), *National Health Accounts: The Private Sector Report 2001*, University of Cape Town, Health Economics Unit.

Department of Provincial and Local Government, (2001), *Planning and Implementation Management Support System*, Pretoria.

Doherty, J., Thomas, S., & Muirhead, D., (2002), *The National Health Accounts Project: Health Financing and Expenditure in Post-Apartheid South Africa, 1996/7–1998/99*, University of Cape Town.

Esmail, N., & Walker, M., (2005), *How Good is Canadian Health Care?* Fraser Institute, Vancouver.

Goodman, C., & Herrick, D., (2002), "Twenty Myths about Single-Payer Health Insurance, International Evidence on the Effects of National Health Insurance in Countries Around the World", National Center for Policy Analysis, Dallas.

Gore, A., (2002, *Future Trends for Medical Schemes in South Africa.* Health Wise Seminar held at Midrand 2002, Sandton: Discovery Health.

Government Communication and Information System, (2002), *South African Year Book 2002–2003*, Pretoria.

Hayek, F., (1976), *The New Confusion About 'Planning'*, Morgan Guaranty Survey.

Hayek, F., (1944), *The Road to Serfdom*, University of Chicago Press, Chicago.

Health Systems Trust, (2003), *South African Health Review 2002*, Durban.

Health Systems Trust, (2004), *South African Health Review 2003–2004*, Durban.

National Department of Health, (2005), The Charter of the Health Sector of the Republic of South Africa (Revised Draft), Pretoria.

National Department of Health, (2002), *Inquiry into the various Social Security Aspects of the South African Health System*, Pretoria.

National Treasury, (2001), *Intergovernmental Fiscal Review 2001*, Pretoria.

National Treasury, (2003), *Intergovernmental Fiscal Review 2003*, Pretoria.

National Treasury, (2001), *Intergovernmental Fiscal Review 2001*, Pretoria.

National Treasury, (2003), *Intergovernmental Fiscal Review 2003*, Pretoria.

Pipes, S., (2002), "The False Promise of Single-Payer Health Care", Pacific Research Institute, San Francisco.

Reisman, G., (1996), *Capitalism* Jameson Books, Ottawa.

Rothbard, M., (2004), *Man, Economy and State with Power and Market*, Ludwig von Mises Institute, Auburn, Alabama.

Statistics South Africa, (2003), *Census 2001: Census in Brief*, Pretoria.

Statistics South Africa, (2005), *South African Statistics 2004/05*, Pretoria.

von Mises, L., (1990), *Economic Calculation in the Socialist Commonwealth*, Ludwig von Mises Institute, Auburn, Alabama.

3 Corruption in public health

Aaby, P. 1995. "Assumptions and Contradictions in Measles and Measles Immunization Research: Is Measles Good for Something?" *Social Science & Medicine* 41(5): 673–686.

Alcazar, L and Andrade, R. "Induced Demand and Absenteeism in Peruvian Hospitals." In Di Tella, R. and Savedoff, W. D. (eds.). 2001. *Diagnosis Corruption*. Washington, DC: Inter-American Development Bank.

Alesina, A., A. Devleeschauwer, W. Easterly, S. Kurlat and R. Wacziarg, 2003. "Fractionalization." *Journal of Economic Growth* 8(2): 155–94. Data: http://www.stanford.edu/~wacziarg/downloads/fractionalization.xls

Anderson, J. 1999. "Corruption in Latvia: Survey Evidence". ECA Region. Washington D.C. World Bank. Processed.

Anderson, J. 2000. "Corruption in Slovakia: Results of Diagnostic Surveys". World Bank and the United States Agency for International Development. ECA Region. Washington D.C.: World Bank. Processed.

Azfar, O. 2005. "Corruption and the Delivery of Health and Education Services." Mimeo. IRIS Center, University of Maryland, College Park, Maryland. Draft.

Azfar, O., and T. Gurgur. 2001. "Does Corruption Affect Health and Education Outcomes in the Philippines?" Mimeo. IRIS Center, University of Maryland, College Park, Maryland. Draft.

Azfar, O., S.Kahkonen and P. Meagher. 2001. "Conditions for Effective Decentralized Governance: A Synthesis of Research Findigs." Mimeo. IRIS Center, University of Maryland, College Park, Maryland. Draft.

Banerjee, A. and E. Duflo. 2005. "Improving Health-Care Delivery in India". M.I.T. Working Paper. Cambridge, MA: Massachusetts Institute of Technology.

Banerjee, A., A. Deaton and E. Duflo (2004) "Wealth, Health and Health Services in Rural Rajasthan." *American Economic Review Papers and Proceedings*. 94(2) 326–330.

Barber, S., F. Bonnet and H. Bekedam. 2004. "Formalizing Under-the-Table Payment to control Out-of-Pocket Hospital Expenditures in Cambodia" *Health Policy and Planning* 19(40 199–208.

Bardhan, P. 1997. "Corruption and Development: A Review of Issues." *Journal of Economic Literature* 35(3) 1310–1346.

Barr, A., M. Lindelow and P. Serneels. 2004. "To Serve the Community or Oneself: The Public Servant's Dilemma." World Bank Policy Research Working Paper 3187. Washington D.C.: World Bank.

Barro, R. J. and J.-W. Lee. 2000. "International Data on Educational Attainment: Updates and Implications." CID Working Paper No. 42. Cambridge, MA: Center for International Development, Harvard University. Data: http://www.cid.harvard.edu/ciddata/Appendix%20Data%20Tables.xls

Belli, P. 2002. Formal and Informal Household Spending on Health: A Multi-country Study in Central and Eastern Europe." Harvard School of Public Health, International Health Systems Group. Mimeo.

Belli, P., and H. Shahriari, and G. Gotzadze. 2004. "Out of pocket and Informal Payments in the Health Sector: Evidence from Georgia". *Health Policy* 70: 109–23.

Belli, P., H. Shahriari, and M. Lewis. 2001. "Institutional Issues in Informal Health Payments in Poland: Report on the Qualitative Part of the Study." HNP Thematic Group Working Paper, World Bank. (February).

Berg, A. 2005. "High Aid Inflows Case Study: Ghana". Paper presented at the International Monetary Fund Seminar on Foreign Aid and Macroeconomic Management. Maputo, Mozambique, March 14–15.

Bloom, G., L Han and X Li. 2001. "How Health Workers Earn a Living in China" *Human Resources for Health Development Journal* 5(1): 25–38.

Brinkerhoff, D. 2004. "Accountability and Health Systems: Toward Conceptual Clarity and Policy Relevance." *Health Policy and Planning* 19(6): 371–379.

Brinkerhoff, D. 2005. "Pro-poor Health Services in Madagascar: Decentralization and Accountability". Paper presented at Global Health Council Annual Conference (may-June).

Brueckner, J. 2000. "Fiscal Decentralization in Developing Countries: The Effects of Local Corruption and Tax Evasion". Department of Economics and Institute of Government and Public Affairs. Urbana, Illinois: University of Illinois.

Carasciuc, L. 2001. "Corruption and Quality of Governance: The Case of Moldova". Transparency International. Monograph.

Chakraborty, S., R. Gatti, J. Klugman and G. Gray-Molina. 2002. "When is "Free" Not So Free? Informal Payments for Basic Health Services in Bolivia. Mimeo. Processed.

Chaudhury, N., and J.S. Hammer. 2004. "Ghost Doctors: Absenteeism in Bangladeshi Health Facilities". *World Bank Economic Review* 18(3).

Chaudhury, N., J.S. Hammer, M. Kremer et al. 2004. "Provider Absence in Schools and Health Clinics". Northeast Universities Development Consortium Conference, HEC Montreal, October.

Chawla, M. 2001. "How Well Does the Health Sector in Georgia Serve the Poor: An Examination of Public and Out-of-Pocket Expenditures on Health". Washington D.C.: World Bank. Processed.

Chawla, M. 2002. "Poland Informal Payments in Health". Washington, D.C.: World Bank. Mimeo. PRocessed.

Chawla, M., et al. 1999. "Provision of Ambulatory Health Services in Poland: A Case Study from Krakow." *Social Science and Medicine* 58:227–235.

Chawla, M., P. Berman, A. Windak, and M. Kulis. 2001. "The Changing Face of the Health Care Providers Market: A Case Study from Poland". Processed.

Cohen, J. C. 2002. "Improving Transparency in Pharmaceutical Systems: Strengthening Critical Decision Points against Corruption". Washington, D.C.: World Bank. Mimeo.

Cohen, J. C. and J.C. Montoya. 2002. "Using Technology to Fight Corruption in Pharmaceutical Purchasing: Lessons Learned from the Chilean Experience" World Bank. Mimeo.

Commission for Africa. 2005. *Our Common Interest: Report of the Commission for Africa*

Commission on Macroeconomics and Health. 2001. *Macroeconomics and Health: Investing in Health for Economic Development*. Geneva: World Health Organization.

Das Gupta, M., V. Gauri, and S. Khemani. 2003. "Primary Health Care Service Delivery in Nigeria. Survey Evidence from Lagos and Kogi". Development Research Group. Washington D.C.: World Bank.

Dehn, J., R.Reinikka, and J. Svensson. 2003. "Survey Tools for Assessing Performance in Service Delivery." In Francois Bourguignon and Luiz Pereira da Silva, eds., *Evaluating the Poverty and Distributional Impact of Economic Policies.* Oxford University Press and World Bank.

Delcheva, El, D. Balabanova, and M. McKee. 1997. "Under-the-Counter Payments for Health Care." *Health Policy*, 42:89–100.

Di Tella, R. and Savedoff, W. D. (eds.). 2001. *Diagnosis Corruption*. Washington, DC: Inter-American Development Bank.

Di Tella, R. and Savedoff, W. D. "Shining Light in Dark Corners." In Di Tella, R. and Savedoff, W. D. (eds.). 2001. *Diagnosis Corruption*. Washington, DC: Inter-American Development Bank.

Eichler, R., P. Auxilia and J. Pollock. 2001. "Output-Based Health Care: Paying for Performance in Haiti." World Bank, Viewpoint, Note 236. Washington, D.C.

Elliott, K. A. 1997. (Ed.) *Corruption and the Global Economy*. Washington, DC: Institute for International Economics.

Falkingham, J. 2002. "Health, health seeking behavior and out of pocket expenditures in Kyrgyzstan 2001". Kyrgyz Household Health Finance Survey. London School of Economics. Monograph.

Falkingham, J. 2000. "Poverty, out-of-pocket payments and inequality in access to health care: evidence from Tajikistan". London School of Economics.

Falkingham, J. 2004. "Poverty, Out-of-Pocket Payments and Access to Health Care: Evidence from Tajikistan." *Social Science and Medicine*, 58: 247–258.

Filmer, D. and L. Pritchett. 1999. " The Impact of Public Spending on Health: Does Money Matter?" *Social Science and Medicine*. 49; 1309–1323.

Fisman, R., R. Gatti. 2000. "Decentralization and Corruption: Evidence across Countries". Development Research Group. Washington D.C. World Bank. Processed.

Gatti, R., G. Gray-Molina, and J. Klugman. 2003. "Determinants of Corruption in Local Health Care Provision: Evidence from 108 Municipalities in Bolivia". World Bank. Processed.

Giedion, U. Morales, L. G. and Acosta, O. L. "The Impact of Health Reforms on Irregularities in Bogot†Hospitals." In Di Tella, R. and Savedoff, W. D. (eds.). 2001. *Diagnosis Corruption*. Washington, DC: Inter-American Development Bank.

Gilson, L. 1997. "The Lessons of User Fee Experience in Africa." *Health Policy and Planning* 12(4): 273–285

Gopakumar, K. 1998. "Citizen Feedback Surveys to Highlight Corruption in Public Services: the Experience of Public Affairs Centre, Bangalore." (September) Mimeo.

Gosden, T., L. Pedersen and d. Torgerson. 1999. "How should We Pay Doctors? A Systematic Review of Salary Payments and their Effect on Doctor Behavior" *Quarterly Journal of Medicine* (92) 47–55.

Gray-Molina, G., de Rada, E. P. and Ya–ez, E. "Does Voice Matter? Participation and Controlling Corruption in Bolivian Hospitals." In Di Tella, R. and Savedoff, W. D. (eds.). 2001. *Diagnosis Corruption*. Washington, DC: Inter-American Development Bank.

Gray-Molina, G., E. Perez de Rada and E. Yanez. 2001. "Does Voice Matter? Participation and Controlling Corruption in Bolivian Hospitals," In *Diagnosis Corruption Fraud in Latin America's Public Hospitals* W. Savedoff and R. Di Tella eds.

Gupta, S., H. Davoodi, and E. Tiongson. 2000. "Corruption and the Provision of Health Care and Education Services". IMF Working Paper. Washington D.C.: International Monetary Fund.

Hotchkisss, D., P. Hutchinson, A. Malaj and A. Berruti. 2005. "Out-of-pocket Payments and Utilization of Health Care Services in Albania: Evidence from Three Districts." *Health Policy* (forthcoming).

Hsiao, W. 2005. Personal communication based on studies in China.

IMF and World Bank. 2005. *Global Monitoring Report.* Washington, D.C.: International Monetary Fund and World Bank.

IMF. 1997. "Good Governance: The IMF's Role". IMF Guidance Note. Washington, D.C.: International Monetary Fund.

Jack, W. and M. Lewis. 2004. "Falling Short of Expectations: Public Health Interventions in Developing and Transition Economies." *Social Science and Medicine* 58(2).

Jaîn, M. H. and Paravinski, D. "Wages, Capture and Penalties in Venezuela's Public Hospitals." In Di Tella, R. and Savedoff, W. D. (eds.). 2001. *Diagnosis Corruption.* Washington, DC: Inter-American Development Bank.

Kaufman , D. and A. Kraay. 2003. Governance and Growth: Causality which way? – Evidence for the World, in brief." Washington, D.C.: World Bank

Kaufman, D, A. Kraay and M. Maztruzzi. 2005. "Governance Matters III: Governance Indicators for 1996–2002." Washington, D.C.: World Bank.

Kaufman, D, A. Kraay and P. Zoido-Lobat – n. 1999. "Governance Matters." World Bank Policy Research Working Paper 2196. Washington, D.C.: World Bank.

Kaufmann, D. 2003. "On Evidence-based Rethinking of Governance and Challenging Orthodoxy." Presentation at USAID, Washington, DC, September 23. http://www.worldbank.com/wbi/governance/pdf/usaid_present092303.pdf

Kaufmann, D. and A. Kraay. 2002. "Growth Without Governance". *Economia* 3(1):169–215.

Kaufmann, D. and S.-J. Wei. 1999. "Does "Grease Money" Speed Up the Wheels of Commerce?" NBER Working Papers 7093. National Bureau of Economic Research, Inc.

Khemani, S. 2004. "Local Government Accountability for Service Delivery in Nigeria." World Bank. Processed.

Killingsworth, J., N. Hossain, Y. Hedrick-Wong et. al. 1999. "Unofficial Fees in Bangladesh: Price, Equity and Institutional Issues." *Health Policy and Planning,* 14(2): 152–163.

Klitgaard, R. 1998. "Strategies against Corruption." Presentation at Agencia Espa–ola de Cooperaci – n Internacional Foro Iberoamericano sobre el Combate a la Corrupci – n, Santa Cruz de la Sierra, Jun 15–16. http://unpan1.un.org/intradoc/groups/public/documents/clad/clad0035403.pdf

Koenig, M. A., M. A. Khan, B. Wojtyniak, J. D. Clemens, J. Chakraborty, V. Fauveau, J. F. Phillips, J. Akbar, and U.S. Barua. 1991. "Impact of Measles Vaccination on Childhood Mortality in Rural Bangladesh." *Bulletin of the World Health Organization* 68(4): 441–447.

Kutzin, J., T. Maeimanaliev, A. Ibraimova, C. Cashin, and S. O'Dougherty. 2003. "Formalizing Informal Payments in Kyrgyz Hospitals: Evidence from Phased Implementation of Financing Reforms." Paper presented at IHEA Conference, San Francisco, California.

La Forgia, G. 2005. *Health System Innovations in Central America: Lessons and Impact of New Approaches*. World Bank Working Paper No. 57, Washington, D.C.: World Bank.

La Forgia, G., R. Levine, A. Dias and M. Rathe. 2004. "Fend for Yourself, Systemic Failure in the Dominican Health System. *Health Policy* 67:173–186.

Leonard, K. 2005. "Getting Clinicians To Do Their Best: Ability, Altruism and Incentives." University of Maryland. Mimeo (Draft)

Lewis, M. 2000. "Who Is Paying for Health care in Europe and Central Asia?" Europe and Central Asia Region. Monograph. Washington D.C.: World Bank.

Lewis, M. 2003. "Health and Corruption in Developing and Transition Countries" Presented at the Transparency International Annual Conference, Seoul, Korea. (May)

Lewis, M. 2005. "Improving Efficiency and Impact in Health Care Services – Lessons from Central America" in *Health System Innovations in Central America: Lessons and Impact of New Approaches*. World Bank Working Paper No. 57, Washington, D.C.: World Bank.

Lewis, M., 2002. "Informal Health Payments in Central and Eastern Europe and the Former Soviet Union: Issues, Trends and Policy Implications" in *Funding Health Care: Options for Europe*. Figueres and Moussiales. editors. Buckingham: Open University Press.

Lewis, M., G. Eskeland, and X. Traa-Valarezo. 2004. "Effectiveness and Impact of Rural Health Care Policies in El Salvador". *Health Policy*. 70(3): 303–325.

Lewis, M., G. La Forgia, and M. Sulvetta. 1992. "Productivity and Quality of Public Hospital Staff: A Dominican Case Study." *International Journal of Health Planning and Management*. 6.

Lewis, M., G. La Forgia, and M. Sulvetta. 1996. "Measuring Public Hospital Costs: Empirical Evidence from the Dominican Republic." *Social Science and Medicine*. 43(2): 221 – 234.

Lindelow, M. and J. Dehn. 2001. "Public Expenditure Tracking Survey of the Health Sector in Mozambique". Washington, D.C.: World Bank. Draft.

Lindelow, M., I. Kushnarova and K. Kaiser. 2005. "Measuring Corruption in the Health Sector: What We Can Learn from Public Expenditure Tracking and Service Delivery Surveys in Developing Countries." Washington D.C.: World Bank

Lindelow, M., P. Serneels, and T. Lemma. 2003. "Synthesis of Focus Group Discussions with Health Workers in Ethiopia." Washington, D.C.: World Bank, DEC Draft paper.

Lindelow, M., P. Ward, and N. Zorzi. 2004. "Expenditure Tracking and Service Delivery Survey", The Health Sector in Mozambique". Final Report. Washington D.C.: World Bank. Processed.

Lindelow, M., R. Reinikka, and J. Svensson. 2003. "Health Care on the Frontlines. Survey Evidence on Public and Private Providers in Uganda". Africa Region Human Development Working Paper Series. Washington D.C.: World Bank. Forthcoming.

McPake, B.,A. D. Asiimwe, F.Mwesigye, et. al. 1999. "Informal Economic Activities of Public Health Workers in Uganda: Implications for Quality and Accessibility of Care." Social Science and Medicine. 49: 849–865

Murrugarra E., and Cnobloch, R. 2003. "Health Status and Health Care Dimensions of Poverty in Armenia". Europe and Central Asia Region, Human Development Department. Washington D.C.: World Bank. Processed.

Narayan, D. 2000. *Voices of the Poor*. Washington, D.C.: World Bank and Oxford University Press.

Partnership for Governance Reform. 2002. *A Diagnostic Study of Corruption in Indonesia.*

Phongpaichit, P., N. Treerat, Y. Chaiyapong, and C. Baker. 2000. "Corruption in the Public Sector in Thailand Perceptions and Experience of Households. Report of a nationwide survey". Political Economy Centre. Bangkok.: Chulalongkorn University. Processed.

Rajkumar, A. S. and V. Swaroop 2002. "Public Spending and Outcomes: Does Governance Matter?" Policy Research Working Paper Series 2840. Washington D.C.: World Bank.

Rauch, J. E. and P. B. Evans. 2000. "Bureaucratic Structure and Bureaucratic Performance in Less Developed Countries." *Journal of Public Economics* 75(1): 49–71.

Reinikka, R. and J. Svensson. 2003. "Working for God? Evaluating service delivery of religious not-for-profit health care providers in Uganda" World Bank Policy Research Working Paper 3058 (May).

Reinikka, R. and J. Svensson. 2004. "The Power of Information: Evidence from a Newspaper Campaign to Reduce Capture." Mimeo (March).

Reinikka, R. and J. Svensson. 2002. "Measuring and Understanding Corruption at the Micro Level." Mimeo (January) Processed.

Reinikka, R. and J. Svensson. 2004. "Local Capture: Evidence from a Central Government Transfer Program in Uganda." *Quarterly Journal of Economics* 119(2): 679–705.

Rigobon, R. and D. Rodrik. 2004. "Rule of Law, Democracy, Openness and Income: Estimating the Interrelationships." NBER Working Papers 10750. National Bureau of Economic Research, Inc.

Rodrik, R., A. Subramanian and F. Trebbi. 2002. "Institutions Rule: The Primacy of Institutions over Geography and Integration in Economic Development." NBER Working Papers 9305. National Bureau of Economic Research, Inc.

Roland, M. 2004. "Linking Physician's Pay to the Quality of Care – A Major Experiment in the UK." *New England Journal of Medicine* 351(14): 1448–1458.

Ryterman, J., J. Hellman and G. Jones et al., 2000. "Corruption in Russia: Interim Report." World Bank. Mimeo (June) Processed.

Sari, A., J. Langenbrunner, and M. Lewis. 2000. "Affording Out-of-Pocket Payments for Health Care Services: Evidence from Kazakhstan." *Euroheath 6,2* (Spring). Geneva: World Heath Organization.

Schargrodsky, E., Mera, J. and Weinschelbaum, F. "Transparency and Accountability in Argentina's Hospitals." In Di Tella, R. and Savedoff, W. D. (eds.). 2001. *Diagnosis Corruption*. Washington, DC: Inter-American Development Bank.

Shahriari, H., P. Belli, and M. Lewis. 2001. "Institutional Issues in Informal Health Payments in Poland: Report on the Qualitative Part of the Study". HNP Working Paper. Washington D.C.: World Bank.

Shishkin, Sergey. 2003. "Informal Payments for Health Care in Russia". Presentation at IHEA 2003 4th World Congress, San Francisco. Processed.

Shleifer, A. and R. W. Vishny. 1993. "Corruption." *Quarterly Journal of Economics* 108(3): 599–617.

Soto, B. 2002. "Corruption and the Colombian Health System Reform." Corruption in Health Services. WHO/I-ADB/Transparency International Report. Mimeo.

Sparrow, M. (1996). *License to Steal: Why Fraud Plagues the American Health Care System*. Boulder, Colorado: Westview Press.

Stempovscaia, E. 2002. "Corruption in the Public Health Service in a Post-Communist Country: Some Elements of corruption in the Transition Period in Moldova." In *Corruption in Health Services*. WHO/IDB/Transparency International Report.

Tendler, J. and S. Freedheim. 1994. "Trust in a Rent- Seeking World: Health and Government Transformed in Northeast Brazil." *World Development* 22(12): 1771–1791.

Thampi, G.K. 2002. *Corruption in South Asia, Insights & Benchmarks from Citizen Feedback Surveys in Five Countries*. Monograph.

Thamrin, Jalan M.H. 2002. "A Diagnostic Study of Corruption in Indonesia". Partnership for Governance Reform in Indonesia. Final Report. Processed.

Thompson, R. 2004. Informal Payments for Emergency Hospital Care in Kazakhstan: An Exploration of Patient and Physician Behavior. Ph.D. thesis. York, UK: University of York.

Thompson, R. and A. Xavier. 2002. "Unofficial Payments for Acute State Hospital Care in Kazakhstan. A Model of Physician Behavior with Price Discrimination and Vertical Service Differentiation". LICOS Centre for Transition Economics. LICOS Discussion Papers.

Transparency International. 2003. *Global Corruption Report 2003.*

Transparency International. 2005. *Global Corruption Report 2005.*

United Nations Millennium Project. 2005. *Investing in Development: A Practical Plan to Achieve the Millennium Development Goals*. Sterling: Earthscan.

Van Rijckeghem, C. and B. Weder. 2001. "Bureaucratic Corruption and the Rate of Temptation: Do Wages in the Civil Service Affect Corruption and by How Much? *Journal of Development Economics* (65) 307–331.

Vitosha/USAID, 2002. "Regional Corruption Monitoring in Albania, Bosnia and Herzegovina, Bulgaria, Croatia, Macedonia, Romania, and Yugoslavia". Mimeo. Processed.

Wagstaff, A. and M. Claeson. 2004. *Rising to the Challenge: The Millennium Development Goals for Health*. Washington, D.C.: World Bank.

World Bank 2000c. "Paraguay: Resultados de los Diagnosticos a Funcionarios Publicos y Ususarios de los Servicios". Washington D.C.: World Bank. Processed.

World Bank 2001a. "Voices of the Misgoverned and Misruled: An Empirical Diagnostic Study on Governance, Rule of Law and Corruption for Peru". Washington D.C.: World Bank. Processed.

World Bank. 1997. *World Development Report. The State in a Changing World*. Washington, D.C.: World Bank.

World Bank. 2000a, "Armenia Institutional and Governance Review". World Bank Report. Washington D.C.: World Bank. Processed.

World Bank. 2000b. "Cambodia Governance and Corruption Diagnostic: Evidence from Citizen, Enterprise and Public Official Survey".. World Bank Report. Washington D.C.: World Bank. Processed.

World Bank. 2000d. "The Ghana Governance and Corruption Survey, Evidence from Households, Enterprises and Public Officials. Africa Region". Washington D.C.: World Bank. Processed.

World Bank. 2001b. "Voice of the Poor and Taming of the Shrew: Evidence from the Bolivia Public Officials' Survey". Latin America and Caribbean Region. Washington D.C.: World Bank. Processed.

World Bank. 2001c. "Kazakhstan Governance and Service Delivery: A Diagnostic Report". Poverty Reduction and Economic Management Unit, Europe and Central Asia Region. Washington D.C.: World Bank. Processed.

World Bank. 2001d. "Diagnostic Survey of Corruption in Romania". Washington D.C.: World Bank. Processed.

World Bank. 2001e. "Bosnia and Herzegovina Diagnostic Surveys of Corruption". Washington D.C.: World Bank. Processed.

World Bank. 2001f. "Honduras: Public Expenditure Management for Poverty Reduction and Fiscal Sustainability." Report No. 22070. Washington D.C.: World Bank.

World Bank. 2002a. "A Strategy to Combat Corruption in the ECA Region". Issues Paper and Progress Report. Washington D.C.: World Bank. Processed.

World Bank. 2002b. "Governance and Service Delivery in the Kyrgyz Republic – Results of Diagnostic Surveys". Poverty Reduction and Economic Management Unit, Europe and Central Asia Region. Washington D.C.: World Bank. Processed.

World Bank. 2003a. "Albania: Poverty Assessment". Europe and Central Asia Region. Washington D.C.: World Bank.

World Bank. 2003b. *Better Governance for Development in the Middle East and North Africa: Enhancing Inclusiveness and Accountability*. Washington, D.C.: World Bank

World Bank. 2003c. *Turkey: Reforming the Health Sector for Improved Access and Efficiency.* Report No. 24358-TU. Washington, D.C.: World Bank.

World Bank. 2004a. *World Development Report. Making Services Work for Poor People.* Washington, D.C.: World Bank.

World Bank. 2004b. *Ethiopia: A Country Status Report.* Report No. 28963-ET. Washington, D.C.: World Bank.

World Bank. 2004c. *The Millennium Development Goals for Health: Rising to the Challenge.* Washington, D.C.: World Bank.

World Bank. 2005a. *Doing Business in 2005: Removing Obstacles to Growth.* Washington, D.C.: World Bank.

World Bank. 2005b. Ethiopia: *A Country Status Report on Health and Poverty.* Washington, D.C.: World Bank.

World Bank. 2006. *World Development Report. Equity and Development.* Washington, D.C.: World Bank.

World Bank. Forthcoming. *Nigeria: Health, Nutrition and Population: Country Status Report.* Washington D.C.: World Bank Draft.

4 The diseases of poverty and the 10/90 gap

Attaran, A., Barnes, K., Curtis, C., d'Alessandro, U., Fanello, C., Galinski, M., Kokwaro, G., Looareesuwan, S., Makanga, M., Mutabingwa, T., (2004), "WHO, the Global Fund, and medical malpractice in malaria treatment," *The Lancet*, 363:9404, pp 237–240.

Barat, L., Palmer, N., Basu, S., Worrall, E., Hanson, K., Mills, A., (2003), "Do Malaria Control Interventions Reach the Poor?: A view Through the Equity Lens," *Disease Control Priorities Project*, Bethesda: National Institutes of Health.

Black, RE., *Where and why are 10 million children dying every year*? The Lancet 2003; 361: 2226–34

Bruce, N., Perez-Padilla, R. & Albalak, R., (2002), "The health effects of indoor air pollution exposure in developing countries", Geneva: World Health Organization.

Carrin, G., (2002), "Social Health Insurance in developing countries: a continuing challenge," *International Social Security Review,* Vol. 55.

Chima, R., Goodman, C. & Mills, A., (2003), "The economic impact of malaria in Africa: a critical review of the evidence," *Health Policy,* 63(1): 17–36

Deolalikar, A., (1995), "Government Health Spending in Indonesia: Impact on Children in Different Economic Groups." In *Public Spending and the Poor: Theory and Evidence*, eds. Van de Walle, D., & Nead, K., Baltimore: John Hopkins University Press.

Department of Health and Human Services, United States, (2002), "Report to the President: Prescription drug coverage, spending, utilization, and prices", April 2002.

de Soto, H., (2001), *The Mystery of Capital*, London: Bantam Books.

Fenwick, A, (2006), "Waterborne Infectious Diseases – Could They Be Consigned to History?" *Science*, 313:5790, pp 1077 – 1081

Filmer, D. & Pritchett, L., (1999), "The Impact of public spending on health: does money matter?" World Bank

Filmer, D., Hammer, J., Pritchett, L., (2000), "Weak links in the chain: a diagnosis of health policy in poor countries," *World Bank Research Observer,* 15(2): 199–224.

Jones, G., & Stetekee R., (2004), *How many child deaths can we prevent this year?* The Lancet, vol 362, 5 July 2004

Kumarasamy, N., (2004), "Generic antiretroviral drugs – will they be the answer to HIV in the developing world?" *The Lancet*, vol 364.

Levison, L. & Laing, R., (2003), "The hidden costs of essential medicines," *WHO essential drugs monitor*, Issue 33.

Levison, L., (2003), "Policy and programming options for reducing the procurement costs of essential medicines in developing countries", concentration paper: Boston University School of Public Health.

Love J., Hubbard T., (2003) "An agenda for research and development," Meeting on the role of generics and local industry in attaining the Millennium Development Goals in pharmaceuticals and vaccines. World Bank: Washington DC, June 2003

Monath, T., (2005), "Yellow Fever Vaccine," *Expert Review of Vaccines*, 4(4):553–74

Medecins Sans Frontieres & Drugs for Neglected Diseases Working Group, (2001), "Fatal Imbalance: The Crisis in Research and Development for Drugs for

Neglected Diseases", September 2001, available at http://www.accessmed-msf.org/documents/fatal_imbalance_2001.pdf

Muheki, C., McIntyre, D. & Barnes K., (2004), "Artemisinin-based combination therapy reduces expenditure on malaria treatment in KwaZulu Natal, South Africa," *Tropical Medicine and International Health* 9, 959–966.

PAHO, (2006), "New malaria treatments guidelines issued," 20/01/2006, available at http://www.paho.org/English/DD/PIN/pr060120.htm.

Poisal, J. & Chulis, G., (2000), "Medicare beneficiaries and drug coverage," *Health Affairs*, 19(2).

Rice, A., West, K., & Black, R., (2004), "Vitamin A Deficiency" (Chapter 4), in Ezzati, M. et al. (Eds.) *Comparative Quantification of Health Risks*. Geneva: World Health Organization.

Shaw, R. & Ainsworth, M., (1995), "Financing heath services through user fees and insurance," World Bank discussion paper 294.

Soderlund, N. & Hansl, B., (2000), "Health Insurance in South Africa: an empirical analysis of trends in risk-pooling and efficiency following deregulation," *Health Policy and Planning*, 15(4):378–385.

Trouiller et al., (2002), *Drug development for neglected diseases: a deficient market and a public-health policy failure, The Lancet*, vol 359, June 22, 2002

Wirth, D., (2001), *Survey for the Drugs for Neglected Diseases Working Group*, Switzerland, May 2001. [Online]. Original survey and letter available: www.accessmed-msf.org. Andra Brichacek, Top 50 Pharmaceutical Companies of 2000, Pharmaceutical Executive, April 2001. Available: http://www.pharmaportal.com/articles/pe/pe0401_062-82.pdf [2001, August 6].

Monath, T. & Nasidi, A., (1993), "Should Yellow Fever vaccine be included in the expanded program of immunisation in Africa? A cost-effectiveness analysis for Nigeria," *American Journal of Tropical Medicine and Hygiene*, 48(2):274–299.

Moran, M., Ropars, A., Guzman, J. Diaz, J. & Garrison, C., (2005), "The New landscape of neglected disease drug development," London School of Economics pharmaceutical R&D policy project, Wellcome Trust: London

Murray H., Pepin, J., Nutman, T., Hoffman, S., Mhamoud, A., (2001), "Recent advances, tropical medicine", British Medical Journal, 320:490–494

PhRMA, (2005), data solicited by author, November 2005.

Saleh, K. & Ibrahim, M., (2005), "Are Essential Medicines in Malaysia Accessible, Affordable and Available?" *Pharmacy World & Science*, 27:6 442–446.

WHO, (1995), *Global prevalence of Vitamin A deficiency*, Micronutrient Deficiency Information System working paper no.2, Geneva: WHO

WHO (1999), *Report on Infectious Diseases: Removing Obstacles to Healthy Development*, Geneva: WHO.

WHO, (2002), *World Health Report 2002*, Geneva: WHO

WHO, (2002a), *State of the world's vaccines and immunisation*, Geneva: WHO

WHO, (2003), *World Health Report 2003*, Geneva: WHO

WHO, (2003a), *Medicines Strategy Report 2002–2003*, Geneva: WHO

WHO, (2004), *World Health Report*, Statistical Annex, Geneva: WHO.

WHO, (2005a), *Preventing Chronic Disease: a vital investment*, Geneva: WHO.

WHO-IFPMA (2001) Round Table, *Working paper on priority infectious diseases requiring additional R&D*, July 2001

Wofford, D., & Shanahan, C., (2004), *Doing Business in 2005*, World Bank.

5 Increasing access to medicines

Adams, C., & Brantner, V., (2003), "New Drug Development: Estimating Entry form Human Clinical Trials," *Federal Trade Commission*, working paper 262.

Attaran, A., (2004), "How Do Patents and Economic Policies Affect Access to Essential Medicines in Developing Countries", *Health Affairs*, 23:3, 155–66.

Barat, L., Palmer, N., Basu, S., Worrall, E., Hanson, K., Mills, A., (2003), "Do Malaria Control Interventions Reach the Poor?: A view Through the Equity Lens," *Disease Control Priorities Project*, Bethesda: National Institutes of Health.

Bate, R., Tren, R. & Urbach, J., (2005), *Taxed to death*, Washington DC: AEI-Brookings Joint Center for Regulatory Studies.

Carrin, G., (2002), "Social Health Insurance in developing countries: a continuing challenge," *International Social Security Review,* Vol. 55.

Castro-Leal, F., Dayton, J., Demery, L. & Mehra, K., (1999), "Public Social Spending in Africa: Do the Poor Benefit?" *World Bank Research Observer*, 14(1):49–72.

CMR International Institute for Regulatory Science, (2004), *The changing regulatory environment: reality and perception*, R&D briefing no. 42.

Danzon, P. & Furukawa, M., (2003), "Prices And Availability of Pharmaceuticals: Evidence From Nine Countries," *Health Affairs*, W3: 521–536.

Danzon, P., Wang, Y. & Wang, L., (2003), *The impact of drug price regulation on the launch of delay of new drugs-evidence from 25 major markets in the 1990s*,
National Bureau of Economic Research, working paper 9874.

Deolalikar, A., (1995), "Government Health Spending in Indonesia: Impact on Children in Different Economic Groups." In *Public Spending and the Poor: Theory and Evidence*, eds. Van de Walle, D., & Nead, K., Baltimore: John Hopkins University Press.

DiMasi, J., (1995), "Trends in Drugs Development Costs, Times and Risks," *Drug Information Journal*, 29.

DiMasi, J., Jansen, R., & Grabowski, H., (2003), "The Price of innovation: new estimates of drug developments costs," *Journal of Health Economics*, 22: 151–185.

Department of Health and Human Services, United States, (2002), "Report to the President: Prescription drug coverage, spending, utilization, and prices."

de Soto, H., (2001), *The Mystery of Capital*, London: Bantam Books.

Dranover, D., & Meltzer, D., (1994), "Do Important Drugs reach the Market Sooner?" *The RAND Journal of Economics*, 25(3): 402–423.

Dussault, G., & Dubois, C., (2003), *Human resources for health policies: a critical component in health policies*, Human Resources for Health.

European Commission, (2003), *Working Document on developing countries' duties and taxes on essential medicines used in the treatment of major communicable diseases*, European Commission, Directorate-General for Trade.

Filmer, D. & Pritchett, L., (1999), "The Impact of public spending on health: does money matter?" World Bank.

Filmer, D., Hammer, J., Pritchett, L., (2000), "Weak links in the chain: a diagnosis of health policy in poor countries," *World Bank Research Observer,* 15(2): 199–224.

Gambardella, A., Orsenigo, L. & Pammolli, P., (2000), *Global competitiveness in pharmaceuticals: a European Perspecitve*, Paper prepared for the Enterprise Directorate-General of the European Commission, November.

Giacotto, C., (2004), "Explaining pharmaceutical R&D growth rates at the industry level: new perspectives and insights," AEI- Brookings Joint Centre for Regulatory Studies.

IFPMA (2004), *The Pharmaceutical Innovation Platform*, Geneva

Kimani, D., (2005), "Malaria, HIV, TB, Diabetes Drugs to Cost 10 per cent more," The East African, 24 January. At: http://allafrica.com/stories/200501260090.html.

Kremer, M. & Glennerster, R., (2004), *Strong Medicine*, Princeton University Press: Princeton.

Kumarasamy, N., (2004), "Generic antiretroviral drugs – will they be the answer to HIV in the developing world?" *The Lancet*, vol 364.

Lichtenberg, F., (2003), "The value of new drugs," *Milken Institute Review*, Fourth Quarter, 2003.

Maskus, K., (2000), *Intellectual Property in the global economy*, Institute for International Economics, Washington DC.

Menon, D., (2001), "Pharmaceuticals cost control in Canada: Does it work?" *Health Affairs, 20(3)* 92–103.

Padma, T., (2005), "India's drug tests," *Nature*, 436, 485. 28 July 2005.

Poisal, J. & Chulis, G., (2000), "Medicare beneficiaries and drug coverage," *Health Affairs*, 19(2).

Rawlins, M., (2004), "Cutting the cost of drug development?" *Nature*, 3:360.

Reekie, D.W., (1997), "How Competition Lowers the Cost of Medicines," *Cuadernos de Derects Europeu Farmaceutico*, 3(8): 35–48. Reprinted in *Pharmacoeconomics*, 14:107–113.

Rozek, R., (2000), "The effects of compulsory licensing on innovation and access to healthcare," *NERA*, September.

Saleh, K. & Ibrahim, M., (2005), "Are Essential Medicines in Malaysia Accessible, Affordable and Available?" *Pharmacy World & Science*, 27:6 442–446.

Sauer, R. & Sauer, C., (2005), "Reducing Barrier to the Development of High Quality, Low Cost Medicines: A Proposal for Reforming the Drug Approval Process," London: International Policy Press.

Shaw, R. & Ainsworth, M., (1995), "Financing heath services through user fees and insurance," *World Bank*, discussion paper 294.

Sherwood, R., (2000), "The economic importance of judges," *Federal Circuit Bar Journal*, 9(4): 619–633.

Soderlund, N. & Hansl, B., (2000), "Health Insurance in South Africa: an empirical analysis of trends in risk-pooling and efficiency following deregulation," *Health Policy and Planning*, 15(4):378–385.

UNAIDS, (2006), *2006 Report on the global AIDS epidemic*, UNAIDS, Geneva, available at http://www.unaids.org/en/HIV_data/2006GlobalReport/default.asp

U.S. Department of Commerce, (2004), "Pharmaceutical price controls in OECD Countries: implications for US consumers, pricing, research and development, and innovation," *International Trade Administration*, December.

Wofford, D., & Shanahan, C., (2004), *Doing Business in 2005*, World Bank.

6 Cost effective means of fighting the diseases of poverty

Attaran, A., Barnes, K., Curtis, C., d'Alessandro, U., Fanello, C., Galinski, M., Kokwaro, G., Looareesuwan, S., Makanga, M., Mutabingwa, T., (2004), "WHO, the Global Fund, and medical malpractice in malaria treatment," *The Lancet*, 363:9404, pp 237–240.

Baird, J., (2000), "Resurgent malaria at the millennium: control strategies in crisis," *Drugs*, (4) 719–743.

Bean, J., (2001), "Can we roll back malaria?" *The Health Exchange*, December 2001.

Black, R.,. Morris, S. & Bryce, J., (2003), "Where and why are 10 million children dying every year?" *The Lancet*, 361:2226–2234.

Blower, S., Ma, L., Farmer, P. & Koenig, S., (2003), "Predicting the Impact of Antiretrovirals in Resource-Poor Settings: Preventing HIV Infections whilst Controlling Drug Resistance", *Current Drug Targets – Infectious Disorders*, 3:4, 345–353.

Bruce, N., Perez-Padilla, R. & Albalak, R., (2002), "The health effects of indoor air pollution exposure in developing countries", Geneva: World Health Organization.

Choi, H., Breman J., Teutsch S., Liu S. & Hightower A., (1995), "The effectiveness of insecticide-impregnated bednets in reducing cases of malaria infection: a meta-analysis of published results," *American Journal of Tropical Medicine and Hygiene* (52) 377–382.

Galiani, S., Gerther, P., Schargrodsky, E., (2002), "Water for life: the impact of the privatization of water services on child mortality," Stanford Institute for Economic Policy Research (SIEPR), Stanford University.

Greenspan, A., (2003), "Market Economies and Rule of Law," New York: Federal Reserve Board.

Goswami, I., (2004), "Changing contours of rural India," *Financial Express*, September 14, http://www.financialexpress.com/fe_full_story.php?content_id=68671.

Gwartney, J. & Lawson, R., (2004), *Economic Freedom of the World, 2004 Annual Report*, Vancouver: Fraser Institute.

Hamel, M., Odhacha, A., Roberts, J. & Deming, M., (2001), "Malaria control in Bungoma District, Kenya: a survey of home treatment of children with fever, bednet use and attendance at antenatal clinics," *Bulletin of the World Health Organization*, 79(11): 1014–1023.

Kasper, W., (2006), *Make Poverty History: Tackle Corruption*, Australia: Centre for Independent Studies.

Malaria Consortium, (2002), "Roll Back Malaria to Date," available at http://www.rbm.who.int/cmc_upload/0/000/015/905/ch2.pdf

Okonski, K., ed., (2006), *The Water Revolution: Practical Solutions to Water Scarcity*, London: International Policy Press.

Paalberg, R., (2006), "Let them eat precaution: why GM crops are being overregulated in the developing world," in Entine, J. (Ed.) *Let them eat precaution*, Washington, DC: American Enterprise Institute.

Paine, J., Shipton, C., Chaggar, S., Howells, R., Kennedy, M., Vernon, G., Wright, S., Hinchliffe, E., Adams, J., Silverstone, A., & Drake, R., (2005), "Improving the nutritional value of Golden Rice through increased pro-vitamin A content," *Nature Biotechnology*, 23, 482–487.

Phillips-Howard, P., Nahlen, B., Kolczak, M., *et al.*, (2003), "Efficacy of permethrin-treated bednets in the prevention of mortality in young children in an area of high perennial malaria transmission in western Kenya," *American Journal of Tropical Medicine and Hygiene*, 68 (suppl): 23–29.

Premji Z., Lubega P., Hamisi Y., Mchopa E., Minjas J., Checkley W. & Shiff C., (1995), "Changes in malaria associated morbidity in children using insecticide treated mosquito nets in the Bagamoyo District of Tanzania," *Tropical Medicine and Parasitology*, 46: 147–153.

Ramiah, I. & Reich, M., (2005), "Public-Private Partnerships and Antiretroviral Drugs for HIV/AIDS: Lessons from Botswana," *Health Affairs*, 24(2): 545–551

Rao, K., Mishra, V. & Retherford, R., (1998), "Knowledge and Use of Oral Rehydration Therapy for Childhood Diarrhoea in India: Effects of Exposure to Mass Media," *National Family Health Survey Subject Reports* (10).

Roberts, D., Laughlin, L., Hsheih, P. & Legters, L., (1997), "DDT Global Strategies, and a Malaria Control Crisis in South America," *Emerging Infectious Diseases*, 3(3): 295–302.

Rosegrant, M., & Gazmuri-Schleyer, R., (1994), *Reforming Water Allocation Policy Through Markets in Tradable Water Rights: Lessons from Chile, Mexico, and California.* Washington DC: International Food and Production Technology Division, EPTD Discussion Paper No. 6.

Salomon, J., Hogan, D., Stover, J., Stanecki, K., Walker, N., Ghys, P. & Schwartlander, B., (2005), "Integrating HIV Prevention and Treatment: From Slogans to Impact," *PLOS Medicine*, 2(1): 50–56.

Sharma, G., (1987), "A critical review of the impact of insecticidal spraying under NMEP on the malaria situation in India," *Journal of Communicable Diseases.* (19) 187–290.

Singh, S., Darroch, J. & Bankole, A., (2003), *A, B and C in Uganda: The Role of Abstinence, Monogamy, and Condom Use in HIV Decline*, The Alan Guttmacher Institute: New York and Washington.

Snow R., Guerra, C., Noor, A., Myint, H. & Hay, S., (2005), "The global distribution of clinical episodes of *Plasmodium falciparum* malaria," *Nature* 434, 214–217 (10 March 2005).

Stover, J., Bertozzi, S., Gutierrez, J., Walker, N., Stanecki, K., Greener, R., Gouws, E., Hankins, C., Garnett, G., Salomon, J., Ties Boerma, T., De Lay, P., Ghys., P, (2006), "The Global Impact of Scaling Up HIV/AIDS Prevention Programs in Low- and Middle-Income Countries", *Science*, 311: 5766, 1474–1476

UNAIDS, (2004), *2004 Report on the global AIDS epidemic*, UNAIDS, Geneva.

UNAIDS, (2005a), *AIDS epidemic update 2005*, UNAIDS, Geneva.

UNAIDS, (2005b), *Intensifying HIV prevention: UNAIDS policy position paper*, Geneva.

UNAIDS, (2006), *2006 Report on the global AIDS epidemic*, UNAIDS, Geneva, available at http://www.unaids.org/en/HIV_data/2006GlobalReport/default.asp.

UNAIDS, (2006b), Evaluation of WHO's contribution to "3 by 5", WHO, Geneva, available at http://www.who.int/hiv/topics/me/3by5evaluationreport.pdf.

WHO, (1995), *Global prevalence of Vitamin A deficiency*, Micronutrient Deficiency Information System working paper no.2, Geneva: WHO.

World Bank, (2002), "Water – the essence of life," Washington DC: World Bank.

7 Counterfeit medicines in LDCs: problems and solutions

Ahmad, K., (2004), "Antidepressants are sold as antiretrovirals in DR Congo", *The Lancet*, 363: 713.

Cockburn, R., Newton, P., Agyarko, E., Akunyili, D., White, N., (2005), "The Global Threat of Counterfeit Drugs: Why Industry and Governments Must Communicate the Dangers", *PLoS Medicine*, 2(4): e100.

Dondorp, A., Newton, P., Mayxay, M., Van Damme, W., Smithuis, F., Yeung, S., Petit, A., Lynam, A., Johnson, A., Hien, T., McGready, R., Farrar, J., Looareesuwan, S., Day, N., Green, M. & White, N., (2004), "Fake antimalarials in Southeast Asia are a major impediment to malaria control: multinational cross-sectional survey on the prevalence of fake antimalarials", *Tropical Medicine & International Health*, 9(12): 1241.

Hanif, M., Mobarak, M., Ronan, A., Rahman, D., Donovan, J. *et al.*, (1995), "Fatal renal failure caused by diethylene glycol in paracetamol exlixir: The Bangladesh epidemic", *British Medical Journal*, 311: 88–91.

Pcoul, B., Chirac, P., Trouiller, P., Pine, J., (1999), "Access to Essential Drugs in Poor Countries – A Lost Battle?" *JAMA*, 281(4)

Raufu, A., (2003), "India agrees to help Nigeria tackle the import of fake drugs", *British Medical Journal*, 326: 1234.

Shakoor, O., Taylor, R., Behrens, R., (1997), "Assessment of the incidence of substandard drugs in developing countries," *Tropical Medicine & International Health* 2(9): 839–845.

White, N., (1999), "Delaying antimalarial drug resistance with combination chemotherapy," *Parassitologia* 41, 301–308.

WHO, (2003), "The quality of antimalarials: a study in seven African countries," Geneva: WHO, available at http://whqlibdoc.who.int/hq/2003/WHO_EDM_PAR_2003.4.pdf

9 The World Health Organisation: a time for reconstitutions

Barro, Robert J. (1967). "Second Thoughts on Keynesian Economics." *American Economic Review*, Proceedings, 69: 54–59.

Bauer, Peter. (2000). *From Subsistence to Exchange*. Princeton: Princeton University Press.

Boettke, Peter J. (1993). *Why Perestroika Failed: The Politics and Economics of Socialist Transformation*. London: Routledge.

Boettke, Peter J. ed. (1994). *The Collapse of Development Planning*. New York: New York University Press.

Borcherding, Thomas E., ed. (1977). *Budgets and Bureaucrats*. Durham, NC: Duke University Press.

Cheung, Steven N. S. Cheung. (1973). "The Fable of the Bees: An Economic Investigation." *Journal of Law and Economics*, 16: 11–33.

Downs, Anthony. (1967). *Inside Bureaucracy*. Boston: Little, Brown.

Easterly, William (2001). *The Illusive Quest for Growth*. New York: St. Martin's Press.

Friedman, Milton and Anna J. Schwartz. (1963). *A Monetary History of the United States* Princeton: Princeton University Press.

Gwartney, James and Robert Lawson. (2004). *Economic Freedom of the World*. Vancouver: Fraser Institute.

Hayek, F. A., ed. (1935). *Collectivist Economic Planning*. London: Routledge.

Ikeda, Sanford. (1997). *Dynamics of the Mixed Economy*. London: Routledge.

Johnson, David B. (1973). "Meade, Bees, and Externalities." *Journal of Law and Economics*, 16: 35–66.

Kealey, Terence. (1997). *The Economic Laws of Scientific Research* London: Palgrave Macmillan.

Lal, Deepak. (1983). *The Poverty of Development Economics*. Cambridge: Harvard University Press.

Littlechild, Steven C. (1978). *The Fallacy of the Mixed Economy*. London: Institute of Economic Affairs.

Meade, James E. (1952). "External Economies and Diseconomies in a Competitive Situation." *Economic Journal*, 62: 54–67.

Morris, Julian, Philip Stevens and Alec van Gelder. (2005). *Incentivising Research and Development for the Diseases of Poverty*. London: International Policy Press.

Niskanen, William A. (1971). *Bureaucracy and Representative Government*. Chicago: Aldine.

Nutter, G. Warren. (1961). *The Growth of Industrial Production in the Soviet Union*. Princeton: Princeton University Press.

Roberts, D et al., (2000). "A probability model of vector behaviour: effects of DDT repellency, irritancy and toxicity in malaria control." Journal of Vector Ecology, 25(1): 48–61.

Roberts, Paul Craig. (1971). *Alienation and the Soviet Economy*. Albuquerque: University of New Mexico Press.

Rothbard, Murray Rothbard. (1963). *America's Great Depression*. Kansas City: Sheed Andrews.

Samuelson, Paul A. and William D. Nordhaus. (1989). *Economics*, 13th ed. New York: McGraw-Hill.

Snow, B et al., (2005). "The global distribution of clinical episodes of Plasmodium falciparum malaria", *Nature* 434, 214–217. Available at: http://www.who.int/3by5/about/initiative/en/index.html, accessed 10 May 2005.

Tullock, Gordon. (1967). *The Organisation of Inquiry*.Durham, NC: Duke University Press.

Wagner, Richard E., ed. (1991). *Charging for Government*. London: Routledge.

Wagner, Richard E. (1997). "Does the World Health Organisation Return Good Value to American Taxpayers?" *Delusions of Grandeur: The United Nations and Global Intervention*. Ed. Ted Galen Carpenter. Washington DC: Cato Institute.

The Campaign for Fighting Diseases

Advisory council

Dr Amir Attaran Amir Attaran holds the Canada Research Chair in Population Health and Global Development Policy at the University of Ottawa. He is also an associate fellow of the Royal Institute of International Affairs, London and a member of Africa fighting Malaria, an organisation aimed at the eradication of the disease. Previously he was an adjunct lecturer in Public Policy at Harvard University, publishing research as part of the Center for International Development and the Carr Center for Human Rights Policy at the John F. Kennedy School of Government.

Professor Lucas Bergkamp is a professor of environmental liability law at Erasmus University Rotterdam, and partner at Hunton & Williams in Brussels, Belgium. He is the author of numerous law review articles, and is a member of the editorial board of several academic and trade journals. He is an expert in the emerging area of biotechnology.

Professor Sir Colin Berry is professor of morbid anatomy and histopathology at Queen Mary, University of London. He has held the position of Dean of the London Hospital Medical College and has served on advisory committees on health and related matters, and has penned more than 200 papers on development, toxicology and vascular biomechanics.

Dr Philip Brown is the former owner of PJB Publications Ltd, the leading business-to-business publisher for the international healthcare industry. He writes and speaks on a variety of issues related to the development and use of pharmaceutical products. Dr Brown is the Chairman of Council of the University of London School of Pharmacy and is the owner of a number of pharmacies and other businesses.

Dr. Alphonse L. Crespo, a Swiss orthopaedic surgeon, is currently Director of Research and member of the Board of Directors of the Institut Constant de Rebecque, an independent think tank founded in January 2005. As well as publishing numerous books and articles Dr. Crespo maintains his professional qualifications, sits on the Editorial Board of *Le Courrier du Mdecin Vaudois* and is a medical consultant for the Swiss Accident Insurance Fund in Lausanne.

Professor William Keatinge is author to more than 200 scientific papers, reviews, chapters and two books, and commentator on the media about effects of cold and heat on human health.

Dr John Kilama is founder and president of the Global Bioscience Development Institute. He has a broad background in the pharmaceutical, agricultural biotechnology and agrochemical chemistry but his areas of expertise include Intellectual Property rights and Biotechnology Strategy development.

Professor Deepak Lal is James S. Coleman Professor of International Development Studies, University of California at Los Angeles, Professor Emeritus of Political Economy, University College London, and co-director of the Trade and Development Unit at the Institute of Economic Affairs, London.

Professor The Lord McColl is Emeritus Professor of Surgery at Guy's Hospital and continues to teach at King's College on the Guy's Campus. He is also Surgeon to the international charity Mercyships and frequently operates in the poorest countries of West Africa.